WIRED

FOR SUCCESS

Auto Electrical Made Easy

By Randy Rundle

Published by

krause publications

700 E. State Street • Iola, WI 54990-0001
Telephone: 715/445-2214

Please call or write for our free catalog of automotive publications. Our toll-free number to place an order or obtain a free catalog is 800-258-0929 or please use our regular business telephone 715-445-2214 for editorial comment and further information.

Library of Congress Catalog Number: 95-77302
ISBN: 0-87341-402-0
Printed in the United States of America

Dedication

This book is dedicated to the antique, classic, and street rod car owner, and for all of you that take the time to drive and enjoy your car.

Contents

Acknowledgments

I would like to acknowledge the following companies for their help in completing this book:

Interstate Batteries

OPTIMA Batteries

Standard Ignition Products

Standard Wire and Cable Products

Delco-Remy Co. Educational Services Division

Antique Automobile Radio, Inc.

John Bryant, Inc.

Dan Poremba, IPM Technical Services

Thanks to all of these companies for providing their time and effort in helping me create this book. Without their help and cooperation, it would have been an impossible task.

Introduction

For some of you, the things you learn in this book will be a reminder of what your grandfather knew when he was a young man. If you ever spent time with him when you were little, you no doubt watched him do some of the things talked about in this book.For the rest of you, the book is designed to give you a basic knowledge of how things worked in the old days. Just as with any trade, there are little tricks and secrets that you learn from owning and driving an old car. By sharing these secrets with you, and at the same time explaining the basic rules of the automotive electrical game, you will be able to maintain your own car, as well as make much needed improvements.

This will give you more confidence as an antique car or street rod owner/driver, and at the same time provide more enjoyment because you have now conquered your fear of auto electricity. After all, the reason we buy and drive antique and street rod cars is for the pride and enjoyment of ownership. You will be even prouder when you can say "Yep, I installed and wired up that radiator cooling fan myself, and boy, it works great. If you get one for your car and need help installing it, I can help you. They are really quite simple to install once you know how."

My goal for you, the reader of this book, is to be able to understand basic automotive electricity as it applies to you and your car. You will not learn all of the theory, rules, and the physics involved. That stuff is boring, especially when you have nothing to relate it to.

In this book you will learn theory only when it has practical applications. For instance, if I told you that a generator armature helps the generator produce current output by breaking the magnetic fields created by the field coils, you would slam this book shut and use it for a drink coaster.

But if I can show you how that really works by using a simple horseshoe magnet and a 16 penny nail, then you can demonstrate this for yourself and actually see and feel what is going on. At the same time you can take that knowledge and apply it to a generator AND understand how a generator produces energy.

My goal as author of this book, is to explain automotive electricity in simple, common-sense terms. I also will present as many real-life examples as possible so you can use what you're learning. Throughout the book you will find "Time-Saving Tips" and "Rundle's Rules" as well as chapter reviews at the end of Chapters 4-8. A Source List at the end of the book contains vendor information. All of these features are provided to save you time and make automotive electricity much easier to understand. After reading this book, you will be "wired for success."

Chapter

1

"The Plumber Follies"

Chapter 1

The Plumber Follies

Because this is the first chapter, it is only fair that we get started off on the right foot. Automotive electricity really is quite simple if someone will take the time to explain how it works and what all of the jargon means. In this book that has become my job.

The information I will give you will be in commonsense, everyday terms that you can understand. It may disappoint some of the trade professionals, but they will get over it. Just smile as you wave to them, to let them know you now know what's going on.

As the old story goes, and it gets repeated often, understanding electricity is easy... "it's just like water flowing through a pipe." Asking for any further explanation, however, will get you more answers and more confusion than you thought possible. With no two stories being the same, you become totally confused.

To add insult to injury, amps, volts, and resistance are not terms your granddad used when he was plumbing. So what gives? Who is telling the truth? How is electricity supposed to be related to plumbing?

Before we can understand how automotive electricity works we have to understand the "jargon," or terms of the trade. There really are no secrets, only a lot of misinformation.

So it is with great pleasure (and credit to David Letterman) that I present the official top six terms used in automotive electricity and their commonsense meaning.

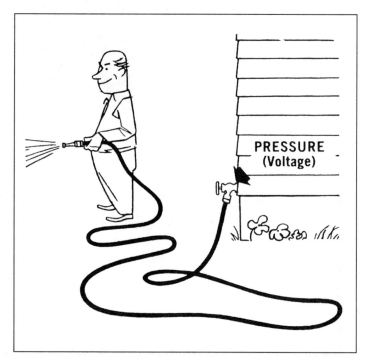

Why not grab the beverage of your choice and take a few minutes to look these over. You'll be seeing lots of these terms in the chapters ahead. It's all part of the job of making sense out of this electrical voodoo.

VOLTS - In the United States, water pressure is measured in pounds per square inch. This is the amount of "push" that is behind the water to force it through the pipe. In electricity, this "push" is measured in volts. The volts are simply the amount of push that is forcing the electrical current through the wires.

AMPERES - Again using water as an example, the quantity of water passing through a pipe at a given point is measured in gallons. In electrical terms it is measured in amperes or "amps," as it is sometimes called. The amps are the "horsepower" that does the actual work. Amps, just like water, are measured such as the amount of current passing through a wire at a given point.

WATTS - A watt is the unit of measurement that tells how much total energy is being used. To figure watts, simply multiply the volts by the amps. As an example, if the heater motor in your car requires 10 amps of electricity and you have a 6-volt system, then the heater motor would have a rating of 60 watts.

EXAMPLE: **Volts x Amps = Watts**

6 x 10 = 60

A watt is a common measurement found on headlamps, for instance. The low beam of each headlamp is rated at 55 watts. So if you divide 110 (55 x 2 bulbs) by the system voltage of 6, we would know that both headlamps working on low beam will require just over 18 amps of electrical energy.

EXAMPLE: $\underline{\textbf{Watts}}$ **= Amps**
                  Volts

$\underline{110}$ **= 18**
  6

CIRCUIT - A circuit is a wire or similar device that provides the path for electricity to flow from point A to point B and back again. In other words, the wire that goes from the battery to the ignition switch, to the heater switch to the heater motor and back to the battery, is called a circuit.

A "switch" in the circuit is used to "break" the circuit and turn off and on an accessory. A switch in the "off" position breaks the path of electricity, preventing the electricity from reaching the accessory. Moving the switch to the "on" position will close the circuit turning on the accessory.

When a **short** develops in a circuit it means that there is an unauthorized break in the wire or the circuit, something that is providing another path for the electricity to follow.

When this happens, the electricity does not follow the path of the original circuit and does not return to the battery. It becomes "lost." This can show up as an accessory that does not work properly, a blown fuse, or as a drain on the battery, which will discharge the electrical energy from the battery.

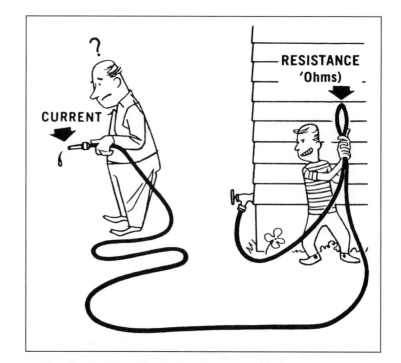

RESISTANCE - Resistance is simply electrical friction. Resistance is the drag or friction created as the electrical current is being pushed through the wires.

Excessive resistance can be caused by poor or loose connections, corroded terminals, or damaged wires.

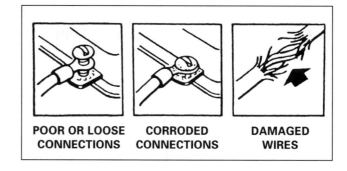

| POOR OR LOOSE CONNECTIONS | CORRODED CONNECTIONS | DAMAGED WIRES |

OHMS - Ohms are how electrical friction is measured. "Ohms of resistance" is equal to the drag on a fishing line in the water. In order to force the electrical current through a wire, the friction or resistance has to be overcome.

BIG WIRES AND LITTLE WIRES - The bigger the physical diameter of the wire, the easier it is for the electricity to flow through it (because there is less resistance). This is why 6-volt wiring harnesses will be made up of primary wire that is twice the physical diameter of the wire used in a 12-volt wiring harness. The 6-volt system requires twice the amps of a 12-volt system to do the same job because the voltage or pressure behind the amps is less.

Battery cable size becomes very important as it relates to automotive electrical systems. If you were to install 12-volt cables on your 6-volt system, you would encounter difficult starting. This is because the amount of amps flowing to the starter from the battery is being reduced by almost 50 percent due to the fact that your battery cable is now 50 percent smaller in physical diameter. Also, there is 50 percent less voltage on hand to push the amps needed through the smaller cable.

Buying a bigger battery will not help. The amps are in your original battery already; the problem is, the path from the battery to the starter is being restricted.

WIRE SIZES - The simple rule is that the "larger" in physical diameter the wire, the "smaller" the gauge size is. (Another trick to try to confuse you). As an example, the cables on your 6-

volt battery were a number 4 gauge from the factory, as compared to the "BATT" wire attached to your voltage regulator, which should be a number 10 gauge.

Generally, battery cables come in sizes ranging from 8, 6, 4, 2, 1, 0, and 00. The most common size of battery cable found on 12-volt batteries will be 8-gauge, and the most common size found on a 6-volt battery will be 4-gauge.

Electrical wiring harnesses will use common sizes such as 10, 12, 14, 16, and 18 gauge, with 16 and 18 gauge being the most common sizes used.

FINAL TRIVIA - *WHILE THIS DOES NOT RELATE DIRECTLY TO AUTOMOTIVE WIRING, DID YOU EVER WONDER ABOUT THE ELECTRIC MOTORS THAT RUN THE POWER TOOLS IN YOUR SHOP? THE GRINDER, DRILL PRESS, ETC., ALL HAVE A HORSE-POWER RATING ON THEM. SO HOW MUCH IS ONE HORSEPOWER OF ELECTRICITY? ABOUT 746 WATTS.*

With this new information you can now figure out how many amps will be required to run the electric motor on the new air compressor you just bought for your shop. All you have to do to find the amps required (besides reading the instructions, but who does that?) is divide the "voltage" by the watts. The result will be the amount of amps needed to run your air compressor's motor. (This is what a house electrician will do so he knows how big of a circuit you need for your compressor. Normally he will add 10 amps as a margin of safety.)

This will also work in reverse to find out how many watts you are using. To do that, simply multiply the voltage times the amps and you will get watts.

EXAMPLE: **Volts x Amps = Watts**

110 volts x 6 amp motor = 660 watts

Knowing how many watts you are using will tell you why your electric meter is spinning around so fast, and why your bill is so high!

COMMON TOOLS OF THE TRADE
(THE ONLY ONES YOU REALLY NEED)

Like most projects, you can buy as few or as many tools as you want to complete a job. But because so many people hate working on electrical projects, the number of tools they have on hand for the job is usually zero!

The following tools are the basics and will allow you to complete 95 percent of your electrical projects. And best of all, you will spend less than $100 dollars total! This money savings will allow you to blow money on the things you really want to buy.

TEST LIGHT - This tool is the most popular and the easiest to use; it is the equivalent of a pair of pliers or a crescent wrench to a mechanic. With a test light, for instance, you can see if an accessory has "power" at the switch, find shorts in a wiring harness, or find the "hot" wire in a group of wires in a wiring harness. The cost is $10 to $15 for one of good quality.

VOLT METER - A volt meter simply checks the voltage at a given point. For instance, if you wanted to know what condition your battery is in, you could use a volt meter to check voltage at the battery posts. You can also check voltage at your starter's battery post to see if all of your battery's voltage is reaching the starter. The cost is $20 to $30 for one of good quality.

AMMETER - An ammeter ("amp meter") will tell you how many amps are flowing through a wire at a given point, just like the one in the dash of your car. There are two commonly used styles of ammeters, although they both do the same job.

One style is called an "inductive" ammeter. It measures the amps by measuring the magnetic current created as the amps are pushed through the wire. This type of gauge is easy to use, as you can simply hold the gauge on top of a wire to get a reading.

Ford cars and trucks used this style of amp gauge in the dash of their cars and trucks during the 1940s and 50s. A metal tab held a loop of wire to the back of the amp gauge so the gauge could provide a reading.

The other style of common amp gauge will have two studs on the back of the gauge, with electrical leads attached. To check the amperage output of your alternator, simply remove the hot lead from the alternator and place the amp gauge leads between the hot wire and the stud on the alternator. You can then start the car and turn on accessories to see if your alternator is working correctly.

In a vehicle using this type of amp gauge, the wire from the generator/ alternator will connect to one side, and the wire from the battery will connect to the other stud. This will allow the gauge to read what is coming into, or going out of, the battery. This style was common in cars and trucks beginning in

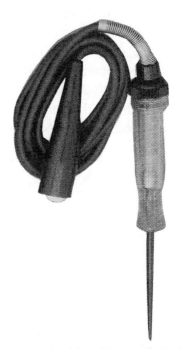

The test light is one of the most popular auto electrical tools.

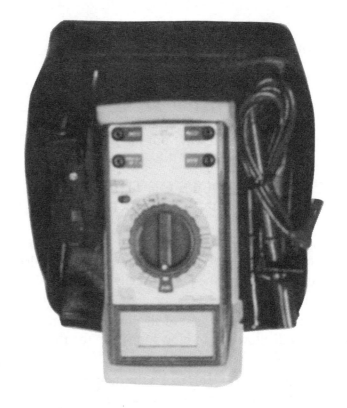

Amp/Ohm Meter.

the 1920s, and is still in use today. The cost is $20-$30.

OHM METER - This meter simply reads the resistance, or the amount of friction developed as the current is being pushed through the wire. This gauge is helpful in locating electrical shorts in a wiring harness system. An ohm meter uses a small battery as a power source to force current through the circuit to be

In dash ampere hour meter, from the 1920s.

Soldering Gun.

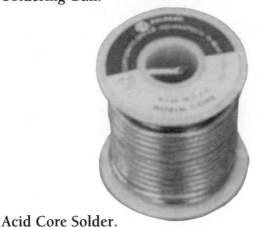

Acid Core Solder.

checked. Any excessive resistance can then be detected.

NOTE OF CAUTION: Because an ohm meter has its own power source, it should **never** be connected to a circuit with system voltage. (System voltage plus battery power will toast your ohm meter.) The cost is $10 to $25.

JUMPER WIRE - This is simply a piece of 18 ga (gauge) wire usually about 14 to 16 inches in length. It will have "alligator clips" on both ends. It can also be used to make temporary wiring connections such as connecting an accessory to a switch to see if it is working. It is also used along with a test light or volt meter to find shorts in a wiring harness.

A jumper wire is something you can make yourself, and will want to make more than one of, as they are quite handy. The "alligator ends" are available at most full-line auto parts stores or Radio Shack stores. The cost is minimal, and you get to choose the wire color(s).

HYDROMETER - A hydrometer is optional and is the last tool you really might want to invest in. They are used to check the specific gravity in the "cells" of a battery. Besides a volt meter, a "hydrometer" is another way of checking the condition of your battery. You will learn how to do that in an upcoming chapter.

"Turkey Baster" used to add water to battery cells.

Buying one is an option, so if you don't want to spend the money and buy one of your own, you can always borrow one from your mechanic neighbor, because now you will know how to use one. The cost is $10 to $15.

Many of the tools we just talked about can be purchased from the local full-line auto parts store such as NAPA or BIG A or CarQuest. In addition, Radio Shack stores are a good source for many of these tools. Shop around. Most store clerks should be able to explain how their tools work. Look for the features you want in your price range. Also ask someone in the trade for their recommendations.

Example of various hydrometers.

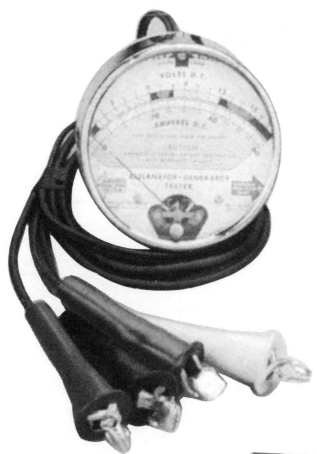

Combination Volt/Amp Meter.

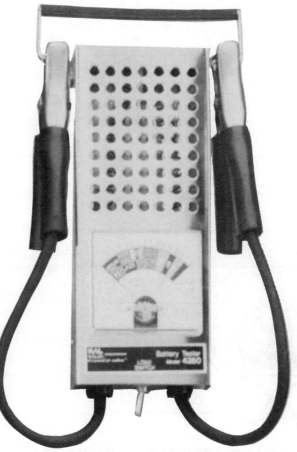

Battery Load Tester.

Chapter 2

"Fitting It All Together"

Chapter 2

Fitting It All Together

Now that we understand the jargon of the trade and we know about the tools of the trade, it's time to discuss where this plumbing story came from. Electricity really is like water flowing through a pipe. From the early years, up through the mid-1950s, with a few exceptions, most antique cars had a 6-volt electrical system. A 6-volt electrical system was chosen because there was not a big demand for electrical horsepower. Not many accessories had been invented yet, and most of the engines were long stroke and low compression, therefore the starters of the era did not require a lot of electrical horsepower to do their job.

The other known advantage of a 6-volt system is the reserve capacity the batteries carried. Because the voltage was low, a larger amount of amperage reserve was on hand to do the job. So even though the starters would not crank very fast, they would crank for a long duration of time. Just when you thought they were on their last legs, you would get two or three more rounds, and the tired old engine with the oil-fouled spark plugs would finally come to life. Six-volt systems worked fine up until the mid-1950s when the electrical demand greatly increased.

By the time the mid-1950s came around, cars were being loaded with accessories. Power windows, power seats, power antennas—all became popular. Another factor that came into play was that more cars and drivers, all going to the same place, created "traffic jams" where cars sat in one place with the motors idling, and with all of the accessories turned on. The simple 6-volt system was being overwhelmed and desperately needed some help.

So the decision was made to switch to a 12-volt electrical system. This was a logical decision for the engineers to make. Let's take a look and see why they chose 12 volts and what rules apply.

One of the most basic rules of electricity applies to this decision: **if you double the voltage or pressure, then you will need only one-half the amps or horsepower to do the same job.**

Using the imaginary car of your choice, if the original 6-volt starter required 250 amps of electrical energy to start the car, then the same car and the same engine, only changing over to a 12-volt system and a 12-volt starter, in theory would require only 125 amps, or **half** the amount of electrical horsepower required by the 6-volt system to start the car. This is because while we are using half as many amps, we are using twice the voltage or pressure to force the amps through the wire.

As a result, the car of the early 1950s, loaded with accessories, that once required an 80-amp 6-volt generator to power those accessories and keep the battery fully charged, can now be supplied with enough electrical energy to run the same accessories and keep the same battery fully charged, while using only a 40-amp generator and 12 volts of pressure.

But as with all things, there is a trade-off. With less amps on hand, there is less reserve cranking capacity on hand. The remaining amps, however, are under greater pressure and in theory will spin the starter motor over much faster, and the reserve will not be needed.

 SO WHAT HAPPENS TO THE SIZE OF OUR WIRING HARNESS IF WE CHANGE OVER TO A 12-VOLT ELECTRICAL SYSTEM?

As the rule states, if we are carrying less amps, the size of our wiring or "pipe" can be smaller, about 50 percent smaller, because we doubled the voltage.

But because we are using less horsepower, we must increase the pressure or voltage, sending the amps through the wiring under greater pressure. In real life, some of our horsepower will be lost via the friction of traveling in the wire under the higher pressure or voltage. This is called resistance, and is part of the trade-off.

As a reminder, the 6-volt system normally has less resistance because it flows more amps, but through a 50 percent larger diameter pipe under half of the pressure.

 TIME-SAVING TIP: Despite the rumors and misinformation, it is NOT necessary to replace the 6-volt wiring harness when changing over to a 12-volt system. If the original harness is in good shape, it will work just fine because, as we have learned, it is designed to carry twice the amp load of the 12-volt system. In other words, it is actually twice as heavy as it needs to be for the 12-volt electrical system.

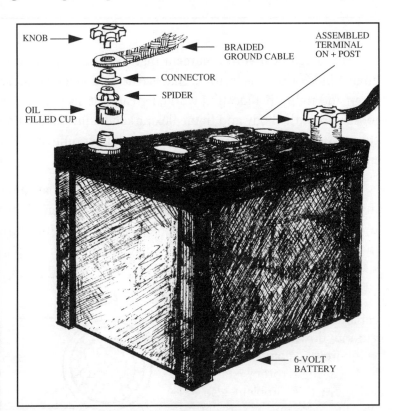

Worn Stopper, by Terminals, 22700 Martha St., Woodland Hills, California, featured in *Popular Science* in 1957, allowed quick disconnect of an auto battery by unscrewing plastic knobs. The knobs screwed into threaded spiders forced over terminals, and were held in oil-filled cups to prevent corrosion. They sold for about $4.

USING WHAT WE JUST LEARNED, IF YOU HAVE DIFFICULTY STARTING YOUR CAR, ESPECIALLY WHEN THE MOTOR IS WARM, HERE IS ONE EASY SOLUTION TO YOUR PROBLEM.

RUNDLE'S RULES:

1) Buy a battery cable that is at least two sizes larger in diameter than the gauge of the original battery cable. Remember, a larger cable will flow a greater volume of amps easier, with less resistance than a smaller cable. What you are doing is increasing the efficiency of your electrical system.

2) Remember also to physically look at the end of the cable to be sure of the gauge size. Some cables are wrapped in thick insulation to give the appearance of a heavier gauge cable.

3) As an added benefit to insure easier starting, the ground cable from the battery should go directly to the starter mounting bolt or as close as possible to the starter. This is because that is where the ground has to go to complete the starting circuit. By moving the battery ground to the starter, you are greatly increasing the efficiency of your starting system by providing a direct path between the starter and the battery.

Wait...I can hear your argument that the battery ground was connected to the frame or engine block from the factory! That is true, and when your car was new and everything was clean and tight, that location worked great! But, as your car gets older, the connections get looser (from the body and frame flexing) and a fine layer of oil and grease settle over everything; your electrical system ground is no longer quite as efficient, and some of your cranking power will be lost.

This is also true for cars built through the 1960s that came with V-8 motors and performance exhaust systems (headers to us). The heat given off by the headers would be soaked up by the starter and solenoid, requiring more cranking amps from the battery to start the motor. In many cases with the small 8-gauge cables and a poor ground, the engine will not start when it is hot.

Increasing the battery cable size and moving the ground down to the starter will cure this common problem. (A high torque starter will cure this problem also, usually at much greater expense.)

Body to frame ground, as well as engine to frame ground, is also very important. Be sure that you have

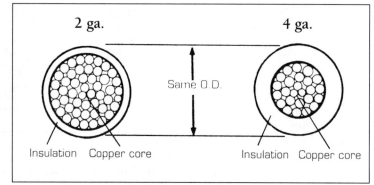

Cross-sectional view of battery cable. The gauge is determined by the cross-sectional area of the copper core.

good clean connections at all of these locations. It is quite common for a newly restored car to have partial or no electrical system ground because of all the fresh paint and detail work. (Paint is an excellent insulator.)

In short, combining the bigger cables with the higher pressure of 12 volts will help your car start much easier. This is true of 6-volt cars also, as the larger gauge of cable will make it easier to flow an even greater amount of amps to the starter from the battery, due to less resistance.

MOVING RIGHT ALONG

Now that we have a basic understanding of how things work and what tools to use, let's go back and check out all the things that make an automotive electrical system possible. You can then learn how to use your new tools. Finally, you can change your last name to Allen, and be on television.

NOTES

Chapter 3

"It All Started with a Pine Tar Box"

Chapter 3

It All Started With A Pine Tar Box

The automotive storage battery is something we pretty much take for granted. And why not, it has been around since the mid-1800s and for the most part looks similar in design to the batteries sold in the 1920s. You would think that after that length of time with no significant changes, that the engineers of the day pretty much got it right the first time. And they did. But first a simple review.

Let's look at the job the battery has been doing all of these years. The battery has the official title of the "electrochemical" device that changes chemical energy into electrical energy. In other words, it stores the chemicals and provides the place for the chemical change to happen, which creates the electricity. And that is the exact same job it had in 1920.

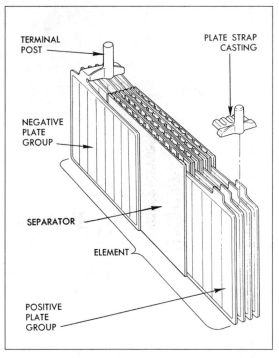

Active parts of a battery

 OK, SO IT CONVERTS CHEMICAL ENERGY INTO ELECTRICAL ENERGY. EXACTLY HOW DOES THAT HAPPEN?

The inside of a battery is made up of three active parts. It is these three parts which cause the chemical reaction that produces the electricity.

Two of those parts consist of "positive" and "negative" plates. A plate is made up of a series of grids. In turn, a grid is simply a framework of cast lead and alloys to which an active chemical is attached. It is this active chemical attached to the grid that is involved in the chemical reaction.

Grid construction is important and is used to determine both the life and the output of a battery. As you might guess, the more area or grid space available, the more chemical that will be exposed to the electrolyte, (the third active ingredient on the inside of our battery), the more powerful the battery will be.

However, thin grid plates will flex more, and are easily damaged by vibration. Also, excessive heat will cause the plates to flex and warp, which makes the chemical attached to the grid flake off, causing the battery to fail.

Grid plate thickness is for the most part determined by the application of the battery, and the environment in which it will be used. Grid plates will usually range in thickness from 3/32nd to 3/16th of an inch.

Ideally, pure lead would be the best grid material. However, because lead is soft, a material called "antimony" is often mixed with the lead to harden and stiffen the grid structure. Only a small amount, just two to eight percent, is needed.

An excess of antimony will cause brittleness, and high electrical resistance that will "block" the electrolyte from reaching the chemical on the grid material. Excess antimony will also cause the battery itself to self-discharge more rapidly.

In recent years, battery engineers have learned that it is also possible to harden the lead grid using a small amount of calcium. Calcium promotes less self-discharge along with low water loss. Using calcium has been a part of the recent technology used to develop the maintenance-free batteries.

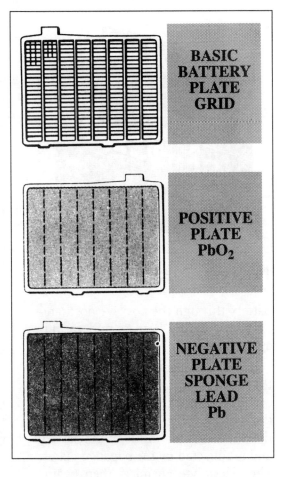

BASIC BATTERY PLATE GRID

POSITIVE PLATE PbO_2

NEGATIVE PLATE SPONGE LEAD Pb

BUILDING A BATTERY

After a series of grids is assembled it becomes a "plate." Once becoming plates, the grids are coated with the chemicals that will be necessary to produce electricity.

The positive plates are coated with peroxide of lead or PbO_2, and will be chocolate brown in color.

The negative plates are coated with sponge lead or Pb, and will be gray in color.

The **electrolyte** is the solution that mixes with these chemicals and produces the electricity. The electrolyte is commonly called **sulfuric acid** or H_2SO_4. The water in the battery is simply the carrier of the sulfuric acid.

A collection of treated plates or grids inside of a battery is called a

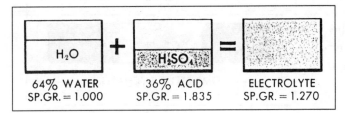

H_2O	+	H_2SO_4	=	ELECTROLYTE
64% WATER SP.GR. = 1.000		36% ACID SP.GR. = 1.835		SP.GR. = 1.270

Formula for electrolyte

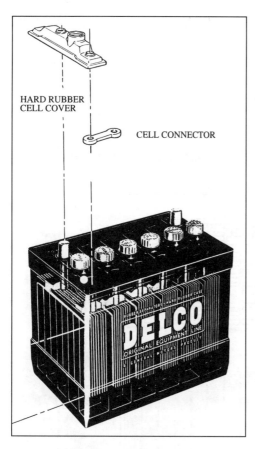

HARD RUBBER
CELL COVER

CELL CONNECTOR

DELCO

1960s battery technology

plate group. Because the positive plate group and the negative plate group are exact opposites, they do not make good neighbors. This makes it necessary to have separators between the plate groups that separate the positive plates from the negative plates.

In the old days, separators were made of hardwood lumber pieces. In later years they were made of hard rubber. Because of modern technology, plastic is commonly used today. Regardless of what they are made of, separators still have the same function as in the old days.

When the chemical reaction takes place inside of the battery, the electrical energy produced will exit the battery by traveling from the positive plates inside of the battery, to the outside of the battery through the positive post, and on to the wiring harness and various accessories.

After the electricity has traveled through the wiring harness and to all of the accessories, it will be returned to the battery at the negative post. From there it enters the inside of the battery and is collected by the negative plates. The electrolyte chemical then begins to break up and the solution becomes sulfur and oxygen.

This leftover sulfur and oxygen solution join up with the chemicals that were originally a part of the positive plates. When the separated electrolyte chemicals mix with the chemicals from the positive plates, the leftover chemical solution is water (H_2O). This weakens the battery and it becomes **discharged**.

Over time, as the "cycling" of the battery takes place over and over, the sulfa-

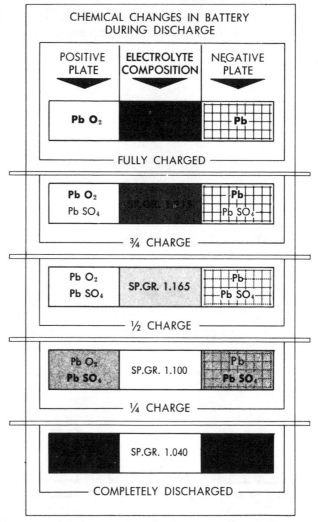

Chemical changes in battery during discharge.

tion that is produced as a result of this charging/discharging process will collect on the bottom of the inside of the battery case. Eventually enough will accumulate to reach the bottom of the plates and short out the battery, causing it to fail.

An inactive, partially discharged battery will speed up this process. Also, a battery low on water will expose the top of the plates to the outside air and will allow sulfation to grow on top of the plates themselves.

The sulfation will also act as an insulator and prevent the electrolyte from reaching the chemical on the grid. This reduces the surface area left for the chemical reaction to take place, and will in turn reduce the output of the battery.

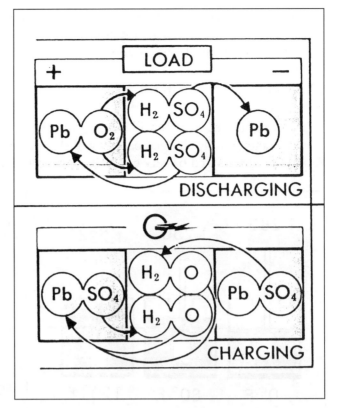

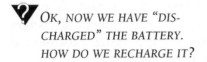 OK, NOW WE HAVE "DIS-CHARGED" THE BATTERY. HOW DO WE RECHARGE IT?

Chemical reactions occurring in the battery cell during charge are basically the reverse of those which occur during discharge.

In order to recharge the battery, the current flowing through the battery must be reversed. This is where the charging circuit comes into play. The generator or alternator produces current mechanically, and sends that current into the battery through the positive post. This is exactly the **opposite way** that the battery released the current it originally produced.

When this electrical current from the generator enters the battery, this starts a chemical reaction that causes the sulfur and oxygen to leave the negative plates and reunite on the positive plates, to form electrolyte once again. When the battery is completely recharged, the electrolyte will again be back to its original solution.

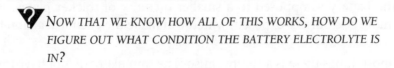 NOW THAT WE KNOW HOW ALL OF THIS WORKS, HOW DO WE FIGURE OUT WHAT CONDITION THE BATTERY ELECTROLYTE IS IN?

The tool most often used to check the condition of a battery is called a "hydrometer." As you might suspect, all that a hydrometer does is measure the acid strength of the electrolyte, or what concentration of acid is present in the water.

A hydrometer does this by measuring the specific gravity or the weight of the solution. Water has been assigned a value of 1 to make it easy to figure the acid-to-water ratio.

Pure sulfuric acid, the active ingredient in electrolyte, weighs 1.835 times more than pure water. This means that if a **gallon of water weighs eight pounds, then a gallon of pure sulfuric acid will weigh 14.68 pounds**.

EXAMPLE: 8 x 1.835 = 14.68

The weight of electrolyte will change with the amount of acid present in the water. Using a hydrometer, a fully charged battery will show a specific gravity reading of 1.275 or 1.300. A partially discharged battery could give a reading of 1.150.

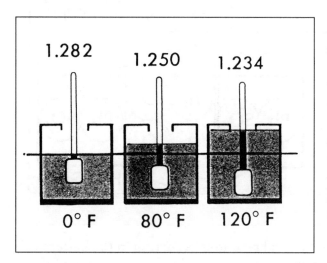

1.282   1.250   1.234

0° F   80° F   120° F

Compensation for specific gravity variations caused by temperature changes.

One more thing. As you might suspect, the outside temperature will affect the readings of the hydrometer. Eighty degrees Fahrenheit is considered the ideal temperature for specific gravity readings.

So to correct for a warmer outside temperature, simply **add four points** to the reading for every 10 degrees above 80° F.

For every degree colder than 80° F, **subtract four points** from the reading.

If you are still wondering why you have to do that, it is because warmer temperatures will cause expansion of the electrolyte, while the colder temps will cause the electrolyte to contract.

OK, WE NOW KNOW HOW A BATTERY WORKS, AND HOW TO CHECK ITS CONDITION. NOW LET'S LOOK INTO WHAT AFFECTS THE FINAL OUTPUT.

The total capacity of a battery is greatly determined by the total amount and size of grid material in the plates. The overall size or thickness is not as important as the total amount of surface area.

The useful capacity of a battery can be increased greatly by placing a large number of thin plates inside the battery as opposed to a smaller quantity of thicker plates. By using thin plates there is more grid surface exposed, which will make the chemical action happen more quickly.

But as with most things there is a compromise. The thin plates do not have the heavy coating of chemical that the thick plates do. As a result, the thin plates will deteriorate faster, and be more likely to be damaged by vibration and excess heat. This will give the battery a shorter life span.

An example of this is heavy construction equipment. These batteries must have thicker plates to be able to stand the rough environment and all of the vibration. As a result, the case will fill faster with these fat grids. This is why you will see construction vehicles have a series of big batteries. Inside of those batteries will be few, but thick, plates. It will take a series of these batteries to get enough grid surface to provide the electrical energy needed to do the job.

There have been a number of different rating systems for battery output over the years. The one most common in the early years up through the late 1950s was called **ampere-hour rating**. This rating system was used mainly during the 6-volt battery era. An ampere-hour rating was actually the storage capacity of a battery. This was figured out by **multiplying the current in amps by the time of discharge**.

EXAMPLE: A battery that will deliver a minimum of 5 amps for a 20-hour period is said to have a 100 ampere-hour capacity (**5 x 20 =100**).

The 12 Volt Era...

When 12-volt systems were introduced, a new rating system was needed to reflect the change that voltage had in rating batteries, since ampere-hour ratings were based mainly on total weight of grid material.

We know that 11 thick plates such as those found in a 6-volt battery cell could weigh the same as 22 thin plates found in the cell of a 12-volt battery.

While they could have the same ampere-hour rating based on the weight of the material, we know that the 66 thin plates found in the 12-volt battery will have more grid surface area and would be a higher output battery than the 6-volt battery it is being compared to by weight. The 6-volt battery will have only 33 plates total.

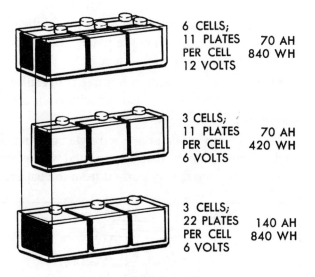

6 CELLS; 11 PLATES PER CELL 12 VOLTS	70 AH	840 WH
3 CELLS; 11 PLATES PER CELL 6 VOLTS	70 AH	420 WH
3 CELLS; 22 PLATES PER CELL 6 VOLTS	140 AH	840 WH

A comparison of ampere-hour capacities of 6- and 12-volt batteries.

In addition to the extra grid surface area, the extra voltage will have a noticeable affect on the battery's total output. None of this would be reflected in the ampere-hour ratings used during the 6-volt era.

As a result, the Society of Automotive Engineers developed and adopted the following updated battery ratings.

1) **Reserve Capacity** - This test measures the time in minutes that a battery can be discharged at the rate of 25 amps and still keep a minimum voltage of 7.5 volts at 80° F. Reverse capacity is measured in minutes. An example would be a 120 minute reserve capacity.

2) **Cold Cranking Amps or (CCA)** - The most difficult job a battery has is to provide electrical energy to the starter to crank over the engine. Since turning over the engine becomes more difficult as the temperature drops, the best way to measure a battery's true cranking energy is to measure the cranking power available at 0° F for 30 seconds while staying above 7.5 volts. An example of a rating would be 800 CCA.

3) **Cranking Amps (CA)** - CA is sometimes referred to as Marine Cranking Amps. MCA measures how much current can be delivered for 30 seconds at 32°F while staying above 7.2 volts.

In the old days, batteries were judged by how many plates they contained. The old rule was "the more plates, the better." As we have just learned, that was not always the best advice.

 OK, NOW WE KNOW HOW A BATTERY IS MADE AND HOW THE OUTPUT IS RATED. NOW WHAT ARE THE DO'S AND DON'TS OF BATTERY CARE, AND WHAT MAKES A BATTERY FAIL COMPLETELY?

•Having a **low electrolyte** level is one of the main causes of battery failure. When the level of electrolyte drops below the plates, the result will be excessive sulfation and buckling of the plates, caused by excess heat.

•The next most common mistake is **overfilling** the battery, which will cause the electrolyte to "boil out" or "gas" excessively when the battery is being charged. This will cause a loss of the electrolyte solution.

Also remember when the electrolyte boils out on top of the battery, it forms the green and white corrosion on the battery posts and wiring connections. This corrosion will act as an insulator and stop the flow of current from the battery posts to the battery cables, as well as to the wiring harness and accessories.

•**Impurities** are another common battery problem. It is always best to use distilled water when adding water to your battery. Any dirt or foreign matter will lessen the effectiveness of the electrolyte solution in the battery.

•**Freezing** happens quite often to a partially discharged battery. The examples below are the temperatures at which the electrolyte inside a battery will begin to freeze, causing damage to the battery. Keep in mind a fully charged battery will not freeze until the temperature reaches -90° F. (Brrrrrr)

•A half-charged battery with a specific gravity of 1.150 will freeze at just 9° F.

•A battery showing a specific gravity of 1.025, an almost totally discharged battery, will freeze at just 30° F.

A hot shower will put your old car's battery into top condition for summertime driving. (Illustration courtesy of John Gunnell)

Believe it or not, cold temperatures will not harm a battery if the battery is kept charged up so the electrolyte does not freeze.

Most frozen batteries cannot be repaired. NEVER TRY TO JUMP-START A FROZEN BATTERY. The battery will explode, causing serious damage to you and your car.

•**Overcharging** of the battery is another common cause of early battery failure. Overcharging is most commonly caused by burnt points in the voltage regulator or cutout, allowing the generator to overcharge, or from overcharging caused by too high an amp setting while being recharged on a battery charger.

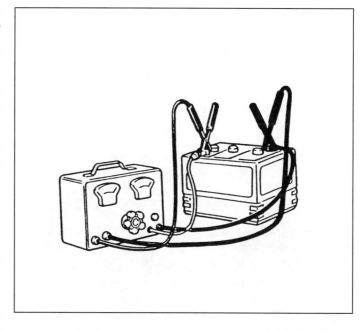

The results of overcharging are warping or buckling of the battery plates, followed by internal shorting of the battery. In addition, a good portion of the electrolyte will be "cooked" away. This will cause most of the chemical attached to the grids to flake and fall off, causing the battery to be useless.

Remember, a long, slow charge from a battery charger is much better for a battery than a fast high-amp "booster" charge. Always **be sure you have the cables connected correctly** before you turn on your battery charger.

It goes without saying, when jump-starting a vehicle, be sure to match negative (black) to negative (black) posts, and positive (red) to positive (red) posts.

Also, when jump-starting a vehicle, hook up your jumper cables to the fully charged battery first. NEVER STAND DIRECTLY OVER THE BATTERY YOU ARE TRYING TO JUMP-START.

Always stand off to one side in case the battery would explode. Remember, the gas that is vented from the battery as it charges is explosive. You should not be smoking or near open flames when jump-starting your car. You do not want to risk damaging your pretty profile as well as that of your car's.

Make your connections to the charged battery first. Then connect the positive jumper cable to the positive post of the dead battery. The last connection should be ground. **It is also suggested that you connect the ground to a metal surface away from the battery— anyplace along the frame is good.**

The idea here is to keep the sparks away from the battery. When you connect the cables to the disabled car, sometimes sparks will occur. If the battery has been "gassing" an explosion could result.

After the car starts, remove the ground cable first, then the positive. After you remove them be sure you do not touch them together. REMEMBER, your cables are still attached to the other battery.

Observe all safety rules, and be sure the brake is set on both vehicles BEFORE you start this process. It is kind of embarrassing if you are run over by your own car.

While this is risky, it can be done, IF YOU ARE CAREFUL! If you are going to do it (and some of you will anyway), here is the safest way. Be sure all of your lights and accessories

The joys of winter

are turned off. Start by connecting to the 12-volt battery first. Then connect the negative to the 6-volt vehicle. Last of all, briefly touch the positive cable directly to the STARTER BATTERY CABLE POST. DO NOT CONNECT DIRECTLY TO THE BATTERY!

It is a good idea to have someone ready to try to start the car when the 12-volt cable touches the starter. **You want to have the 12 volts connected to the 6-volt car for the least amount of time possible!**

Remove the cable as soon as the car is started. If the car fails to start, DO NOT leave the cable connected to the starter. AGAIN, DO NOT connect directly to the 6-volt battery! The same safety rules apply: Do not get run over by your own car.

 RUNDLE'S RULES:

If your car is positive ground, and some were (the positive post of the battery is ground), be sure that you match up the jumper cables to the correct terminals. Always positive to positive and negative to negative. **NO EXCEPTIONS!** Or you may end up like Alice Kramden and go straight to the moon.

REMEMBER THIS HAPPENING?

Here is a battery problem straight from the archives:

 IS IT POSSIBLE TO INTERNALLY REVERSE THE POLARITY OF A BATTERY?

It was possible in the old days, as a result of a heavy discharged battery, to actually "reverse" the polarity of the battery internally.

This was due to overheating from a high charging rate. Sometimes it would occur in just one or two cells, and in severe cases all of the cells will be reversed. In a reversed polarity battery, the grid plates take on each other's chemicals.

A battery with reversed polarity will tend to overheat easily, contain a large amount of sulfation on the plates, and will not take a charge, or will only hold a charge for a short time.

The cure for reversed polarity was a long, slow charge in the correct direction of charge. Sometimes up to two weeks was required. It also may be necessary to "cycle" the battery: Charge it for a few days then install a load on the battery to discharge it completely. Then start the charging process over again.

With some time and patience and lots of good luck, a few of the batteries with reversed polarity were saved. However, not many, and the odds are not in your favor.

 CAN A HYDROMETER TELL ME ANYTHING ELSE ABOUT THE CONDITION OF A BATTERY BESIDES THE CONDITION OF THE ELECTROLYTE?

Besides the overall condition of the electrolyte, you can also check the specific gravity in each cell of the battery. The specific gravity readings of all of the cells should not vary more than half a point (.5). If there is more than a .5 difference between the highest and the lowest cell reading, that is a sign that you have a defective cell in the battery, and the battery itself may need replacing.

 *TIME-SAVING TIPS: There is an easy way to check to see how good your battery connections are between the battery and the starter. **Simply turn on your headlights before you crank over your engine**. If the headlights go completely out when the engine is cranking, you have high resistance in the starting circuit. This can be caused by dirty cables, or a loose cable or wiring connection. If the headlights dim but the engine cranks over and starts right away, you're in good shape.*

 IS THERE ANYTHING NEW IN BATTERY TECHNOLOGY AFTER ALL OF THESE YEARS?

The latest technology in automotive batteries belongs to OPTIMA Batteries, Inc. of Denver, Colorado. By combining traditional lead acid chemistry with innovative construction techniques, OPTIMA Batteries, Inc. has developed what they call a "SpiralCell" design. It is a sealed, maintenance-free battery with outstanding performance characteristics.

The OPTIMA Battery Co., once a division of Gates Rubber Co. of Denver, Colorado, invested twenty years of research and development into these batteries, resulting in the issuance of 20 patents to OPTIMA Batteries, Inc.

OPTIMA BATTERIES

First a little history about OPTIMA Batteries, Inc., then we will compare an OPTIMA battery to a conventional automotive battery and identify the similarities and differences.

In 1973, Gates Rubber Co. of Denver, Colorado, the same company known for the manufacture of automotive belts and hoses, develops a spiral cell battery design to be used for batteries that power portable power tools and small appliances. The batteries are a big success.

In 1984, after 10 years of production of the single spiral cell design batteries, a project team is established by Gates to look into applying the SpiralCell technology to automotive-type batteries.

In 1987, limited production begins of a new type of automotive battery. Although further testing is still going on, the SpiralCell technology has successfully been incorporated for use in an automotive-type battery.

In 1990, the project is declared a success and Gates incorporates the new division as OPTIMA Batteries, Inc.

In 1992, The Gylling Group of Scandinavia, one of the largest importers of the new OPTIMA battery, purchases the company from the Gates Rubber Co.

In 1993, public demand rapidly increases for the new OPTIMA battery. Ground is broken for a new modern OPTIMA Battery manufacturing plant in Denver, Colorado, to meet the growing demands for the new battery.

To have 20 patents issued during the development of a battery, a product that has remained unchanged for 75 plus years, is quite unusual. Let's take a look at a new OPTIMA battery and compare it to a regular automotive battery.

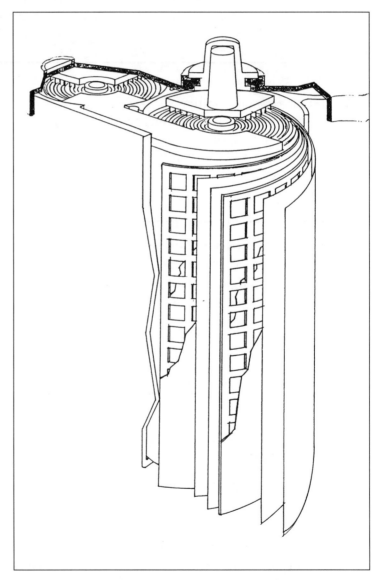

The OPTIMA SpiralCell.

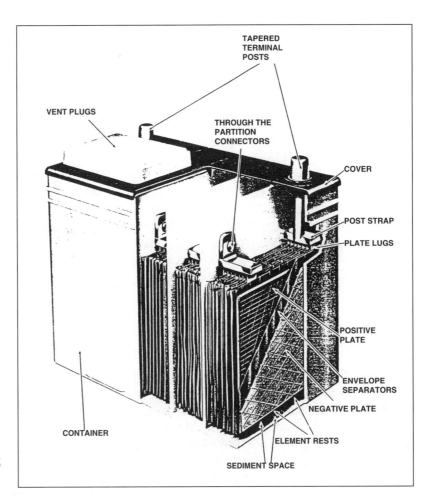

TAPERED TERMINAL POSTS

VENT PLUGS

THROUGH THE PARTITION CONNECTORS

COVER

POST STRAP

PLATE LUGS

POSITIVE PLATE

ENVELOPE SEPARATORS

NEGATIVE PLATE

ELEMENT RESTS

CONTAINER

SEDIMENT SPACE

Conventional Flat Plate Battery.

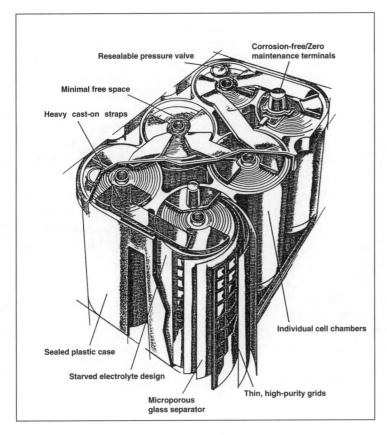

Resealable pressure valve

Corrosion-free/Zero maintenance terminals

Minimal free space

Heavy cast-on straps

Individual cell chambers

Sealed plastic case

Starved electrolyte design

Thin, high-purity grids

Microporous glass separator

OPTIMA SpiralCell Battery Design.

OPTIMA VERSUS CONVENTIONAL BATTERIES

PLATE / GRID CONSTRUCTION	
OPTIMA	**Conventional Battery Design**
Pure lead plates are used to make grid for the cells of the **OPTIMA** battery. Two long bands of grid are wound into a tight spiral configuration, then pressure-inserted into an individual cylinder within the case. This design provides the mechanical strength for the cell, eliminating the need for alloys in the lead. Using lead without alloys extends the life of the **OPTIMA** battery by reducing grid corrosion. Alloys added to the grid of conventional flat plate batteries accelerate corrosion of the plates and, ultimately, shorten the life of the battery. Heat will further accelerate corrosion of the alloys in conventional batteries. The **OPTIMA**, however, with pure lead grid, will resist corrosion and last longer in high temperature environments. The use of pure lead also enhances the electrical conductivity in the cell, contributing to the low internal resistance of the **OPTIMA**. This low resistance allows the **OPTIMA** to deliver high amounts of power quickly to meet the demands of vehicle electrical systems and on-board electronic components. Another advantage of the pure lead used in the **OPTIMA** is a low self-discharge rate. The alloys in conventional batteries act to chemically accelerate the reaction between the active material and the grid, causing a loss of electrical charge. Also, when a conventional battery is stored for a long period of time without recharging, corrosion of the alloys in the grid accelerates. This corrosion forms a boundary layer of nonconductive material between the active lead paste and the grid. This results in a loss of capacity in the battery.	In conventional batteries, a series of flat grids are used in each cell. To improve strength and stiffness (needed for manufacturing, handling, and operation) flat grids have additional materials added, such as antimony and calcium. These alloys in the lead increase corrosion, self-discharge, internal resistance, and promote shedding of the active material (lead paste applied to grid). Additional alloys such as tin, cadmium, and selenium are added to counteract these effects. When a conventional battery is used in extreme high temperature conditions, corrosion of the grid is accelerated. When the grid of a conventional battery corrodes it loses conductivity. The corroded grid also begins to shed the active material (lead paste) more rapidly. This reduction in conductivity and loss of active material results in a loss of power in the battery. This power loss is not immediately apparent but becomes noticeable when demand is highest on a battery, such as starting a car in very cold weather. The loss of active material also shortens the lifespan of the battery. While conventional batteries are adversely affected by heat, the effects of heat on a pure lead **OPTIMA** battery are minimal. Use of alloys in the grid causes trade-offs in terms of performance versus construction benefits. For example, antimony improves castability and paste adherence, but it lowers electrical conductivity and increases the rate of self discharge.

CELL DESIGN

OPTIMA	Conventional Battery Design
Individual cells of the **OPTIMA** contain only two plates, one positive and one negative. These thin pure lead plates are wound into a tight spiral, separated by an absorbent glass material. The separator is very thin, allowing for very close plate spacing. The close proximity of the plates enhances the flow of current and lowers the internal resistance. The porous separator material retains the electrolyte like a sponge, preventing the active material on the plates from drying out.	The cell of a conventional battery contains several plates connected together and suspended in a pool of electrolyte. Alloys are added to the lead grid to increase its strength and stiffness. Stiffness and strength are required for the plates to retain the active material during operation and to make the plates easier to work with during manufacturing.
The tightly wound spiral provides the lead plate with mechanical strength to enable the use of a very thin pure lead grid. Using thinner plates allows more winds in the spiral. This increases the amount of surface area in the cell, which in turn increases the amount of power which can be generated from a battery. The plate surface area of an **OPTIMA** cell is much larger than a similar size conventional battery.	While the alloys do add strength to the grid, they also contribute to corrosion, higher internal resistance, and shedding of active grid material.
After the cell is wound, it is pressure-inserted into an individual chamber with a tight interference fit. This design increases the structural strength of the cell and retains all of the active material on the grid, preventing it from falling off or shedding from the grid.	Sufficient space between the plates in the cell is required for shedding of the active material to prevent electrical shorts. This material falls from the plates and accumulates at the bottom of the case.
Since the **OPTIMA** does not shed active material, it does not need extra space between the plates and below the cell as required in a conventional battery. The **OPTIMA** can take advantage of all of the available space inside the case to maximize the plate size and increase the power of the battery.	This spacing requirement results in a battery that is larger in size, with a lower energy density (energy per pound) and a higher internal resistance than the **OPTIMA**.
Another feature of the tightly wound cell is its resistance to vibration. There is no free space between the plates and separator material. This prevents movement of the plates which causes plate to plate shorting and shedding of the active material.	For the cells to remain operational they must not dry out. The electrolyte must always completely cover the grids in the cell. For this reason, the electrolyte in the conventional battery is filled well above the top of the cell.
	The flat, suspended grids do not have sufficient means to retain the active lead material throughout the life of the battery. When a conventional battery is used in harsh conditions such as high temperatures or high vibration, shedding of the active material increases. This leads to premature battery failure. Typically, the battery fails due to loss of active material or plate to plate shorting.

ELECTROLYTE

OPTIMA	Conventional Battery Design

OPTIMA

The OPTIMA battery is designed as an absorbed electrolyte, recombinant battery. All of the electrolyte is absorbed (like a sponge) within the separator material between the plates in the SpiralCell.

The electrolyte consumes approximately 95% of the voids in the separator material. The remaining 5% is left as open space, for gas passages. Unlike a conventional battery, gas does not collect above the cell in an OPTIMA to create an explosion hazard. During the charging procedure, oxygen is emitted by the positive plate and hydrogen is emitted by the negative plate. These two gases combine to form water, which then recombines back into the electrolyte solution. A result of this absorbed recombinant system is that the battery can be totally sealed. Since the electrolyte is contained in the separator, it does not leak, even if the case is ruptured or broken in an accident.

Since the electrolyte cannot escape via leakage or gassing, the plates will not dry out and cause loss of capacity.

The OPTIMA never needs water and does not gas. Therefore, it can be mounted anywhere in the vehicle. However, good engineering practices make it appropriate to not install the OPTIMA in an airtight space, but to provide some means of ventilation in the event that the vehicle's charging system fails, causing an abusive overcharge. This overcharge could cause the internal safety valves to release some of the pressure within the battery case, resulting in the escape of some of the gas (primarily oxygen and hydrogen).

Another benefit of the sealed, no-gassing design is the elimination of corrosion to battery cables, connectors, and vehicle components.

Conventional Battery Design

A conventional battery is described as a flooded system. Flooded means that there is an excess of electrolyte in the battery above the level of the plates. This excess electrolyte is required to prevent the plates from drying out (causing sulfation of the active material and leading to a failure of the sulfated part of the plate, which reduces the capacity of the battery).

Unlike the OPTIMA, which recombines the gases back into the electrolyte, gases in a conventional battery collect in the free space above the plates; these gases are ultimately vented out of the battery. When a battery is overcharged, gassing increases. The gas being vented (hydrogen and oxygen) is very combustible. If it is ignited by a flame or spark, it can lead to a rapid combustion of the gases. The result is a battery explosion, which can be extremely hazardous.

A portion of the gas which is vented causes corrosion to the battery cables and connectors. This corrosion is often noticeable by the appearance of a white powder or blue fuzz on the terminals.

The conventional battery case must allow for venting of gases. These vents also provide passages for the electrolyte to escape if the battery is tipped over or tilted. If the battery case of a conventional battery is cracked or ruptured, the acid within the battery will escape. Loss of the acid will cause the conventional battery to fail. The escaped acid also poses a risk to people, equipment, and the environment.

FEATURE	FUNCTION	BENEFIT
SPIRAL CELL DESIGN	Greater plate surface area	✓ Increases starting power (CCA - cold cranking amps). ✓ Faster recharging.
	Stronger mechanical design	✓ Withstands vibration, increasing life. ◆ Eliminates shedding of active material. ◆ Reduces internal shorting.
	Pure lead grid	✓ Reduces corrosion for longer life. ✓ Lower internal resistance, which increases conductivity for more starting power and quicker recharging.
	Thinner plates / grid	✓ Higher CCA, for better starting. ✓ Faster recharging.
	Closer, consistent plate spacing	✓ More effective chemical reaction, providing increased starting power. ✓ Faster recharging.
	Reduced battery size	✓ Higher power-to-weight ratio. ◆ Produces power equivalent to conventional batteries several times its size. ✓ Allows it to fit in more vehicles.

ADDITIONAL FEATURES AND BENEFITS

Unique to OPTIMA batteries is the 72-month warranty and a two-year free replacement warranty. They can be shipped by UPS or other carrier (including the airlines) **without a hazmat** (hazardous materials) permit required.

For information about purchasing Optima Batteries See the source pages at the back of the book.

NOTES

Chapter 4

"Let's Go Visit the Generator Family"

Chapter 4

"Let's Go Visit The Generator Family"

Now that we understand the basics of how a battery works and how it is constructed, we can move on to the generator, which is the second most important part of the electrical system.

To sound bona fide, I might as well give you the official job description of the generator. It is "a machine that converts mechanical energy, supplied by the engine, into electrical energy used for either recharging the battery or supplying power to the electrical system."

While that description seems a little confusing, if you follow along a little further we will make sense out of it all. Come on, it'll be better than you think.

THE WORK SCHEDULE FOR THE GENERATOR FAMILY

When the engine speed is at idle or at low rpm, the generator has little or no output, and the battery provides all the electrical energy needed for the electrical system.

When vehicle speed reaches about 20 mph or engine rpm reach about 1200, the generator will begin to charge. The output will help the battery with some of the electrical load. (This speed is known as the generator "cut-in" speed.)

At higher engine rpm of about 1800, the generator is capable of providing all of the electrical current needed to run the accessories, as well as recharge the battery as needed.

Generators will usually provide their maximum output at about 1800 to 2300 rpm engine speed. Normally the pulley diameter of a generator is designed so the engine will spin the generator at, or close to, its ideal rpm, (the rpm at which the generator operates most efficiently.) This rpm is matched to the rpm at which the engine will spend most of its time.

 IN MOST OLDER CAR APPLICATIONS, THE GENERATOR ARMATURE TURNS ABOUT TWICE FOR EVERY RPM THE ENGINE TURNS.

When a generator spins at high speeds (above 3500 rpm engine speed) the output of the generator will actually drop off quite a bit, as the brushes are lifted off of the armature by centrifugal force. If heavier brush springs were used (a great idea), it would cause excessive brush wear at the slow speeds.

An interesting note: Did you ever wonder why over the road trucks get such long life out of their generator brushes as compared to a car? Here are the reasons. One is the constant rpm that make it easy to match the correct engine to generator speed.

The other factor is called air gap. This is when the brushes lift off of the commutator just slightly due to the centrifugal force. The brushes will then experience minimum wear because the brushes are not physically touching the commutator and the loss in output will be slight.

Cars driven in town will wear out generator brushes at a much faster rate than those that spend their life traveling up and down the highway. The same principle applies.

 WHILE WE ARE ON THE SUBJECT OF BRUSHES...BUICK CARS OF THE LATE 1940S AND EARLY 1950S HAD AN INTERESTING SAFETY FEATURE.

They had what they called a "brush protected generator." The "field" wire of the charging system was routed through the ignition system. When the brushes in the generator got too "short" from wear, the field wire would "ground out" the ignition and the car would not start.

While this was a good idea in theory, it left a lot of early-day Buick owners stranded without warning (and very unhappy). The servicemen of the day carried a jumper wire in the tow truck. If this was the problem (a simple check), they used the jumper wire to bypass the generator to ignition circuit. If the car started, they simply drove it back to the dealership and installed new brushes in the generator. And the customer was happily on his way.

 HEY, HOW COME THERE ARE SO MANY DIFFERENT SIZE PULLEYS USED ON THE SAME STYLE OF GENERATOR?

As we learned earlier, the pulley size is matched to the rpm at which the engine will spend most of its time running. In-town delivery trucks had a small diameter pulley so the armature turned faster at the low engine rpm, increasing the output at the slow speeds.

MAKING ELECTRICITY

All generators "make" electricity in much the same way. Let's take a look and see what parts make up a generator and what job each of those parts has to perform. As I have done before, I will give you the official description of what a generator does, then explain things in common English.

Generator operation is based on the principle of electromagnetic induction. This means that voltage is generated when any conductor is moved at right angles through a magnetic field. When voltage is produced in this manner, it will cause the current to flow in the conductor if that conductor is a complete circuit. Whew! Got all that? Now let's explain that in commonsense terms, starting with the internal parts.

ARMATURE - An armature starts out as a bare hardened steel shaft. To this shaft is added a series or group of non-insulated copper wires wound close together. They in turn will form

How a generator develops voltage.

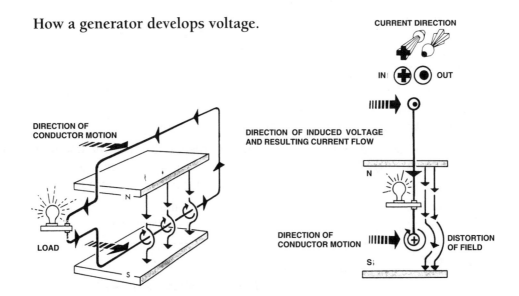

what is called a loop. The loops of wire are then embedded in a series of slots in an iron core. This iron core is then attached to the armature shaft. This shaft spins and helps to generate the electrical current. As you might guess, the size of the wire and the number of wires in the loop will affect the output of the generator.

COMMUTATOR - The commutator is a series of segments or bars that are also attached to the armature shaft at the rear of the armature. It is the wire ends from the loops of the armature windings in the iron core that are attached to the commutator. When this is done, a complete circuit is formed.

FIELD COILS - Field coils are the windings or the group of wires that are wrapped around the pole magnet. It is the job of the field coils to take the current drawn to the pole magnet, and make it stronger. (Field coils are the windings that are attached to the inside of the generator housing.) This increased strength in current will force even more current to be drawn to the pole magnets, which will continue to build up current.

This is how the current produced by the generator is built up and increased, until it can be used by the battery and the accessories.

BRUSHES - After the generator develops the current, it is the brushes that carry the current to the

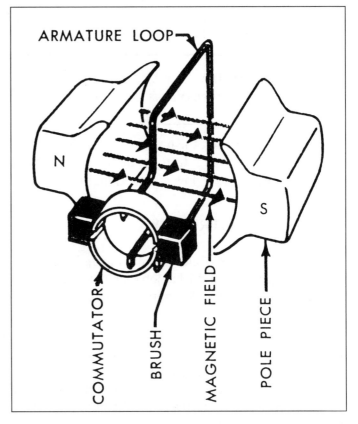

The ends of the armature loop are securely attached to a split ring called a commutator.

"field" circuit and the "load" circuit, so the electricity can be used by the battery and the accessories. This process is called "commutation." The brushes will ride on the commutator segments of the armature. Brush holders hold the brushes in position by way of spring tension.

Most automotive generators will contain two brushes, one that is grounded to the frame of the generator, one that will be insulated from the frame.

The insulated brush is the positive brush and is connected to the "A" terminal of the generator, and to one end of the field coils. The other end of the field coil is connected to the insulated "F" terminal of the generator.

BEARINGS AND BUSHINGS - At either end of a generator you will find a bushing or a bearing. They have the job of making the armature shaft run true in the housing between the field coils and pole shoes.

Bushings will be made of copper or brass and are soaked in oil before they are installed. The brass or copper bushing material is porous and able to absorb the oil like a sponge. This provides the lubrication between the shaft and the bushing. They can also be re-oiled from the oiling tube on the outside of the generator.

Some heavy-duty generators will use ball bearings instead of bushings for the armature shaft to ride in. This is done to support a radiator fan or other accessory.

BUILDING A WORKING GENERATOR

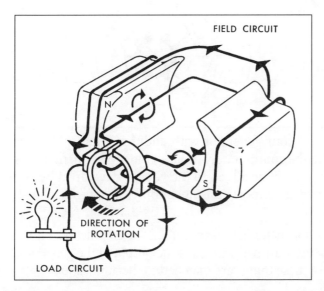

This illustration depicts the relationship between the magnetic field from a permanent magnet, the direction of motion of a conductor cutting through this magnetic field, and the current flow direction from the voltage.

An assembled generator will look something like this: The electrical rule that applies to a generator states that "electrical voltage will be generated when any conductor is moved at right angles through a magnetic field."

To demonstrate this theory to yourself take a simple horseshoe magnet and stand it on its side. (It will have a north pole and a south pole, just like in your generator.)

Now take a piece of plain copper wire and move it back and forth between the poles of the magnet. You will be breaking the magnetic field, which will produce a magnetic current inside of your wire. This is exactly what the armature does to the field coils.

When current is produced this way, it will cause current to flow in the conductor if it is a complete circuit. (Remember the armature with the loops of wire embedded in the slots of an iron core? Didn't the ends go down and connect to the commutator to form a complete circuit?) Okay, so you're lost....

First let's look at a simple generator with an armature that has only one turn or loop of wire and two pole pieces. These pole pieces (actually magnets) will always have some "magnetism" left over from the last job they did.

However, these magnets are weak because of the magnetic field between them. (Remember these two magnets are exactly opposite of each other. That is the cause of the weak current. They will tend to cancel out each other.)

If we place the armature between these two magnets and then spin it in a clockwise direction, a weak voltage will be "generated." Remember, the rule of generators says that any current generated will flow to the conductor if it is a complete circuit. Because the armature is a complete circuit, the current will flow to the armature and then to the field coils where the voltage will be increased.

The rotating armature cutting through the current produced by the field coils forces even more current through the field coils that makes still more stronger voltage. This is how the voltage generated by the loop is increased into voltage that can be used by the battery and the accessories.

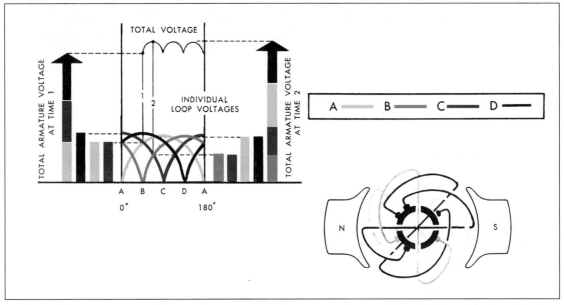

Now, if we were to add a real armature to our generator with additional loops of wires imbedded in an iron core and connected to the commutator, what is going to happen? That's right. Any voltage generated by any one loop will be added to the voltage developed by any of the other loops. By having multiple loops, an almost constant supply of voltage is developed, finally!

As you might guess, the strength of the magnetic field, the number of conductors on the armature, and the speed at which the armature is turned will affect the output of the generator. Just like the internal parts of a battery, all of these things are matched to the application.

OK, SO OUR GENERATOR IS CHARGING. WHAT HAPPENS IF WE SPIN THE ARMATURE REALLY FAST TO PROVIDE A HIGH OUTPUT FOR A HEAVY ELECTRICAL LOAD?

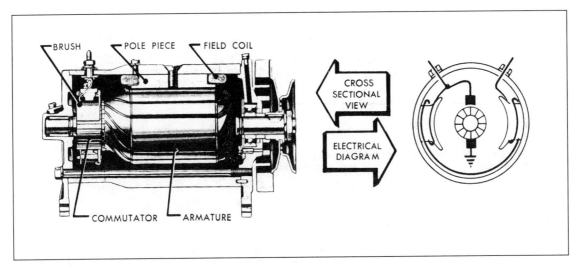

BRUSH   POLE PIECE   FIELD COIL

CROSS SECTIONAL VIEW

ELECTRICAL DIAGRAM

COMMUTATOR   ARMATURE

Right. Things are going to get hot, in part because of the resistance or electrical friction and in part due to the mechanical friction. What will happen to our generator then?

The high heat can melt the "varnish" and damage the insulation used to hold the loops or conductors in the armature slots. Also, the soldered connections of the armature coils and the commutator bars will melt from the heat. When this happens, it is commonly called "throwing the solder" out of the generator. Besides losing all of the solder, the bars of the commutator separate from the shaft that holds everything together; in simple terms, everything just flies apart, and the generator is ruined.

To prevent this damage, a current regulator is necessary. Just as it sounds, a current regulator limits the amount of current the generator is allowed to produce for both the electrical demand of the accessories, and the safe limit of current the generator can produce without damage to the generator itself.

Another source of internal heat that has to be dealt with is called "iron loss." The iron core of the armature will act as a large electrical conductor, and will "cut" magnetic "lines" of energy as the armature spins. As a result, the armature core itself will generate unwanted current. The current developed by the core of the armature is mixed with the current developed by the regular conductors of the armature.

This creates excess heat inside of the generator that is not wanted. To overcome this problem, the iron core of an armature is made up of thin sections of steel material that is laminated together. By doing this, the lamination or varnish will act as an insulator and help to prevent the flow of core current to the regular conductors of the armature.

Last on our parts list is the fan. It is mounted behind the pulley and has the job of keeping the generator cool. In some heavy-duty applications, the fan gets a little help from the engine intake where some of the air intake from the engine is used to cool the generator.

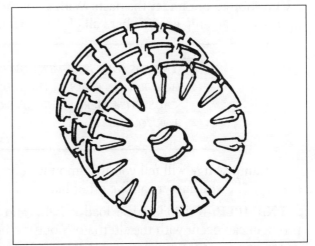

To overcome the problem of excess heat, the iron core of an armature is composed of thin sections of steel material that is laminated together.

TIME-SAVING TIP*: Before we go on, here's a quick reminder to check the
wiring between the regulator and the generator. While this sounds like a no-
brainer, you would be surprised how many times the wiring gets switched by
accident. So as a simple review, and in order for everything to work properly,
things should be connected as follows.*

1) The positive wire from the generator will be connected from a post on the generator (marked either "B" for battery or "A" for armature) and should be connected to the (armature) terminal of the regulator.

2) The field terminal of the generator should connect to the field terminal of the regulator.

3) And finally, the wire that travels down from the amp gauge in the dash to the regulator should connect to the "BATT" terminal of the regulator.

Did you know...The amp gauge only tells you what is going into or what is being drawn out of the battery? It is not connected directly to the generator to tell you if the generator is actually charging or not charging as commonly believed. (This idea comes from the belief that the generator has to be working if the gauge shows a charge.)

Volt meters are also sometimes used instead of an ammeter in the dash of a vehicle to show the condition of the charging system. Volt meters became quite common in the 1960s with the introduction of alternator charging systems.

This was done so no "heavy" current had to be carried up to the dash. By using a volt meter, a much smaller gauge of wire could be used with less danger of electrical fire when a wire shorted out under the dash. With a volt meter, only minimal amps were on hand, as opposed to an amp gauge where all of the generator's output passed through the gauge.

 *THERE IS SOME ARGUMENT OVER WHICH **GAUGE** IS MORE
ACCURATE IN READING THE TRUE CONDITION OF AN ELECTRI-
CAL SYSTEM. HERE IS THE DIFFERENCE; YOU CAN THEN DECIDE
FOR YOURSELF.*

An **amp gauge** will tell you the amount of amps passing into or being drawn out of the battery. The **volt meter**, on the other hand, will tell you the "pressure" behind the amps.

EXAMPLE: If the electrical load is light, and there is not much resistance, in theory a problem can occur with the alternator's output; however, it will not show up on the voltage gauge because the amp demand is low, so the pressure will remain strong. But when the electrical load increases, then the voltage will drop, exposing the problem. From a safety standpoint, some engineers believe the minimal amps is better.

This problem will occur more often with cars of the 1960s and with alternator charging systems. (We will get into alternators in an upcoming chapter). An alternator can have a blown diode that will take away (in most cases) one-third of the alternator's charging ability. But if the amp load is light, the voltage will not drop until the amp load increases.

Chapter 4 Review

1) The **cut-in speed** of a generator is the rpm that a generator begins to provide an output, typically about 1200 rpm vehicle engine speed or about 20 mph.

2) **Generator pulley diameter** is determined by the rpm at which the vehicle engine spends most of its time, and the rpm at which the generator operates most efficiently. In other words, the goal is to spin the generator at the rpm it is most efficient while the vehicle engine is running at the rpm it is most efficient .

3) **Throwing the solder** out of a generator means that because of high rpm and excessive heat caused by a high amp load, the solder that holds the segments to the armature has melted. The centrifugal force of the spinning armature has caused the segments to break away from the armature. In short, you have just toasted your generator.

Chapter

5

"Keeping Track of the Generator's Output"

Chapter 5

Keeping Track Of The Generator's Output

Now that we understand how a generator manufactures electricity, we need to figure out how to control the output of current from the generator. As we said in the last chapter this is done by the use of a voltage regulator.

Let's start at the beginning and see how this happens. Inside the voltage regulator is a set of contact points, much like those found in an ignition distributor. To these contact points is connected a wire from the field coils. When the points in the regulator open and close it will start and stop the flow of current to the field coils, battery, and accessories.

NOW THAT WE HAVE A BRIEF UNDERSTANDING OF WHAT THE REGULATOR DOES, LET'S TAKE A FEW MINUTES AND TALK TERMINALS. THE TERMINALS ON A REGULATOR ARE CLEARLY MARKED. BUT SOMETIMES THEY STILL DON'T MAKE SENSE...UNTIL NOW.

▼ TERMINAL TALK

BATT - This is the battery terminal. This terminal connects the voltage regulator to the amp gauge in the dash, on its way to the battery.

GEN OR ARM - This terminal is always connected to the armature post on the generator.

F or FLD - This terminal is always connected to the field post of the generator.

IGN - This is a terminal used mainly before the war (1944). This terminal was used on the early regulators that controlled the voltage of the entire electrical system at the ignition switch. In the old days, it was believed that controlling the voltage at the ignition switch was the best way to furnish an even voltage to the entire electrical system. Later on, the voltage was controlled by the battery terminal of the regulator and this ignition terminal disappeared.

It will not be necessary to have this terminal and with the replacement regulator you won't use it, but that ignition wire will still be "hot," so you need to fold it back into the original harness and wrap it with black electrical tape in order to insulate the end well to prevent a short. In case someone wants to do a 100 percent restoration in another lifetime, everything else will match up perfectly for them.

Meanwhile, when our original generator begins charging and produces enough current to begin recharging the battery, it will travel up through the regulator to the contact points. Beside the contact points is a shunt coil. A shunt coil is made up of many windings of a fine wire that is shunted (wires connecting two points in an electric circuit that has the ability to turn away part of the circuit) across the generator. The current here is not allowed to reverse.

When the voltage is strong enough, the magnetism developed from this shunt coil will close the contact points and allow the current to pass through the series windings and on to the battery and accessories.

In turn, when the generator slows down or stops, current begins to flow in reverse from the battery to the generator. This reverses the direction that the current travels through the series windings. This will cause the magnetic field in the series windings to reverse. But as we learned earlier, the magnetic current from the shunt coil is not allowed to reverse. So instead of helping each other out, they work against each other. When this happens, the resulting magnetic field is no longer strong enough to overcome the spring tension on the contact points. The points are opened, stopping the flow of current to the field coils.

Just when you thought things couldn't get any more difficult, and we had everything figured out, there is one more factor to consider for regulator control. That is temperature compensation. Because a cold battery is harder to charge than a warm one (due to higher resistance), the regulator must allow for this. To do that, a regulator is built with a bi-metal "thermostatic" hinge. What this means is the material the contact point arm is made of is temperature-sensitive to cause the regulator to regulate to a higher voltage during colder weather in order to charge a cold battery.

CURRENT REGULATION

Besides the voltage being regulated, the current output (amps) of a generator is also regulated by what is called a current regulator. The current regulator is built inside of the voltage regulator and works in much the same way as the voltage regulator.

The main difference you will notice is that located on the inside of the voltage regulator, the current side of the regulator is made up of wire that is thicker (heavier gauge), and there are less turns or wraps of wire on the coil. Remember, the current regulator has to carry all of the amps the generator is producing.

Ok, do these regulators work together or separately?

They are unfriendly and will never work together. One or the other will do the work depending on the load. For instance, if the generator is spinning fast, the battery has a good charge, but most of the accessories are turned on, then the voltage regulator is the one doing the work.

If, on the other hand, the generator is turning slowly, the battery is in need of a charge, and all of the accessories are turned on, it will be the current regulator doing the work.

This type of circuit where the regulator is a part of the field circuit is called an "A" circuit. An "A" circuit is easily identified because the contact points are always located after the field coils. This type of circuit is common to the General Motors family of vehicles.

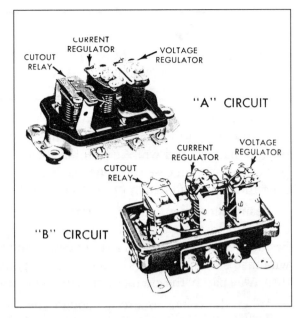

 OK, MY SHOP MANUAL SAYS I HAVE A "B" CIRCUIT REGULATOR. HOW IS THAT DIFFERENT FROM AN "A" CIRCUIT REGULATOR?

The voltage regulator and current regulator are units in the external circuit used to "sense" either high voltage supplied to the electrical system or high current supplied to the external loads.

A "B" circuit regulator works in much the same way that an "A" circuit type regulator does. The only difference is the contact points are located before the field coils instead of after. There is no advantage to either location and they both work equally well.

"B" circuit regulators are common to Ford cars and trucks.

CHECKING REGULATOR OUTPUT

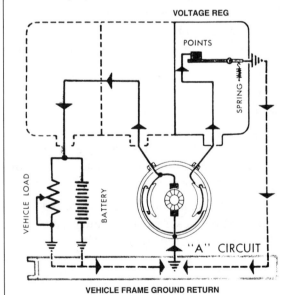

This illustration shows the various factors involved in voltage regulation and the manner in which it is done.

 "SO DO YOU CHECK AND ADJUST "A" AND "B" CIRCUIT REGULATORS THE SAME WAY?"

No, They are both checked differently. If you have to adjust the regulator at some point in time, it is best to follow the directions in your shop manual. The secret is to know how the regulator works; then reading those directions will make sense.

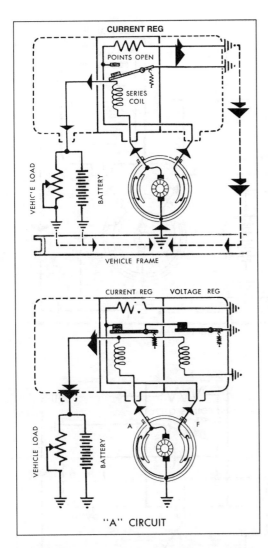

"A" CIRCUIT

A simplified circuit employing both current and voltage regulators is illustrated. The regulator or contact points are located "after" the field coils ("A" circuit). The field circuit is attached to the insulated brush inside the generator.

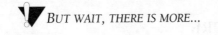 BUT WAIT, THERE IS MORE...

The "A" and "B" circuit are by far the most common types, but not the only types of regulator circuits. There are a few others you may encounter. They include Third Brush, Bucking Field, and Split Field .

 OK, ALL I HAVE IS A GENERAL REPAIR MAN-UAL, HOW DO I KNOW IF I HAVE AN "A" CIRCUIT OR A "B" CIRCUIT REGULATOR?

Simple. All you have to do is check the connections at the brushes and the fields. If the generator field coil is connected to the insulated brush at the back of the generator, you have an "A" circuit.

If the generator field coil lead is connected to either the grounded brush (a brush that goes to ground) inside of the generator, or is connected to the inside of the generator frame itself, you have a "B" circuit. From there all you have to do is follow the directions given in the repair manual.

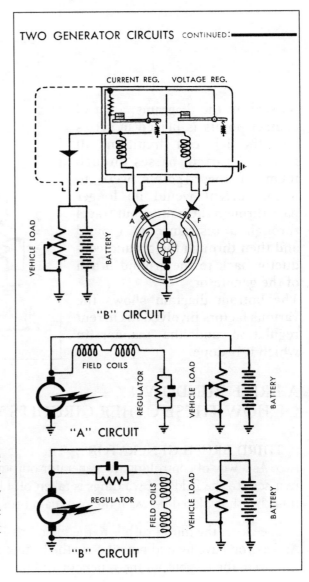

TWO GENERATOR CIRCUITS CONTINUED:

"B" CIRCUIT

"A" CIRCUIT

"B" CIRCUIT

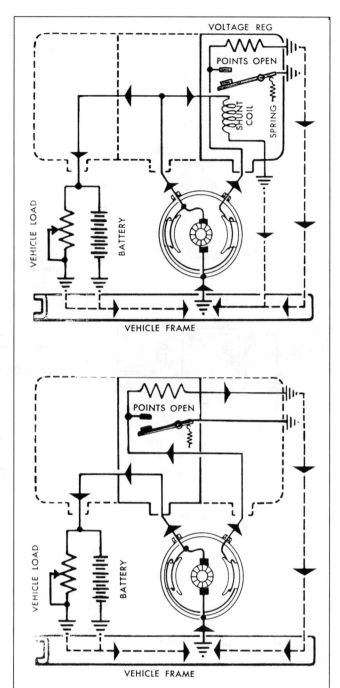

As seen in the diagrams, a set of contact points is placed in series with the field coil circuit and all field coil current passes through them. If these points were to open, current would no longer pass through the points, but travel through a resistance to ground and then through the ground conductor back to the ground brush of the generator.

The bottom diagram shows the various factors involved in current regulation and the manner in which it is done.

A BRIEF RUNDOWN
OF HOW THESE OTHER CIRCUITS WORK

THIRD BRUSH GENERATORS - This type of generator uses three brushes instead of two. As a way of controlling the generator output, the field circuit is connected so the current sent to the field coil windings is taken off of the commutator by this third brush. The third brush is placed between the two main brushes and is adjustable.

The closer the third brush is to the main brush, the more output the generator will have. And as you have figured out by now, the further away from the main brush the third brush is moved, the less output the generator will have.

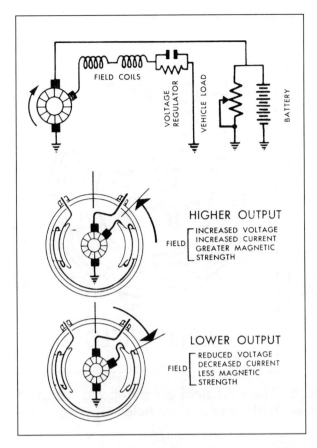

FIELD COILS

VOLTAGE REGULATOR

VEHICLE LOAD

BATTERY

HIGHER OUTPUT

FIELD { INCREASED VOLTAGE
INCREASED CURRENT
GREATER MAGNETIC
STRENGTH

LOWER OUTPUT

FIELD { REDUCED VOLTAGE
DECREASED CURRENT
LESS MAGNETIC
STRENGTH

Third Brush type generators use three brushes instead of two. The closer the third brush is to the main brush, the more output the generator will have.

This third brush system works similarly to a voltage regulator. When the third brush is moved away from the main brush, the current to the field windings is reduced and the output drops.

Third brush generators were used a lot on farm tractors and cars of the early days. The advantage was that they did not need a voltage regulator. In cars, for instance, when you turned on the lights at night, you also "turned up" the third brush in the generator to increase the output.

The bad side was if you forgot to return the third brush to its original setting the next morning, it would overcharge during the day and boil all of the water out of the battery.

Because most of the early generators were low output of about 20 amps max, this setup worked pretty well. There were not many accessories to run and the electrical load was light.

CUTOUTS - These were simple early regulators. The cutout had a set of single contact points and a small shunt coil mounted inside a little metal box that mounted to the top of the generator.

When the battery was low, the points closed and generator current was allowed to pass on to the battery. When the battery became fully charged, the magnetic field developed and opened the points, stopping the flow of current to the battery.

Most of the cutouts were used on cars and trucks of the late 1920s and early 1930s. They were also quite common on farm tractors of that era. Most were used on generators that had a 20 amp output or less.

While they worked okay, cutouts were affected by moisture and vibration. Moisture would cause the points to stick together and cause overcharging. Sometimes vibration would cause the cutout to lose its ground, causing the generator not to charge. On a rare occasion, the points would stick together after they had "arced" a number of times. When the vehicle was turned off and the points would stick together, it would run the battery down in about three to four hours, while also welding the points together.

TECH TIP: *A company called Fifth Avenue Antique Auto Parts located at 415 Court Street in Clay Center, KS 67432 (Ph. 913-632-3450) offers a modern solid state cutout. The cutout they offer will work with a positive or negative ground system as well as 6 or 12 volts. A solid state cutout will eliminate most of the common problems associated with the early style cutouts. This modern style cutout is internally grounded and does not depend on an outside ground. Solid-state construction means no more sticking points.*

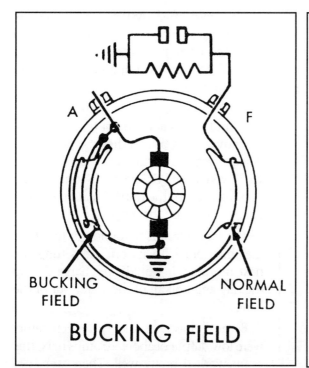

BUCKING FIELD

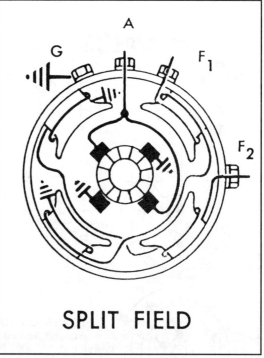

SPLIT FIELD

A bucking field coil is a shunt coil of high resistance that controls voltage on a bucking field generator.

The split field generator was designed with an additional field coil circuit.

THE OTHER STYLE OF GENERATOR/REGULATORS INCLUDE:

BUCKING FIELD GENERATORS - Some generators will have additional turns of wire on the armature to enable them to develop voltage at idle and low speed. An example is some of the marine applications that are 32-volt systems and require the extra output at the slow speeds, in order to produce 32 volts at the higher rpm. When these generators are operated at high rpm, it is possible for them to produce more than the required voltage. When this happens, the regulator can no longer control the voltage. This means trouble in paradise.

The solution to this problem is what is called a Bucking Field Coil. (Pay attention here because this is pretty tricky.) This is a shunt coil regulator just like in a normal regulator except that it has high resistance. It is also connected to one of the pole pieces of the generator that in turn is connected "directly across the brushes of the armature."

The trick here is that the shunt coil is wound backwards and has the opposite effect of a normal shunt coil. At low speeds, the magnetic field of this shunt coil is small compared to the normal output. But at high speeds, when the output of the generator is high and the resistance is high, the reverse windings will tend to cancel out the extra voltage. Pretty slick, huh?

 WHAT ABOUT THE POINTS IN A REGULATOR; DOES IT MATTER HOW MANY AMPS PASSES THROUGH THEM?

So glad you asked. As a matter of fact, it does. Each and every time the points open and close to break the current, a small "arc" of electricity occurs. This arc of electricity will burn off a little of the contact surface each time. The more amperes present, the bigger the arc and more of the contact surface will be lost (just like it does in a set of ignition points).

SO IF THE AMPERAGE THAT PASSES THROUGH THE CONTACT POINTS IS KEPT LOW, THEN THE LIFE OF THE POINTS WILL BE EXTENDED. OK, SO HOW MUCH IS TOO MUCH?

In general, the engineers say 6-volt systems should handle 2 amps as the max for the field circuit. For the 12-volt system, 1.5 amps is the maximum limit. What all of this means is that when the engineers design a charging system, they have to design the regulator first because of the design limits. This will insure that they will have a reliable charging system.

SPLIT FIELD GENERATORS -This is another special application generator. When the engine in a car spends most of its time idling or at low rpm, the generator does not turn fast enough for any current to be produced. Soon the battery will become discharged. So a way was devised to increase the output of a generator at idle and low rpm.

The answer is a split field generator. As you might guess, this generator has two field circuits. The magnetic field is increased by using a second field coil circuit. Generator output can begin at low rpm to keep the battery charged and supply power for the accessories.

This is done by placing a second set of brushes, field coils and pole shoes (magnets) inside of the generator. For all practical purposes, it is like two generators in the same case. Some of the applications that use this style of generator include city buses and home delivery vans.

REGULATOR POLARITY - Some regulators are designed for use with negative ground systems, while others are designed to be used with positive ground systems. Using the wrong regulator on an application (which happens fairly often) will cause the regulator points to pit and burn badly, resulting in a short regulator life. Not polarizing a generator can also cause these same problems.

 OK, SO HOW CAN I TELL BY LOOKING AT A REGULATOR WHAT POLARITY IT IS?

Normally, when they were new, most regulators were marked. The other way to tell is that positive ground regulators will have copper-colored current and voltage regulator coils, while the negative ground regulators will have cadmium- or straw-colored coils.

GENERATOR POLARITY - This is simply the direction the current is flowing between the battery and the charging system. As we learned earlier, the pole pieces in a generator will store up magnetism. When a generator produces voltage, the left-over magnetism will cause the current to flow in the direction it last traveled.

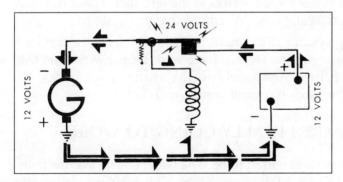

An illustration of what happens when the generator is of the opposite polarity from that of the battery. The plus and minus signs indicate the direction of current flow.

When a generator has been removed for repair, the magnetism is sometimes lost in the pole pieces. So when the generator is reinstalled, it must be "polarized." This means the magnetism must be reinstalled in the pole pieces to insure the current travels to the battery in the right direction.

61

Remember our example in the battery chapter? We said in order to recharge the battery, we had to deliver current to the battery in the opposite way it left the battery. When we polarize a generator, we are matching the flow of current to the battery.

OK, SO IF I FORGET TO POLARIZE MY GENERATOR, WHAT WILL HAPPEN?

Just as we learned earlier in this chapter, it will cause the points in the voltage regulator to stick and burn. It can also run your battery down, as well as cause serious damage to the generator itself.

HOW DO I POLARIZE MY GENERATOR?

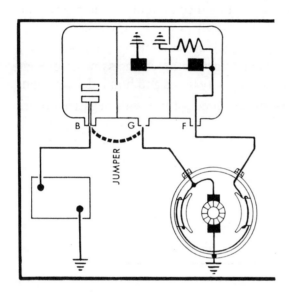
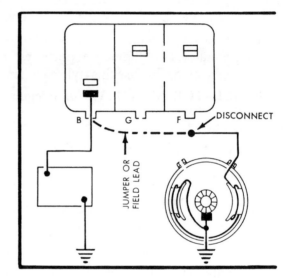

Polarization of "A" circuit generators.   Polarization of "B" circuit generators.

To polarize an "A" circuit charging system you can use your jumper wire. First connect one end to the field terminal of the regulator. Now strike the "BATT" terminal with the other end. Once or twice will do, just until you see a few sparks at the terminal. That's it, you're done! (FYI: General Motors products typically used "A" circuit charging systems.)

To polarize a "B" circuit charging system, disconnect the Field wire from the regulator and strike it on the "BATT" wire of the regulator. DO NOT use your jumper wire to do this; it will burn the points inside of the regulator. Again, only briefly, when you see sparks, you are done! (FYI: Ford products typically used "B" circuit regulators.)

TOOL TIME - YOUR TOOLS ARE FINALLY GOING TO WORK

The old reliable '50 Chevrolet ain't what she used to be. The battery is always dead, and driving home at night you kind of hope for a full moon. Okay, so it is pretty obvious the charging system is not working. You even consider taking the Weber grill out of the trunk.

The question is, what is at fault? You have already checked out the battery so it has to be either the generator or the regulator. How do you check? What if your neighbor isn't home so you can't borrow his volt meter, can you still find the problem with just a jumper wire, the only electrical tool you have? Yes, you can! Here is how.

How to Perform the Full Fielding the Generator Test

• First round up your jumper wire. To check the regulator, start the car with the garage door open, brake set, etc. Turn the idle speed up to about 1000 or 1100 rpm. (This is the speed that your generator will begin to charge, also known as the cut-in speed.)

• Start by checking the ground of the regulator. One end of your jumper wire will connect to the frame of the regulator; the other end to a good ground. If things begin to charge again, you have found your problem--poor ground. (This is quite common.)

• If you still have a no-charge condition, connect one end of your jumper wire to the field terminal of the regulator, and the other end to a good ground (like the intake manifold or the engine block). What you are doing is bypassing the regulator to see if the generator is working.

• Now look at your dash gauge. If the dash gauge shows an increase in the output, the chances are quite good that your regulator is at fault. But if there is no increase in output, the chances are good that your generator is at fault.

To be sure, you can remove the jumper wire ground from the engine block, and strike it against a metal surface. No sparks will confirm that the generator is indeed not working.

This test should take just a few minutes at most, then you will want to remove your jumper wire. The test you have just completed is called **Full Fielding the Generator.** What you just did was allow the generator to charge at its maximum capacity for a brief time, just as if there was not a regulator attached in the circuit, to see if the generator was still working.

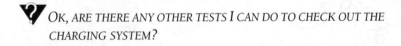

OK, ARE THERE ANY OTHER TESTS I CAN DO TO CHECK OUT THE CHARGING SYSTEM?

You also can hook up your volt meter to the "A" terminal on the generator. With the car running at a fast idle, if you have a low reading of 2-4 volts, and increasing the rpm doesn't increase the voltage, the chances are good you have an open field circuit (broken wire). It could be inside of the generator itself or outside of the generator in the wiring harness or other connections.

An open circuit in the armature windings will cause severe arcing between the brushes and the commutator. This arcing of the commutator and brushes can be seen at the back of the generator while the generator is working. Another giveaway to this condition is that it will take about twice the rpm to get the normal output from your generator.

An armature with a grounded circuit will also have a low output. A grounded armature circuit means that the normally insulated part of the armature is now touching the ground or return side of the winding, causing a short.

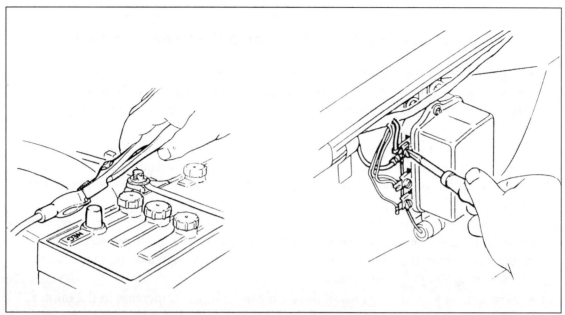

1. When working on regulators, it is always wise to first remove the battery ground strap lead from the battery post. This prevents any short circuits or accidental grounds from occurring.

2. Then remove the lead or leads connected to the battery or "BATT" terminal of the regulator.

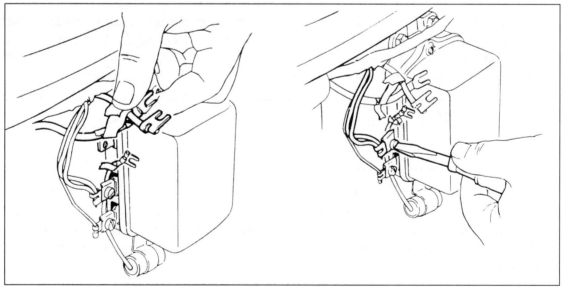

3. To aid in correctly rewiring to the replacement regulator, code the wires in some manner that will aid in proper installation. In this case, one piece of tape has been used to identify those wires that came off the first, or battery, terminal.

4. Then remove the lead or leads connected to the generator, or "ARM," terminal of the regulator.

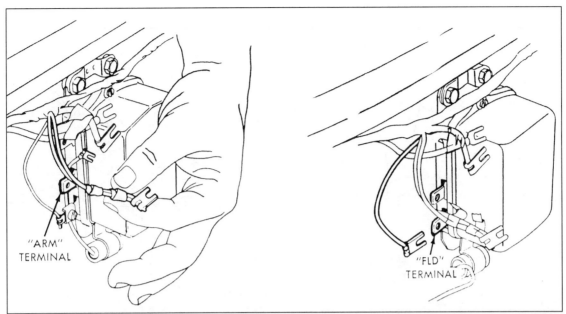

5. Code the lead or leads in some manner to facilitate correctly rewiring the new unit. In this case, two strips of tape have been used to denote those leads removed from the second, or "ARM," terminal.

6. Then remove the lead from the Field or "FLD" terminal of the regulator. Since this is the remaining lead, no coding or tape is necessary.
Note that the condenser is never attached to this terminal.

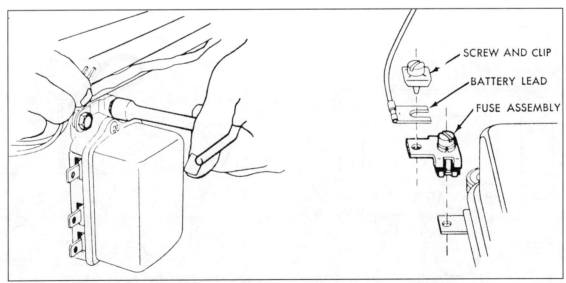

7. The position of any leads attached to either the mounting screws or attached to the base of the regulator should be noted to insure the proper reassembly process, before removing the regulator. With all wires disconnected, the regulator can be removed from its mounting.

8. Some regulators have a fuse attached to the "BATT" terminal. This should be removed for use with the new replacement regulator.

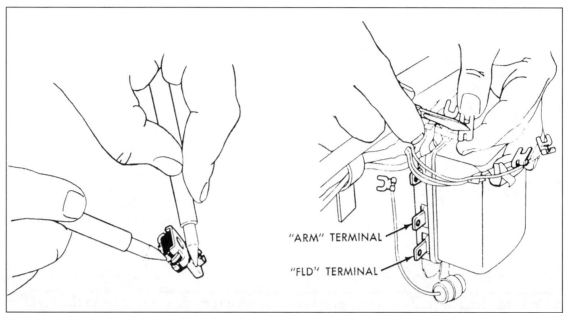

9.Before using the fuse on the replacement regulator, it should be tested for continuity with a test lamp. This is to make sure the fuse is not defective or "blown," which would result in an open circuit.

10. After replacement regulator has been remounted into position, scrape all lead connections or terminals clean to provide a good metal-to-metal contact when reconnected to the regulator terminals.

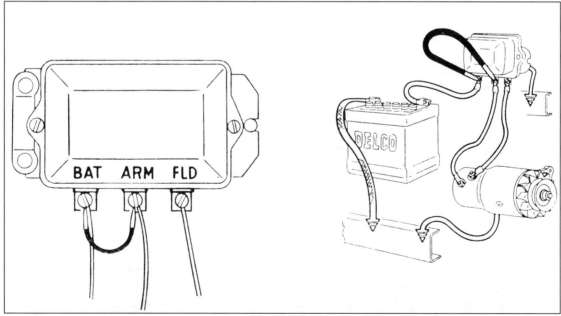

11.After all leads are reconnected and before the engine is started, the generator should be polarized by momentarily connecting a jumper wire between the "GEN" and "BATT" terminals of the regulator. Just a touch of the jumper to both terminals is all that is required.

TESTING "B" CIRCUIT REGULATORS

The tests for a "B" circuit regulator will be outlined in your shop manual and will be similar to those for an "A" circuit. The results you get will also help you to determine which part of your charging system is at fault. Again, most of these tests are easy to perform if you first understand how things work.

 CAN I CHECK THE GENERATOR BY ITSELF OFF OF THE CAR TO SEE IF IT WORKS?

Yes, you can. This is called "motoring" the generator, and is a simple test. (This test can also be done on the car, if you loosen and remove the fan belt first). All that it requires is a fully charged battery of the same voltage as your generator.

Using battery jumper cables, connect the positive post of the battery to the armature "A" terminal of the generator.

Now connect the battery ground cable to the negative post on the battery and the frame of the generator. A working generator should run or spin just like an electric motor.

If you hook up your ammeter for this test, (positive to positive, negative to ground) a 6-volt generator should draw from 4-6 amps, while motoring.

Excessive amp draw tells you the generator needs some work. Be sure you hook up the battery cables to the generator correctly or you will reverse the polarity of the generator.

As a reminder, it is always a good idea to polarize a new or rebuilt generator after it is installed on the car but before the car is started. This will allow a surge of current to flow through the generator, which will remind it which way the current is supposed to flow. And don't forget to check the water in the battery after all of this playing around. Overcharging generators will boil the water out of a battery in a short time.

One final thing: undercutting. While we are not getting into the actual repair of your generator, as that is best left to the repair shops, there is a term used quite often when repairing generators and starters. You will hear about having to "undercut" the armature. What is that anyway, and does it hurt? No.

As the brushes wear on the commutator, the "fillings," or the part of the brush that wears off, will collect in the space between the commutator bars. In addition, dirt and grease, along with these fillings, will collect on the commutator bars themselves. A dirty commutator will cause poor generator performance.

The solution to cleaning dirty commutator bars is placing the armature in a metal lathe and polishing the commutator bars with 00 sandpaper. Another way is by using a special cutting tool to remove a small amount from the surface of the bars.

After the commutator bars are clean, the grooves between the bars must also be cleaned. Again a special tool is used to cut a 1/32-inch groove between the commutator bars. This process will restore the commutator bars to like-new condition.

This process is also done to starter armatures as well, for the same reason: To clean the surface area so the brushes can make good contact with the armature.

Chapter 5 Review

1) Generator to regulator connections:

The "A" terminal of the generator will always connect to the "ARM" armature terminal of the regulator.

The "F" terminal of the generator will always connect to the "FLD" field terminal of the regulator.

The "BATT" terminal of the regulator will always connect to the wire coming down from the "AMP" gauge.

An "IGN" terminal was common on pre-1944 regulators. These regulators ran the entire electrical system output through the ignition switch. This style of regulator can be replaced with a newer style, which we learned to do in this chapter.

2) "A" or "B" circuit?

"A" circuit regulators will ALWAYS have the contact points located AFTER the field circuit.

"B" circuit regulators will ALWAYS have the contact points located BEFORE the field circuit.

2a) Another way to tell the difference is check the generator itself. If the generator "F" terminal wire is connected to the insulated brush at the back of the generator, you have an "A" circuit.

If, on the other hand, the generator "F" terminal wire is connected to the grounded brush or is grounded by a bolt or screw to the inside of the generator case, you have a "B" circuit charging system.

3) To polarize an "A" circuit charging system you can use your jumper wire. First connect one end to the field terminal of the regulator. Now strike the "BATT" terminal with the other end. Once or twice will do, just until you see a few sparks at the terminal. That's it, you're done! (FYI: GM products typically used "A" circuit charging systems.)

4) To polarize a "B" circuit charging system, disconnect the "Field " wire from the regulator and strike it on the "BATT" wire of the regulator. DO NOT use your jumper wire to do this; it will burn the points inside of the regulator. Again, only briefly; when you see sparks, you are done! (FYI: Ford products typically used "B" circuit regulators.)

NOTES

Chapter 6

"Cranking Motors...or 'Starters' to the Rest of Us"

Chapter 6

Cranking Motors...Or "Starters" To The Rest Of Us

It should come as no surprise that the theory of how a starter works is much the same as how the generator works. This means all the time and effort you spent learning how a generator works will not be wasted. We, of course, know that a starter has only one job, to crank over the engine so the engine can start. Let's look at what is the same.

A starter, internally, is built much like a generator. Inside you will find an armature, pole shoes (magnets) and field coils. You will also find a commutator end of an armature, and brushes just like a generator.

 BEFORE WE CAN TALK ABOUT THE DIFFERENCES, WE NEED TO TALK ABOUT MOTOR PRINCIPLES, OR THE THEORY OF HOW A STARTER MOTOR WORKS.

If you will remember the armature and pole shoe arrangement we had for our generator, to that we are going to add a "horseshoe" shaped magnet. With this arrangement there will be two magnetic fields, one created by the "conductor" current and one created by the horseshoe magnet.

Since magnetic lines leave the north pole and enter at the south pole (trust me on this) the direction of the current of the horseshoe magnet would be upwards. The conductor current we create with a rotating magnetic field is in the clockwise direction, just as it did in the generator.

The result is a heavy concentration of magnetic current on the left-hand side of the wires, where the two magnetic currents come together and become stronger.

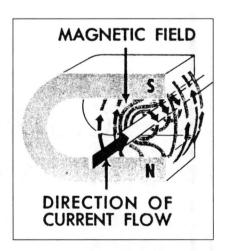

Direction of current flow in a magnetic field.

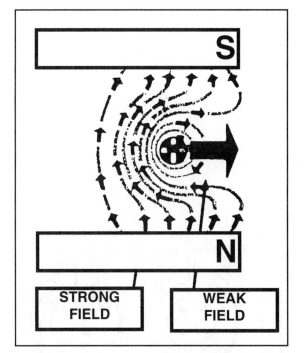

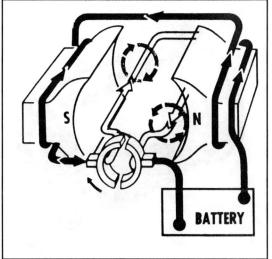

A basic motor is illustrated. A loop of wire is located between two iron pole pieces and is connected to two separate commutator segments, or bars. Riding on the commutator bars are two brushes, which are connected to the battery and to the windings located over the pole pieces.

With this arrangement, current flow can be traced from the battery through the pole piece windings to a brush and commutator bar, through the loop of wire to the other commutator bar and brush, and then back to the battery. The resulting magnetic fields impart a turning or rotational force on the loop of wire as illustrated.

The magnetic current left over on the right-hand side is just the opposite of the conductor current, so they will cancel each other out.

The strong current of the horseshoe magnet and the strong current from the conductor will combine. Because the weaker currents on the right-hand side have canceled each other out, the left-hand current is where the cranking motor will actually get its cranking power.

NOW THAT WE KNOW HOW THINGS WORK , LET'S ADD A COMPLETE ARMATURE AND FIELD COILS TO OUR STARTER MOTOR. WE CAN THEN DEVELOP THE CURRENT FOR A COMPLETE STARTING MOTOR.

One of the main differences of a starter is that it requires a lot of current for a short time, as opposed to a generator, which works with a small amount of current over a longer period of time.

Because of this, there are two types of field coils used in starters. They are series and shunt. The current that flows through a series coil also flows through the armature windings. The current that flows through a shunt coil bypasses the armature and flows directly back to the battery.

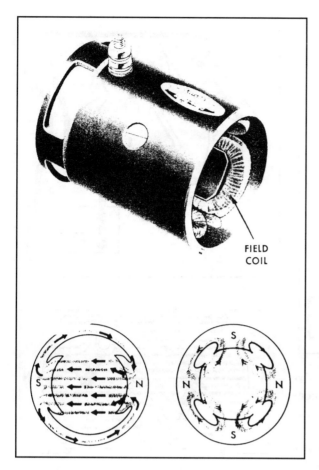

FRAME AND FIELD ASSEMBLY

The frame and field assembly consists of field coil windings assembled over iron pole pieces which are attached to the inside of a heavy iron frame. The iron frame and pole shoes not only provide a place onto which the field coils can be assembled, but also provide a low reluctance, or low resistance path for the magnetic flux produced by the field coil windings.

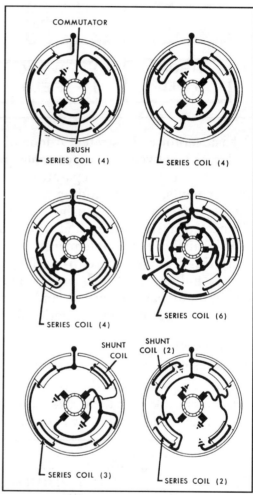

A number of wiring diagrams showing the various types of field coil connections are illustrated. By tracing the current flow through the windings, and by using the "Right Hand Rule," it is seen that the polarity on the face of each pole shoe over which the coil is wound alternates around the field frame. That is, the polarities alternate north, south, north and south.

The **shunt coil** can be easily identified because of its direct connection to ground. Shunt coils will also be made up of a number of turns of smaller wire, just like in a generator.

Because of the extra current necessary for the starter to do its job, a starter will need at least two sets of brushes. Sometimes three sets are required for heavy-duty applications.

A shunt coil does for a starter, just like it does for a generator (controls the output). As we learned about generators, if there is not some control of the output, overcharging will occur and damage to the electrical system will result.

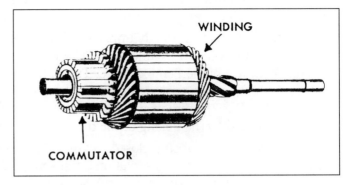

For a starter, if the electrical current output is not regulated, the

Typical armature assembly.

starter motor will spin out of control, causing damage to itself, just like a generator. So the job of the shunt coil is to control the output of the starter.

The **series coils** have the job of increasing the current output of the pole shoes, much like the field coils in a generator. The turning force or "torque" of a starter is determined for the most part by the current available to the series coils, and their position inside of the starter, along with battery cable size, battery capacity, and current carrying capacity of the motor brushes.

In some applications it is necessary to add an **equalizer bar** across two or more brushes to equalize the voltage at the brushes.

OK, WE KNOW THE STARTER IS LIKE A "MOTOR." NOW HOW DO WE GET THE MOTOR TO CRANK OVER THE ENGINE?

This is done through the **motor drive**, or starter bendix as it is commonly called. The motor drive is assembled on the armature shaft and is the part that actually comes into contact with the flywheel (the big gear on the back of the motor), and cranks over the engine. There are a number of different types of drive mechanisms used on cranking motors, and these are covered in the sections that follow.

All drives, regardless of type, will contain a pinion that slides along the armature shaft, and engages to the flywheel. Every starter will also have a gear reduction between the starter and flywheel of about 15:1. This gear reduction will give the starter the strength to crank over the engine.

After the engine is started, the starter drive is designed to disengage from the flywheel. This protects the starter from having to spin as fast as the engine after it is started. (This would be darn fast at a 15:1 ratio!)

The **Bendix drive** shown at right is one of the most common types of starter drives in use.

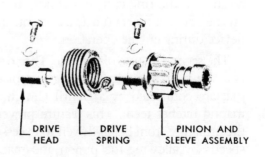

A partially exploded view of a typical inertia drive consisting primarily of a pinion and sleeve assembly, a drive spring, and a drive head.

75

So common, in fact, that when a starter drive goes out or fails, we tend to say the bendix is out of the starter. The Bendix drive is actually a type of starter drive called an "inertia" drive.

Although there are a variety of different types of Bendix drives which may differ considerably in appearance, each drive operates on the principles of inertia to cause the pinion to engage the engine ring gear when the motor is energized.

The drive pinion is normally unbalanced by a counterweight on one side, and has screw threads or splines cut on its inner bore. These screw threads match the screw threads cut on the outer surface of the Bendix sleeve. The pinion and sleeve assembly fits loosely over the armature shaft, and is connected through the drive spring to the drive head, which is keyed to the shaft. Thus, the pinion and sleeve assembly is free to turn on the armature shaft to the extent permitted by the flexing of the drive spring.

When the starting switch is closed and the motor windings are energized by the battery, the armature starts to revolve. This rotation is transmitted through the drive head and drive spring to the sleeve, and these parts increase in speed with the armature. The pinion, however, being unbalanced and having a loose fit on the sleeve, does not increase in speed with the armature due to its inertia. The net result is that the spiral splined sleeve rotates within the pinion, and the pinion moves endwise along the shaft to engage the ring gear. When the pinion reaches its stop on the sleeve, cranking takes place, with the initial shock being taken up by the spring.

When the engine begins to operate, the pinion is driven by the ring gear at a higher speed than the armature. This causes the pinion to rotate in the same direction as the sleeve but at a higher speed, and the pinion is driven back out of mesh with the ring gear teeth. For as long as the operator keeps the motor energized with the engine running, the motor free wheels. The motor start switch, therefore, should be released immediately after the engine has started.

A Folo-Thru Bendix drive is illustrated, top, with the pinion and barrel assembly in the cranking position and partially cut away to show the internal construction. This drive operates in the same manner as the type previously discussed, and has two additional features.

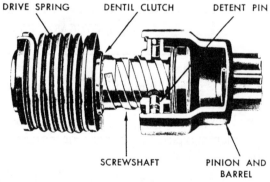

DRIVE SPRING   DENTIL CLUTCH   DETENT PIN

SCREWSHAFT   PINION AND BARREL

A spring-loaded detent pin that moves into a notch cut in the spiral spline serves to lock the pinion in the crank position. This feature prevents unwanted disengagement during false starts. When the engine starts and reaches sufficient speed, centrifugal force causes the detent pin to move out of the notch, and the pinion then is driven out of mesh with the ring gear. A second pin rides on the spiral spline and acts as an anti-drift device during engine operation.

The second feature of the Folo-Thru drive is a sleeve or screwshaft having two pieces that are connected by a **Dentil Clutch**, or mating ratchet teeth. This feature prevents the armature from being driven to excessive speeds by allowing the pinion and mating sleeve to overrun the ratchet teeth until the detent pin has disengaged the notch.

A drive (see illustration ar right, bottom) that is used on some of the smaller motors

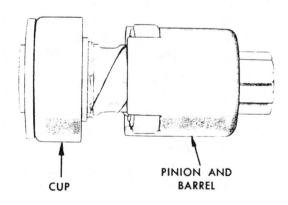

CUP   PINION AND BARREL

is the **rubber compression type**. This drive has the mating ratchet teeth feature, but uses a rubber cushion located inside the cup to take tip the shock of initial cranking. A small spring located over the screwshaft inside the pinion and barrel assembly prevents the pinion from drifting into the ring gear during engine operation.

Another Bendix drive is the **friction-clutch type** that is used on some of the larger cranking motors. This type of drive uses, instead of a drive spring or rubber cushion, a series of flat spring-loaded clutch plates inside the housing that slip momentarily during engagement to relieve shock. A meshing spring is located inside the drive to allow the pinion to clear a tooth abutment condition. An antidrift spring is located over the spiral spline.

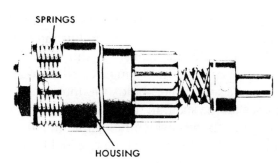

Lost yet? Kind of? Okay. This arrangement makes the pinion and sleeve assembly free to turn on the armature shaft.

When the solenoid is closed or the foot pedal is pushed (in the case of the older cars), this sends current to the motor windings making the armature spin. This rotation of energy is sent to the drive head and spring, then on to the sleeve. All of these parts begin to spin faster along with the armature.

The pinion, because it is unbalanced by the counterweight, does not speed up. So the sleeve inside of the pinion has to speed up by itself. This will cause the pinion to move away, to the end of the armature shaft.

When the pinion reaches the end of the line, it will be engaged to the flywheel and engine cranking will take place. The pinion spring is there to absorb some of the shock of coming to the end of the line.

When the engine starts, the pinion is driven by the flywheel at a higher speed than the armature. This will cause the pinion to rotate the same direction as the sleeve, but at a much faster speed. This will cause the pinion to be pulled back and the pinion will become disengaged.

The spinning process that engages and disengages the starter is called inertia. This is why these starters are called **inertia drive starters**.

This type of starter drive was one of the most common types in use up through the mid-1950s, and is still in use today with a few improvements. Also shown on the next few pages are a few different variations of the inertia drive.

DYER DRIVES - These are the next most common type of starter drive you will encounter.

The Dyer drive pinion is moved into mesh with the ring gear by a shift lever that is either manually operated or operated by a solenoid. This type of drive is used on large motors and features positive engagement of the pinion with the ring gear before the switch can be closed between the battery and motor. This feature avoids spinning meshes which are damaging on high horsepower motors with rapid armature acceleration.

The Dyer drive mechanism consists essentially of a shift sleeve, pinion guide, pinion spring, pinion,

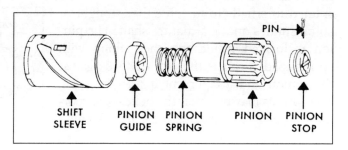

SHIFT SLEEVE   PINION GUIDE   PINION SPRING   PINION   PINION STOP   PIN

pinion stop, and cotter pin. The pinion guide is a close fit on the spiral splines of the armature shaft, while the pinion (which has internal splines matching the armature splines) fits loosely on the armature shaft splines. An exploded view showing the major components is illustrated at the bottom of the previous page..

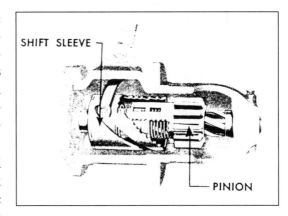

A cutaway view of a Dyer drive in a partial view of the motor assembly is illustrated at right. The drive mechanism is shown in the "at-rest" position. The spring located between the guide and pinion holds the internal teeth of the pinion and guide against the spiral splines on the shaft. In this position, the pinion guide teeth are located in milled notches in the spiral splines, which holds the pinion and guide assembly at the at-rest position. The only way the assembly can be released from this position is by movement of the shift lever.

Movement of the shift lever causes the shift sleeve, pinion guide, pinion spring and pinion to be moved endwise along the shaft so that the pinion meshes with the ring gear teeth. Since the guide and pinion have internal splines matching the shaft splines, these parts rotate as they are moved endwise along the shaft by the shift sleeve. If a tooth abutment should occur, the pinion spring allows further movement of the pinion guide which continues to rotate the pinion until the abutment is cleared. The spring then causes the pinion to mesh with the ring gear. Continued movement of the shift lever closes the switch and cranking takes place, with the pinion held in place by the pinion stop.

When the armature begins to rotate, friction between the pinion guide and shift sleeve causes the sleeve to move back to its original position on the shaft, with the shift lever button following the groove in the shift sleeve. As the engine starts, the ring gear drives the pinion faster than the speed of the armature, and the pinion, spring, and guide are moved back to the at-rest position with the guide held in place by the notches in the shaft splines. Another cranking cycle cannot be started without first moving the shift lever back to the at-rest position.

An important adjustment on Dyer drive motors involves the amount of pinion travel against the pinion spring with the shift lever in the cranking position. This measurement is made by energizing the solenoid or moving the shift lever by hand to the crank position with the motor windings de-energized, and then pushing the pinion back by hand against the spring and noting the full extent of its travel.

Other styles of starter drives you might encounter are shown below. They include roll clutch drive and sprag clutch drive. No matter the style, the basic theory is the same.

ROLL CLUTCH DRIVE

The Roll Clutch drive pinion is moved into and out of mesh with the ring gear by a shift lever which is either manually operated or operated by a solenoid switch. The Roll Clutch drive has a shell and sleeve assembly which is splined internally to match either straight or spiral splines on the armature shaft. The pinion is located inside the shell along with spring-loaded rollers that are wedged against the pinion and a taper cut inside the shell. The springs may be either the helical or accordion type, and four rolls are used. A collar

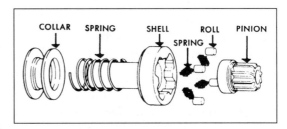

78

and spring located over the sleeve are the other major clutch components. An exploded view and a cutaway view are shown.

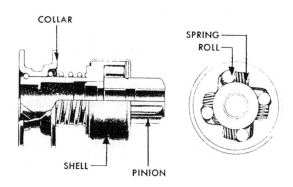

When the shift lever is operated, the shift lever buttons located inside the collar move the collar endwise along the shaft, and the spring pushes the pinion into mesh with the ring gear. If a tooth abutment should occur, the spring compresses with lever movement until the switch is closed, at which time the armature starts to rotate and the tooth abutment is cleared. The compressed spring then pushes the pinion into mesh, and cranking begins with torque being transmitted from the shell to the pinion by the rolls, which are wedged tightly between the pinion and taper cut into the shell.

When the engine starts, the ring gear drives the pinion faster than the armature rotation, and the rolls are moved away from the taper, allowing the pinion to overrun the shell. The start switch should be opened immediately when the engine starts to avoid prolonged over-run. When the shift lever moves back by return spring or manual action, the pinion is moved out of mesh and the cranking cycle is completed.

An important service check on roll clutches involves the clearance in the crank position between the pinion and housing or retainer with the pinion pushed back toward the shift lever. Proper clearance is needed to prevent rubbing of the collar against the shift lever during motor operation and to insure proper engagement before cranking begins.

SPRAG CLUTCH DRIVE

The Sprag Clutch drive is constructed and operates in a manner somewhat similar to the Roll Clutch drive, except that a series of sprags, usually 30 in number, replace the rolls between the shell and sleeve. The sprags are held against the shell and sleeve surfaces by a garter spring. The shell and collar assembly is splined to the armature shaft, and the pinion is spiral splined to the sleeve with a stop collar on the end of the sleeve. A cutaway view is shown.

Movement of the shift lever against the collar either manually or by a solenoid causes the entire clutch assembly to move endwise along the splined shaft, and the pinion teeth to engage the ring gear. If a tooth abutment should occur, continued movement of the shell and spiral splined sleeve causes the pinion to rotate and clear the tooth abutment. The compressed meshing spring then forces the pinion into mesh with the ring gear. If sufficient rotational movement is not imparted to the pinion to clear the abutment before the two retainer cups meet, the shift lever movement is stopped by the retainer cups and the operator must start the engagement cycle over again. This feature prevents closure of the switch contacts to the motor with the pinion not engaged and resulting damage caused by spinning meshes. On the second attempt the pinion will engage in a normal manner.

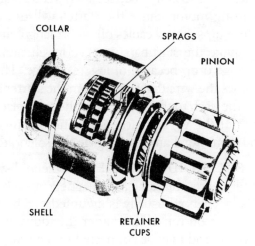

With the pinion engaged and the switch closed to energize the motor windings, the cranking cycle begins. Torque is transmitted from the shell to the sleeve and pinion through the sprags, which tilt slightly and are wedged between the shell and sleeve. When the engine starts, the ring gear drives the pinion and sleeve faster than the armature, and the sprags tilt in the opposite direction to allow the pinion and sleeve to overrun the shell and armature. To avoid prolonged overrun, the operator should immediately open the start switch as soon as the engine starts.

This Sprag Clutch drive is used primarily on larger cranking motors, and is designed to carry the high torque transmitted by the armature. Like the Roll Clutch drive, **an important service procedure is the proper adjustment of pinion clearance in the crank position, and this adjustment is accomplished as covered in the appropriate service bulletin.**

MAGNETIC SWITCHES AND SOLENOIDS - These are the final link in building our working starter. Keep in mind that some of the older applications used a foot pedal that stuck through the floor and mechanically engaged the starter. But by the mid-1950s, most all of the starters used some kind of electrical switch or solenoid. Let's look at some of these.

A magnetic switch (like used on many Fords) is made up of windings mounted on a hollow cylinder. Inside of the hollow cylinder is a plunger with a contact disk attached to it, just like those found on a set of contact points, only heavier.

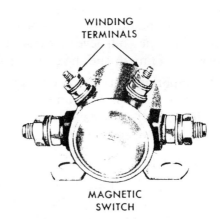

When the windings of the hollow core are energized, the magnetic current travels to the plunger causing it to move, and the contacts to close. This will cause the contact disc to be held tight against the two main switch terminals, and completes the circuit. As you have figured out by now, when the windings are no longer energized, a return spring causes the plunger to return to its original position.

A magnetic switch is often chosen for those applications that need a circuit of short length and low resistance between the battery and the starting motor. Since the starter will draw 100-plus amps, heavy cables of a short length are used to make the starting system more efficient. Less voltage drop because of less resistance. This also allows the wire that travels from the starter switch on the dash to the starter to be the same size as the rest of the wiring harness because it only has to carry minimal amps to engage the solenoid.

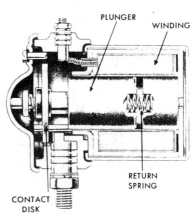

SOLENOID SWITCHES - A solenoid switch is built nearly the same as a magnetic switch except that a solenoid usually is mounted in a horizontal position on top of the starter. In addition, a shift lever or rod may be connected to the plunger.

A typical switch is shown, along with a cross-sectional view of one of the larger models. Some models have one switch terminal with the other winding end grounded internally to the switch case, and others have two switch terminals to which the winding ends are connected.

When the windings are energized and the plunger contacts are drawn together, the shift lever or rod will be moved and the starter will become engaged. At the same time, current is being sent to the starter windings. When this happens together, cranking over of the engine takes place.

The round hollow part inside of a solenoid is called a **plunger**. If you look at the terminal end of a plunger, you will see the top big post is the battery terminal. The other big post directly below that is the motor post and is connected to the starter itself. The other terminals you will find are the "I" terminal, which stands for ignition, and "S" terminal, which is the starter terminal that is energized by the start switch on the dash.

The "I" terminal has a special job. In the early days it was learned that when starting the car, the majority of current from the battery was used by the starter. As a result, the current left for the ignition coil was minimal.

(As we will learn in the next chapter, the ballast resister used on the ignition coil is there to reduce the voltage at the coil approximately two volts to extend the life of the contact points in the distributor.)

When the starter was cranking over the motor, the voltage dropped even further, causing a weak ignition and hard starting. The cure became the "I," or sometimes labeled "R," terminal. It allows the ignition current to bypass the **ballast resistor** during starting only (while the solenoid is engaged). After the car was started, the voltage was again routed through the ballast resistor.

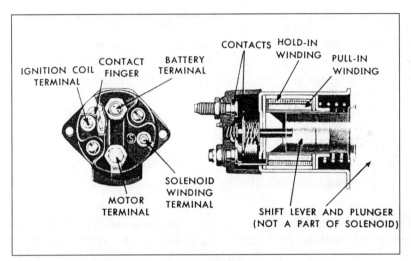

A cross-sectional view of a typical solenoid.

Some of the old foot pedal "button" style of starter switches, like those found on GM cars and many early farm tractors of the early 1950s, used this same type of starter switch with this side terminal. An 18-gauge wire was connected from the battery side of the ignition coil to this stud and served the same purpose as the "I" terminal on the solenoid.

This style of **starter button** can be used as a replacement for the plain style without the stud, and can help, if you are experiencing hard starting. The starter button with the side terminal is Standard ignition brand part number SS-521. This style of switch should be available at your local full-line auto parts store.

Some of you know or have experienced GM products that do not start well when the engine is warm. This is common to large cubic inch V-8s as well as cars with headers or exhausts that fit close to the starter. The excess heat from the headers will be absorbed by the starter and solenoid. This is called "heat soak." In some applications, a heat shield was placed around the starter to help this out. Another cure would be to move the solenoid up and away from the heat and mount it up on the firewall or fender, just like a Ford car or truck does.

But is that possible? Yes. Use Standard replacement solenoid 12V (SS-581), which will be a Ford style solenoid. It will have an "I" terminal and an "S" just like the GM style, so all of the connections will be the same. The only thing you have to do to the solenoid on the starter is connect the "I" and "S" terminals together using a short jumper wire made from 18-gauge wire, and two solderless terminals that will provide the permanent connections.

The rest of the connections to the new terminal will be just the same as they were for the old one. Now your starter solenoid will be out of the heat, which should make your car start better.

 IMPORTANT: *Another note of "havoc" for your reference file. Some of the Ford cars of the late 1940s and early 1950s had a positive ground electrical system (which we will get into in the next chapter). This means that the negative wire is the "hot" wire.*

This also means that the starter solenoid trips from the ground side, and not the positive side, as do nearly all of the rest of the magnetic switches you will encounter.

The replacement magnetic switch you buy for this application will need to have an insulated base. Your shop manual should remind you of this. When you go to the local auto parts store you want to be prepared; you may have to "educate" the counterperson when you get there.

Most of the auto parts counterpeople today are young, and they have no idea there were two types of magnetic switches used in "the old days." It's true, insulated switches were not used for all that many years. (Nonetheless, they will not interchange!) So knowing this will save you some social embarrassment and aggravation that you don't deserve.

AND NOW FOR THE CREATIVE STUFF -

We have covered the most common magnetic switches and solenoids used. But a few of the engineers had a different idea about how to start a car. A few of those ideas got into production. They include the following:

POLARITY SWITCHES - These were quite common on many makes of cars and trucks prior to the late 1940s. The idea was simple. By reversing the polarity to the ignition contact points, each time the vehicle was started (only on the primary side), it would extend the life of the contact points by keeping the surface of the contact points clean of carbon residue or "tracking." This kept the carbon burned off the contact points. This was not necessary in later years when condensers improved and the "after sparks" that caused the carbon tracking were eliminated. Chevrolet cars during the 40s used this setup.

VACUUM STARTING SWITCHES - About 1940, the Delco-Remy Company invented a vacuum switch to control the starter. It hooked into the line of the regular starting solenoid control circuit. The purpose of this vacuum switch was to protect the starting motor from damage by preventing it from accidentally becoming engaged while the engine was already running.

The vacuum switch was operated off of the manifold vacuum and the opening of the throttle. When the throttle opened, it allowed the contacts of the switch to close, completing the starting circuit. As soon as the engine started, the vacuum from the engine manifold "latched" open the contact points, and prevented the starter from being engaged as long as the engine was running.

Buick cars built between 1940-1947 used this type of starter switch, along with a special Stromberg carburetor.

Buick 1940-47 with Stromberg Carburetors

This type switch requires no attention in normal service other than to compensate for manufacturing tolerances in the switch, rotor, and throttle shaft. This is taken care of by special timing washers, supplied by the Stromberg Carburetor Co., which vary the position of the rotor on the throttle shaft, thus establishing the relationship between the throttle shaft and lock-out lever. The washers are numbered and each number represents a difference of three angular degrees in throttle shaft rotation.

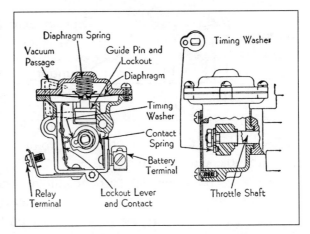

A felt gasket, located beneath the cover plate, is a protection against dust entering the unit. The gasket is porous enough to allow breathing, which is caused by the movement of the diaphragm. Gaskets of any other material should never be substituted.

To check for minimum clearance between cold idle cam and idle screw, proceed as follows:

1. Set idle screw for 8 mph, hot idle.

2. Turn on ignition and start engine. Release throttle, then open throttle until distance between idle screw and cold idle cam in fast idle position is approximately 1/4 inch. Turn off ignition, then release throttle slowly until this distance is 3/64 inch. Do not allow idle screw to drop closer than 3/64 inch to cam as this would void the test.

3. Now turn on ignition switch and open throttle from 3/64 inch position to start. Car should start.

4. Repeat this cycle several times. If engine starts each time, the vacuum switch is timed for starting in all positions of the cold idle cam.

5. If engine fails to start more than once on the above test, it will be necessary to use a higher number timing washer to allow engine to start.

To check for maximum clearance between cold idle cam and idle screw, proceed as follows:

1. Set idle screw for 8 mph, hot idle.

2. Turn on ignition and start engine. Release throttle, then open throttle until distance between idle screw and cold idle cam in fast idle position is approximately 1/4 inch. Turn off ignition, then release throttle slowly until this distance is not less than 1/8 inch. Do not allow idle screw to drop closer to the cam than 1/8 inch as this would void the test.

3. Turn on ignition, and open the throttle from 1/8 inch position to attempt starting. Car should not start. If the car does start, it indicates that the maximum clearance is above the specified high limit and it will be necessary to use a lower numbered timing washer. After changing to a lower numbered washer, repeat the check for minimum clearance as described above.

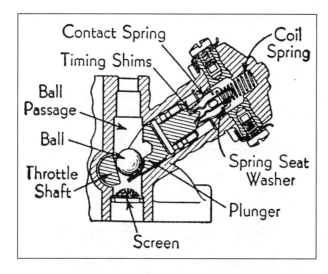

Contact Spring
Timing Shims
Ball Passage
Ball
Throttle Shaft
Screen
Coil Spring
Spring Seat Washer
Plunger

Buick cars built between 1939-1954, along with Packard cars built between 1942-1954 using a **Carter carburetor**, also used a special starting switch called a **Carter carstarter**.

Buick 1939-54 and Packard 1942-54 With Carter Carburetors

The starting switch, on the following page, is incorporated in the carburetor. When the accelerator is depressed with the engine stopped, a steel ball which rests on milled portion of throttle shaft is forced against a plunger, which raises a W-shaped copper contact spring until it makes an electrical connection between two brass blocks in the bakelite top of the switch. This closes the solenoid relay circuit.

As soon as the engine starts the manifold vacuum raises the steel ball up away from the shaft and plunger to a seat in the casting, where it remains as long as the engine runs.

As soon as the ball is raised, the coil spring pushes down on the W-shaped contact, forcing the contact and plunger down, which breaks the connection, opening the starting solenoid relay circuit. The ball cannot return to the starting position until the engine stops, and the throttle is returned to the idle position.

SERVICE NOTES-The W-shaped contact spring rests on two or more brass shims with square holes. These shims determine the point at which the switch contact is made. Contact should be made when the throttle valve is opened between 30 and 45 degrees. If not enough of these shims are in place, contact will not be made soon enough. Too many will cause the switch to function too soon (before 30 degrees) in which case, there is danger that the switch may be in contact all the time.

In disassembling the switch, carefully remove these shims and put them aside in a safe place so they all will be returned to their proper position.

Between the W-shaped spring and the coil spring is a round washer with a square hole. This washer must not be confused with the timing shims. Neither the W-shaped spring nor the coil spring should be stretched or otherwise altered or the operation of the switch will be affected.

When reassembling the switch to the carburetor, be sure the plunger is placed in the position shown, above. If the piston is installed wrong side up, the switch will not function.

Never apply oil or grease to any of the switch parts as dust will collect and eventually cause the switch to stick.

In making the electrical connection, the red or hot wire should be attached to the terminal screw nearest to the center of the carburetor.

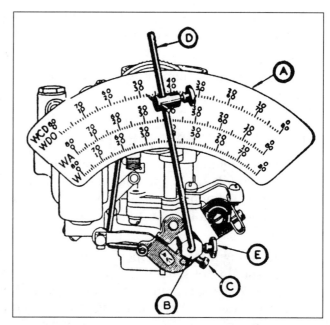

Carstarter Gauge

It is good practice to use **Carstarter Gauge T-109-155S** after the switch has been reassembled. When any new switch parts are installed, it is essential to do so to make certain that the contact is not made before 30° throttle opening and is made before 45° opening.

In using Gauge T-109-155S, shown right, for determining the degree of throttle opening at which switch contact is made, proceed as follows for WDO series carburetors:

Attach plate "A" to the climatic control housing and tighten in position. Connect block "B" to the throttle shaft lever by means of the screw, as shown, being sure the block is tight. Back out throttle lever adjusting screw "C". Hold choke valve open to release fast idle block, close throttle valve tight, and set shaft "D" so that the pointer rests on the line marked zero next to WDO at the left of the plate. Tighten adjusting screw "E". With the carburetor on the car and the switch connected, the switch should make contact when the throttle is opened so that the indicator has passed 30°, but engine must start before pointer has reached 45°. If it does not, the shims mentioned above must be increased or decreased in number until the desired result is obtained. (On 1947 and 1948 Buick carburetors that use the late style throttle connector rod with the bend at the top of the rod, disconnect upper end of rod before installing the protractor gauge T109-155S.)

When the carburetor is on the bench, it is necessary to attach a battery and a bulb in series by wires to the two switch terminals. The point of contact of the switch can then be determined by the lighting of the bulb.

Keep in mind that while both Stromberg and Carter systems work on the same principle, they are of two separate designs and not much will interchange. It's best to refer to your owner's manual for the fine details of making adjustments.

EARLY FORD STYLE - These starting switches are similar to magnetic switches we talked about earlier. The only difference is that they have a metal "cap" covering the plunger inside of the switch. The engineer that designed this style of solenoid must have been a believer in the KISS (Keep It Simple, Stupid) principle.

When the push button dash switch completes the circuit to the solenoid magnetic switch, heavy battery current energizes the magnetic coil which draws in the solenoid plunger. The contact disc which is mounted on the plunger is pulled toward the terminals until the circuit is completed to the starting motor.

When this circuit is completed, the major portion of the magnetic coil is short-circuited and only a small portion is required to maintain contact with the terminals, thereby releasing practically all the battery current to drive the starting motor. The starting motor will continue to run until the dash switch is released.

As a safety feature, should the switch fail to operate electrically, it can be operated manually by removing the metal cap on one end of the switch and pushing the plunger in by hand.

If you have survived everything so far, I am quite proud of you. The remaining chapters of the book will be easier because you now have a basic understanding of how things work, and everything will start to fit into place, beginning with the next chapter.

Chapter 6 Review

1) **Starter drives** are often referred to as Bendix drives, which is actually a common type of inertia starter drive.

2) **Starter solenoids**, while firewall mounted (like Ford) or starter mounted (like GM), will all have the same basic wiring connections.

"I," or sometimes called "R," terminal comes from the battery and provides a hotter spark during engine cranking.

"S" terminal is the wire that comes from the ignition switch itself. This is the terminal that engages the starter when we turn the key to the start position.

"B" terminal is where the battery cable from the battery connects to the starter.

3) Keep in mind that Ford used a positive ground electrical system during the late 1940s and early 1950s. Along with this they also used a **positive ground starter solenoid. The ground wire is the "hot" wire on this solenoid, and is what engages the starter. This will be opposite to 90 percent of all other solenoids you encounter.** If you have one of these on your Ford, you must replace it with one just like this one.

You will want to be prepared to educate the counterperson at the auto parts store who has never seen such a solenoid and will ask you if you are "nuts" because they didn't make 'em like that. Your Ford solenoid will be insulated from its mounting bracket.

4) Another type of Ford starter solenoid had a little metal cap on top of the solenoid. If it fails to work for some reason, you can remove the metal cap and manually force the plunger down to engage the starter.

> 5) **Time-Saving Bonus Tip**: If a solenoid of either type fails to work, you can manually bypass the solenoid and start your car, but you must be careful. Using a pair of pliers or a big screwdriver, touch both the **battery terminal** and the **"S" terminal** at the same time. Be prepared, because **sparks will fly** and your **engine will turn over**. But, if you're in the way, it is curtains. So plan ahead—car in neutral, etc., etc.

For those of you not paying attention here...DO NOT use your jumper wire to do this! You are playing with battery cranking amps of 200 plus amps. Your 14-gauge jumper wire will not last long trying to carry that many amps. And, the alligator clips will also be red hot! If you think "Chef Bob's Hotter-than-Hell Taco Sauce" was hot last Saturday night, brother, you ain't seen nothing yet, until you try and abuse your jumper wire.

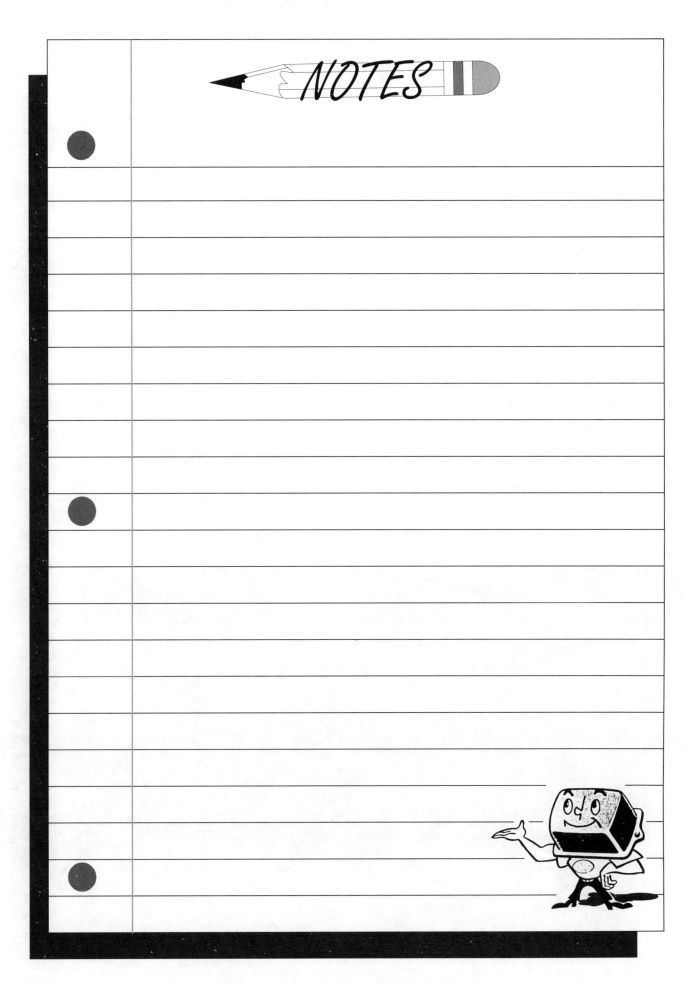

NOTES

Chapter 7

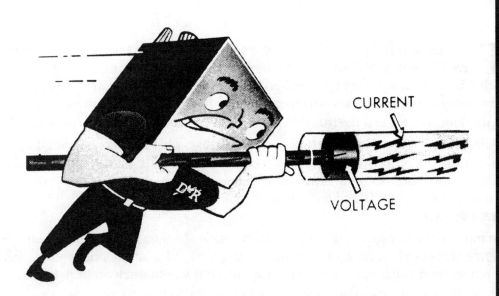

CURRENT

VOLTAGE

"Wire and Cable 101"

Chapter 7

Wire And Cable 101

This is the chapter you have all been waiting for. Wiring seems to be the thing people have the most problems with, but most of those problems are due in part to incorrect information from a well meaning brother-in-law, or other handy relative. With that in mind we are going to learn about a wiring harness, how they are made, how to pick the size of wire you need for the job, and the true difference between a 6-volt and a 12-volt wiring harness.

First, let's look at a piece of primary wire, just like what is in your wiring harness. The insulation is the outside coating that protects the wire inside. In the "good old days" this insulation was made of cotton. Then a coating of clear varnish was added to protect the cotton from the elements. The cotton insulation had a "tracer" color sewn into it so it was easier to trace the wires.

In modern times, primary wire has a coating made of a durable vinyl insulation. The vinyl covering works well because of its resistance to grease, oils, battery acid, and the fact that it will not support combustion (help your car burn if it was to catch on fire). In addition, the wide range of colors available make it easy to trace wires in a circuit.

All automotive wiring is stranded—in other words, it is made of a series of fine wires "twisted" together. This will allow the wire to bend and flex as needed when it becomes a part of the car's wiring harness. The movement of the chassis and frame, along with the route the harness travels, makes this necessary.

Solid wire like that used in house wiring cannot be used for automotive wiring because it would break in half from the twisting and flexing required of

Automotive primary wire is available in many colors.

an automotive wiring harness. House wiring normally does not move or flex except in the case of tornadoes or hurricanes, in which case that is the least of your worries.

As we have learned in previous chapters, copper is one of the best conductors of electricity and is the best choice for the manufacturing of primary wire. We also learned that the bigger the gauge number, the smaller in physical size the wire is.

The other factor that we must consider is the distance the wire has to carry the current to complete the circuit. The greater the distance, the bigger in physical size the wire has to be (in order to overcome the resistance of the circuit).

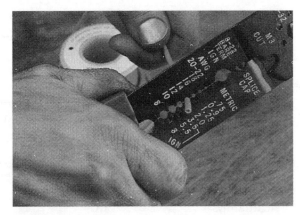

Stripping back primary wire insulation using crimping pliers.

For example, a 12-amp load that has to travel a distance of 10 feet will require an 18-gauge wire for the circuit. If the same 12-amp load had to travel a distance of 100 feet to complete a circuit, a primary wire size of 8-gauge should be used.

The chart below will show the different amp loads and the correct gauge of wire to use, based on the distance the current has to travel.

12 VOLT SYSTEM		TOTAL LENGTH OF WIRE USING GROUND RETURN									
AMPS. APPROX.	CANDLE-POWER	10'	20'	30'	40'	50'	60'	70'	80'	90'	100'
1.0	6	18	18	18	18	18	18	18	18	18	18
1.5	10	18	18	18	18	18	18	18	18	16	16
2	16	18	18	18	18	18	18	18	16	16	16
3	24	18	18	18	18	18	16	16	16	14	14
4	30	18	18	18	16	16	16	14	14	14	12
5	40	18	18	18	16	14	14	14	12	12	12
6	50	18	18	16	16	14	14	12	12	12	12
7	60	18	18	16	14	14	12	12	12	10	10
8	70	18	16	16	14	12	12	12	10	10	10
10	80	18	16	14	12	12	12	10	10	10	10
11	90	18	16	14	12	12	10	10	10	10	8

12 VOLT SYSTEM		TOTAL LENGTH OF WIRE USING GROUND RETURN									
AMPS. APPROX.	CANDLE-POWER	10'	20'	30'	40'	50'	60'	70'	80'	90'	100'
12	100	18	16	14	12	12	10	10	10	8	8
15	120	18	14	12	12	10	10	10	8	8	8
18	140	16	14	12	10	10	8	8	8	8	8
20	160	16	12	12	10	10	8	8	8	8	6
22	180	16	12	10	10	8	8	8	8	6	6
24	200	16	12	10	10	8	8	8	6	6	6
30	240	14	10	10	8	8	6	6	6	4	4
36	290	14	10	8	8	6	6	4	4	4	4
50	400	12	8	8	6	4	4	4	2	2	2
100	800	8	6	4	4	2	2	1	0	0	2/0
150	1200	6	4	2	2	1	0	2/0	2/0	3/0	3/0
200	1600	6	2	2	1	0	2/0	3/0	4/0	4/0	4/0

A 6-volt system, because of the lower voltage, is good for only half the distance of travel per gauge. For instance, a 6-volt system with a 12-amp circuit traveling 10 feet will require a primary wire gauge size of 16 instead of 18 used in the 12-volt system.

Primary wire is normally sold on spools in lengths ranging from 10- to 1,000-foot rolls. A wide variety of colors are available including red, white, yellow, blue, green, black, brown, orange, and purple, to name a few. The old cotton wrapped wire is still available in limited supply from many antique auto parts suppliers, also through Standard brand wire and cable, available at your local full-line auto parts store selling Standard Ignition products.

Example of braided and lacquered wire available through Standard wire and cable products.

Let's use a 1950 Chevrolet car as an example. They are simple to understand and they have a typical electrical load and wiring harness.

Electrical Load	Amps
ignition	1.6
headlamps	14.0
taillights	2.3
dash & instrument cluster	2.5
heater motor	8.0
factory tube-type radio	7.0
Total	35.4

This does not include any extras such as electric fuel pumps, an electric radiator cooling fan, or any other goodies that we modern travelers "must" have to complete our journeys. Take a few minutes and add up the amp load on your own car. You might be surprised how many amps your system requires.

Now, we learned that 6-volt systems run on half the voltage or pressure of the 12-volt system. This means that a 6-volt system will carry more amps in the wiring harness than a 12-volt system does. This means that the primary wire used in the harness will have to be bigger in physical size to carry the higher amp load.

A 12-volt system on the other hand, has twice the voltage or pressure of the 6-volt system. Because of that the 12-volt system will require only half as many amps as a 6-volt system to do the same job.

EXAMPLE: A 6-volt system that requires 14 amps to run both headlamps can power those same headlamps using only 7 amps if the voltage is doubled to 12 volts. In addition the primary wire size can be smaller physically because the 12-volt system is carrying less amps.

As you have figured out by now, instead of using a half dozen different wire sizes in a wiring harness, engineers determined the gauge needed for the longest circuit and used that size throughout the harness. This made it much easier and cheaper to build a wiring harness. All this brings us to an important point.

TIME-SAVING TIP: If you decide to change a vehicle's electrical system from a 6-volt to a 12-volt system, you DO NOT have to replace the wiring harness (unless it is in poor condition), because the 6-volt system is designed to carry TWICE the amp load you will need to run the 12-volt system. In other words, the 6-volt wiring harness is twice as heavy as you need for the new 12-volt system.

This brings us to another important crossroads. What determines or helps you decide whether or not to change your vehicle's electrical system over to a 12-volt system? How about some of these answers:

Because my neighbor did it to his car.

Everyone else in the car club does it.

This guy I talked to on the phone at the auto parts store says "that's the way you have to do it."

These answers are quite common, but not the way you decide if you should change your electrical system to a 12-volt system. You need to base your decision on some facts. First you need to understand the strengths and weaknesses of the system you now have, and identify the actual problem, then you can make your decision based on some sort of merit.

The basic complaints of the 6-volt system are based on three things, all related. First, dead batteries, followed by slow cranking/hard starting, and yellowish dim headlights. But, are these symptoms the fault of the 6-volt system or the parts making up the system?

As we learned earlier, the generator provides little or no output at idle, so the battery is providing the energy at idle and low engine rpm. When the generator does begin to charge, its job is more difficult because it has to provide current for what accessories that are now being used PLUS recharge the battery for what was used earlier.

If our Chevrolet car has an average amp load of 20-25 amps, that is already over half of the generator's total output of 40 amps, just to run a few of the accessories. Then there is the recharging of the battery left to do also. This is why, when you drive these older cars, you always see the amp gauge showing "charging like the dickens" but the battery is still always in need of a charge.

The other thing to keep in mind is that the generator's rating of 40 amps is based on highway speeds and is the maximum output of that generator. So at the slower speeds the generator's output is not near maximum. Therefore, in theory we could have a bigger amp load than the generator can produce current for.

The early engineers believed that even though we had all of those accessories on our car, we would not turn them all on at the same time. While this was true, we also do not have maximum generator output at all times either. So we quite often come up short.

> To give you an idea how this works, every time you start your car with a 6-volt generator system you need to drive your car 10 miles at highway speeds to allow the generator to recharge the battery for that one start! So if you do a lot of short trips or town driving, it's easy to see why the battery is always run down.

As for the headlights, you can see, literally, when the generator begins to charge. As you pull away from the stoplight at night your lights will suddenly get brighter when the generator begins to charge.

This same thing happens in reverse. When you pull up to the stoplight and the engine's rpm drops, the lights are no longer powered by the generator and they get dim. As a result, you can't see where the heck you're going. So, you cuss the 6-volt system and consider changing everything over to a 12-volt system.

Let's take a closer look at this problem. If we check the voltage in the battery, we will find that about 5.0-5.5 volts is quite common for a 6-volt system. We know the starter will require the same amount of amps for starting regardless of whether the battery is fully charged or not. So if the starter takes a big bite out of the battery supply to turn over the engine, what is left will go to the ignition. That will leave us with a yellow spark (instead of a bright blue) which will tell us the ignition is getting short-changed.

With a weak spark, the engine will have to be cranked over a few extra times before it starts, dragging the battery down further. Perhaps we have just found the source for part of our problem.

It looks like we are trying to run our 6-volt system on 5.0 volts. It is no wonder things are not working well. This would be the same as trying to run a 12-volt system on 10 volts. Our actual problem, it seems, is not 6 volts, but rather the lack of it. To work effectively all 6-volt electrical systems should have a minimum of 7 volts in the battery, just like a modern 12-volt charging system will have 13-14 volts in the system. This is so the minimum voltage will be available, even at the far ends of the wiring harness.

This is why modern alternators will have an output of 14 volts, so the nominal voltage in the battery will always be above 12 volts. IF we could do the same for a 6-volt system, then that 6-volt system would work just as good as the modern 12-volt system does now.

What all of this means is that we want to be sure we are fixing the actual problem, rather than treating the symptoms. It is very much like if you go to the dentist with a toothache and a cavity. The dentist gives you an aspirin for the pain, and sends you home. The pain goes away, but the cavity is still there. You have cured the symptom, but have not fixed the actual problem.

Symptom or Problem?

In some instances, that same thing happens with automotive electrical systems; many of the symptoms are treated to cover up the actual problem. Here are a few common ones:

Eight-volt batteries are commonly used on 6-volt systems to help the vehicle start better. At first this seems like a good idea. But in order to keep that 8-volt battery fully charged, it is going to have to have at least 9 volts from the charging system.

In order to do that, the common trick is to "turn up the regulator" to make the generator charge more. When that happens, all of the lights and accessories will burn out due to the excess voltage. If the regulator is not turned up, the battery will only be recharged to the amount set up for the 6-volt battery.

Sometimes you are tricked into thinking this will work (and it does for awhile). When the battery is new, it will have a full charge, and things will work great. But over time the voltage will drop to the level of recharge allowed by the regulator, and things will be back where they were before. And if your generator system isn't keeping up with the 6-volt battery, how is it supposed to keep up an 8-volt battery?

Another bad thing about an 8-volt battery is that it really raises heck with the original factory tube-type radios, and even more damage is done to a restored radio that has had the solid state parts installed. If you want your radio man to talk bad to you, just tell him about your 8-volt battery plans.

6/12 batteries are something else I am not sold on. The theory behind these batteries is to divide a big 6-volt battery in half, thus creating two smaller 6-volt batteries inside of the same case. Then a Ford type starter solenoid is mounted to the top of the batteries to connect them together, thus providing 12 volts for starting only. No damage is supposed to occur to your main harness.

But again this is treating a symptom. If your original charging system cannot keep the original 6-volt battery charged, how is it going to keep this one charged? And you still have not solved the problem of dim headlights.

⚡ **TIME-SAVING TIPS:** "JUST TURN UP THE REGULATOR" is one of the better solutions, especially if you do a lot of in town driving or parades, but again this does nothing for the lights. And you have to be careful you don't go too far (about 7.5 volts maximum), or you will overcharge the battery and "cook" all of the water out of it.

"PUT A SMALLER DIAMETER PULLEY ON THE GENERATOR so it will run faster, and have more output at idle." This, too, will help if you do a lot of city driving or parades; however, be careful when you go back out on the highway. That poor generator is going to get spun at warp speed at 50 mph, and might even pass you by.

Keep in mind that if you decide to change your 6-volt system over to a 12-volt system, not everything will easily follow along. Let's look at what is required to change a 6-volt system over to 12 volts. Then you can apply this knowledge to your application.

CHANGING OVER TO A 12-VOLT ELECTRICAL SYSTEM

1) First you will need a 12-volt battery with the same or more cold cranking amps as your 6-volt battery.

2) Your next job is to decide which type of charging system you are going to use. You have the choice of either a generator or an alternator type charging system. The alternator would be my choice for reasons we will get into in the next chapter. Whatever you decide, you'll need to round up the necessary parts and pieces.

3) You will also want to update to a modern internal resisted 12-volt coil. This will eliminate the need for the external ballast resistor. No other change is necessary to the distributor points or the condenser. (It's true.) The ignition system runs on 2 volts less than system voltage. This is done to extend the life of the contact points, just like in a regulator.

4) You will need to change all of the dash bulbs, along with the headlight bulbs and taillight bulbs, and all others including park lights, dome lights, etc. Your first trial run will show you the ones you missed. Also, do not forget the turn signal flasher; it, too, must be changed to a 12-volt unit.

5) Last are the gauges. The fuel gauge is one of the most important and easily fixed. The best solution is to use one of the transistorized voltage drops available from Fifth Avenue. These transistorized voltage drops will work with any of the gauges that are electrical EXCEPT the amp gauge, which is not affected by the voltage change anyway.

In most cases (except some Ford applications) the temp and oil gauges are mechanical. **The amp GAUGE is not voltage sensitive**. But do not forget your radio, which should be converted to 12-volt by your radio man. It will last about four seconds on 12-volt, and will emit a colorful "voltage cloud" to remind you of your error. Also don't forget the dash clock and any other related accessories.

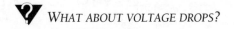 *WHAT ABOUT VOLTAGE DROPS?*

To understand when to use a ceramic voltage drop, we must first understand how a ceramic voltage drop works. A voltage drop is actually a resistor that is rated by the "ohms of resistance" it is able to create. This resistance prevents all of the system voltage from passing through the resistor, thus reducing the voltage. In other words, a resistor just creates excessive friction, reducing the efficiency of the electrical system.

As with everything, there is a trade-off. The more precise your voltage drop must be, the more expensive it is to manufacture. Also, the more easily it is damaged by excess voltage.

Typically, automotive resistors will have a 40+ percent error rate. This means that the resistor that is rated to carry up to a 4-amp load and is designed to reduce 12 volts incoming to 6 volts outgoing, will reduce the incoming 12 volts to approximately 6 volts plus or minus 40 percent, depending on the incoming voltage. This means the current on the output side of the resistor can vary between 3.6 volts and 8.4 volts, depending on the electrical load of the system. It is easy to see why this variation in voltage can easily damage certain accessories.

❓ *SO WHY NOT BUILD A MORE PRECISE RESISTOR?*

Computers and many modern transistorized devices do use a more precise resistor, but their voltage is pretty consistent. The changes in electrical loads of automotive systems vary greatly, and this would destroy the more precise resistors. To give an example of how a voltage drop will affect an accessory, let's install one in the power wire of the heater motor.

The load (with the battery fully charged) will be light, so the voltage drop will work exactly as designed during the daytime hours. But the evening hours will create quite a change. The headlights/taillights will be on as well as various accessories creating as much as a 25-amp load. The resistor, however, has no way to compensate for this change in electrical load. As we learned earlier, the output is directly affected by the input voltage.

Another case study...suppose you have done a lot of town driving. Your battery is low, and holds about an 80 percent charge. Because of the extra output required to recharge the battery, the output side of the resistor may have as high as 8.4 volts during the daytime when the amp load is light, whereas in the evening hours it may be as low as 3.6 volts due to the increased amp load. This variance in voltage would destroy most precision resistors, which is why most automotive resistors have such a high error factor.

This change in voltage puts quite a strain on the heater motor and all of the rest of the electrical accessories as well. The transistorized accessories especially do not deal with this well, and will be damaged in a short time. Low voltage can be just as damaging as high voltage, to an electrical accessory.

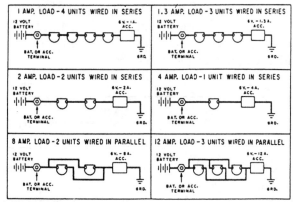

9500007   Used on 4530, 4531, 5158, 5500
"REDUCES 12 VOLTS TO 6 VOLTS"
TO INSTALL

1—CHECK AMP RATING OF ACCESSORY TO BE INSTALLED. YOU MUST HAVE THIS INFORMATION BEFORE INSTALLING ACCESSORY.

2—SELECT THE DIAGRAM WHICH MATCHES THE AMP. RATING OF ACCESSORY. **DAMAGE TO THE REDUCER AND/OR ACCESSORY** WILL RESULT IF WRONG DIAGRAM IS USED.

3—CONNECT ONE OR MORE VOLTAGE REDUCERS IN SERIES OR PARALLEL AS SHOWN IN DIAGRAM.

IMPORTANT NOTE
UCER IS DESIGNED FOR 1.5 OHMS RESISTANCE AT 4 AMP. MAXIMUM LOAD. OVERLOADING WILL DAMAGE REDUCER AND/OR ACCESSORY.

FORM R-10   PRINTED IN U.S.A.

Instructions for installing the ceramic type voltage drop resistor.

For example, when there is not enough voltage, the accessory does not have enough power to work correctly, and it becomes difficult for that accessory to do its job. Excess heat will also be generated, adding to the problem. On the other hand, excess high voltage destroys accessories just the same because the rated voltage has been exceeded. A simple example of this is your headlights. You know what happens to them if the voltage is too high, right? They burn out.

Many of the 6/12 power inverters work in this same way. Through a series of windings much like those inside of an ignition coil, the incoming voltage is stepped up to 12 volts based on an input of exactly 6 volts.

The same thing happens to these power inverters that happens to the voltage drops. When the incoming voltage is increased, the output voltage is also increased, sometimes exceeding the rated voltage of an accessory. This voltage difference will soon damage such transistorized accessories as stereo radios and cellular phones. This is why most of these transistorized accessories will say in their instructions that they must be run from a regulated power supply.

Again, there are two companies that offer a power supply capable of providing the regulated current necessary to run transistorized accessories. They are Fifth Avenue Antique Auto Parts and Antique Automobile Radio, Inc. Complete addresses for these two companies can be found in the Source List at the end of the book.

My suggestion to you, if you think you need to use a voltage drop, is to use them on non-transistorized accessories. By the way, **do not use a ceramic resistor on fuel gauges**. Fuel gauges work off of ohms of resistance, just as a resistor does, and the two mixed together will give you false readings, causing you to have to walk home on a quarter of a tank. The difference between the dash gauges and the rest of your accessories is that dashes are delicate and usually function on one-fourth of an amp or less. Excess voltage can damage and will burn out your dash gauge.

 SO HOW DO YOU REDUCE VOLTAGE TO THE ELECTRICAL DASH GAUGES?

✔ RUNDLE'S RULES:

One of the easiest ways is to use a regulated voltage drop. These voltage drops are all transistorized and do not use resistors to reduce the voltage. As a result, the incoming voltage can vary between 8 and 20 volts, and the output voltage will always remain at a constant 6 volts.

These are simple inline voltage drops that mount directly to the back of the gauge to which you are reducing the voltage. Commonly referred to as "Runtz," these voltage drops require only a simple two-wire installation, and are available through Fifth Avenue Antique Auto Parts.

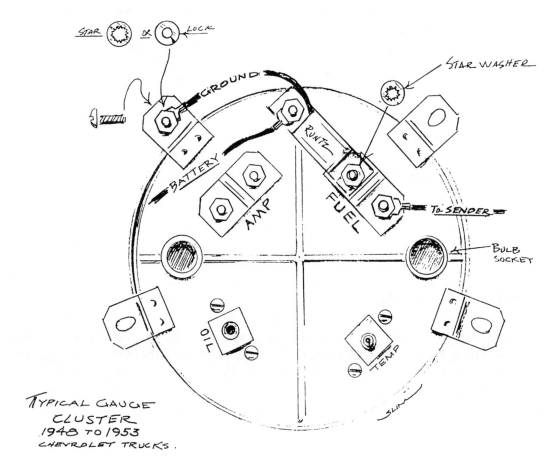

STAR ⊗ or ⊙ LOCK

STAR WASHER

GROUND

RUNTZ

BATTERY

AMP

FUEL

TO SENDER

BULB SOCKET

OIL

TEMP

SLIM

TYPICAL GAUGE
CLUSTER
1948 TO 1953
CHEVROLET TRUCKS.

A Runtz transistorized voltage drop installed on a fuel gauge.

WIRING HARNESS 101 -
How To Shop for a Replacement Harness

If you do need to replace a wiring harness, be sure to buy one of good quality. They will cost more up front, but it is money well spent. Look for good quality copper primary wire, soldered terminal ends, and color coded wiring; things should look much like the original factory harness. In addition, see if the new harness is "finished" by being placed in a wire loom or assembled in some manner.

LOOK at the instruction sheet; it is quite often a good judge of the quality of the harness. The instructions should be complete, easy to read, and the different parts of the wiring harness itself should be easily identified from the instruction sheet.

See if the new wiring harness is color coded to match the original wiring diagram. Remember if it's you and your brother-in-law doing this, and neither of you can make sense of the instructions, you're in big trouble!

In most cases some of the dash light sockets will come as part of the harness. Look at the contacts at the bottom of the socket: are they brass, copper, or aluminum? Look at the insulation on the wiring itself. Good quality wiring will be soft and pliable and easily formed along the wiring harness path.

All of these things will make installing your harness easier and will make a difference in the life of your harness. Remember, as your grandpa would say, "It only costs a nickel more to go first class." When it comes to buying a wiring harness, no truer words were ever spoken.

1951-52 CHEVROLET
All Sedans and Convertibles
WIRING HARNESS ASSEMBLY
WH170

NOTE: Wire numbering method is used to help simplify wiring harness installation. Each of the numbered wires are keyed to the below listed wire functions. We advise not removing the wire identifying numbers until after wiring harness installation and check-out procedures have been completed. Refer to attached sheet for wiring schematic information. **(Pertaining to direction signals if used.)

WIRE NO.	WIRE DESCRIPTION
1	Ammeter (+) terminal to starter solenoid switch "BATT" terminal.
2	Ammeter (+) terminal to dash starter switch.
3	Ignition switch "AUX" terminal to ignition coil (+) terminal.
4	Ammeter (-) terminal to voltage regulator "BATT" terminal.
5	Ammeter (-) terminal to lighting switch "BATT" terminal.
6	Ammeter (-) terminal to ignition switch "BATT" terminal.
7	Ignition switch "BATT" terminal to dash cigar lighter.
8	Ammeter (+) terminal to horn relay "BATT" terminal.
9	Horn relay "H" terminal to horns.
10	Horn relay "S" terminal to steering column horn button.
11	Generator armature terminal to voltage regulator "G" terminal.
12	Generator field terminal to voltage regulator "F" terminal.
13	Lighting switch to headlight beam foot control switch "B" terminal.
14	Lighting switch to front parking lights.
15	Headlight beam foot control switch "L" terminal to front headlight "Low" beams.
16	Headlight beam foot control switch "U" terminal to front headlight "High" beams.
17	To dash headlight "High beam" indicator light.
18	**Lighting switch to stop light switch to rear stop lights. (Note: Both "No. 18" wires are used in tail light harness assembly if not equipped with direction signal lights.)
19	Ignition switch "AUX" terminal to gasoline gauge dash unit.
20	Lighting switch instrument light switch to instrument lights.
21	Lighting switch to rear tail lights.
22	To rear license plate light.
23	Lighting switch to interior dome light and switch.
24	Dome light switch to door courtesy light switches.
25	Gasoline gauge dash unit to tank unit.
26	Lighting switch instrument light switch to clock light.
27	Dash starter switch to power glide transmission neutral safety switch, and to starter solenoid switch.
28	**Direction signal switch to right front direction signal light.
29	**Direction signal switch to left front direction signal light.

Typical written directions for installing replacement wiring harness.

WHAT ABOUT REVERSING THE POLARITY, IS THAT DIFFICULT?

In the early days of the automobile, the ignition system was powered by a magneto. The lights were "gas" lamps powered by kerosene. There wasn't much to an electrical system.

Then along comes World War I. When the manufacturers began building vehicles for war, the government began requesting that a battery ignition be provided. So the logical way to build an electrical system at that time was the simple way. The engineers knew that electricity actually flowed from negative to positive, so negative would be the output and the positive would be the return. With no accessories involved, this made sense.

Things remained pretty much unchanged until the mid to late 1940s. With more cars and more accessories being sold, it was easier and made more common sense if the current flowed from the positive post, and returned via the negative post. This was easier to understand and also provided a way for the current to be easily measured. By flowing the current in the reverse direction, the resistance or friction could be measured, thus providing a unit of electrical measure, voltage. General Motors lead the push to negative ground with the Cadillac models beginning in 1946.

During this era it was not uncommon to see both positive and negative ground cars offered. Even GM offered both. For instance, Chevrolet pickups were negative ground, but in contrast the GMC pickups were positive ground.

Thus, when the majority of the car manufacturers made the switch to 12 volt in the mid-1950s, they also standardized, and began building negative ground electrical systems. It was GM that led the fight for both negative ground and the switch to 12 volts in the early 1950s. GM was a powerful company during those years and sooner or later usually got its way.

WHAT IS THE PHYSICAL DIFFERENCE BETWEEN A NEGATIVE AND A POSITIVE GROUND ELECTRICAL SYSTEM?

A negative ground system, as the name suggests, means that the battery output flows from the positive post of the battery, out through the wiring harness and accessories, where it is then returned to the battery via the negative post.

A positive ground system works just the opposite or backwards of a negative ground system. The positive ground system flows the output from the battery, out through the negative post where it travels out through the wiring harness and returns to the battery via the positive post.

Neither system has any advantage over the other. There is no reason to reverse the polarity of your system unless you are also updating the charging system or want to take advantage of a negative ground accessory. To change just for the sake of changing will gain you little.

HOW DO YOU REVERSE THE POLARITY ANYWAY? WHAT DO YOU HAVE TO CHANGE?

Reversing the polarity is quite simple. There are only two things you have to do to reverse the polarity, to make your system negative ground.

1) Reverse the cables at the battery. The negative cable will now go to the negative (-) post of the battery. The positive cable will now go to the positive (+) terminal on the battery.

2) Your amp gauge is your last duty. You need to simply reverse the wires connected to the studs on the back of the gauge. If you fail to do that it will not hurt the gauge, it will just read backwards. (The negative will be the + reading.)

If you have a Ford car, many of them used an "inductive" style ammeter, (like we learned about in the first chapter). There will be a loop of wire held to the back of the gauge by a small clip. Simply remove the wire from the clip, reverse the loop half a turn and replace the wire back in the loop. Now your gauge will read correctly.

You will need to replace the positive ground voltage regulator with a negative ground regulator, then polarize the regulator to the generator. If you update to an alternator, it will be designed for a negative ground system already.

Keep in mind any transistorized accessory will not work with the polarity reversed; most everything else will work just fine. The majority of non-transistorized radios will be okay. However, as you will learn in the upcoming radio chapter, there are a few radio models that will not work on reverse polarity.

Check with your radio man for details. Also there are some in-dash clocks that are polarity sensitive. It's best to review all of your accessories, and if you have any doubt ask someone! Most any technician in a given field, especially the radio repair guys, would much rather have you ask before you destroy something, rather than after!

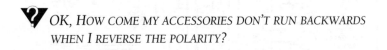

OK, How come my accessories don't run backwards when I reverse the polarity?

Why indeed? I get asked this question a lot. It is because you are not changing anything internally inside of your accessories.

Using your starter as an example, if your system was originally positive ground, the negative cable from the battery was connected to the starter. The negative cable delivered battery current to the starter, but if you reverse the polarity, the positive cable becomes the battery cable. The output is still flowing in a circle, and it doesn't matter which direction it flows; the end result will be the same. Remember, as long as there is power from the battery delivered to the starter, it will work regardless of which way the current was delivered to the starter.

It is just like your headlamps. We do not have to buy positive ground or negative ground headlamps, do we? No, we just buy headlamps, and as long as there is power to those headlamps they will work. Some things such as radios are polarity "challenged" but it is due to the way the components inside are built and the job they perform.

BY THE WAY - We also need to spend a little time learning how to read a wiring diagram. I know, some of you thought I might forget about this part and you wouldn't have to learn any of this. Well, I didn't forget, so come on. It'll be better than you think. Really.

Our first task is to look over the symbols on the chart below. The symbols are like a road map telling you what path the current is going to travel down. This will come in handy, for example, when your heater motor only works part of the time.

You can use the wiring diagram to follow the path of power from the battery to the switch and on to the motor. The wiring diagram will tell you the color of the wire to look for in the harness. This way, you can check for power at various points along the wiring harness (using your test light) until you locate where the power is no longer being delivered.

Below is the wiring harness for a 1950 Chevrolet car. Take a few minutes to study the diagram, and you will see it starting to make sense. Pick one of the simple circuits like the heater motor and trace the power supply from the battery to the heater motor itself. As you then practice by tracing out the rest of the circuits, it will all start to make sense.

We talked about wiring harnesses earlier in this chapter, and the importance of quality wiring terminal ends. This next page shows how a primary wire terminal is made and what features to look for when you go to buy them.

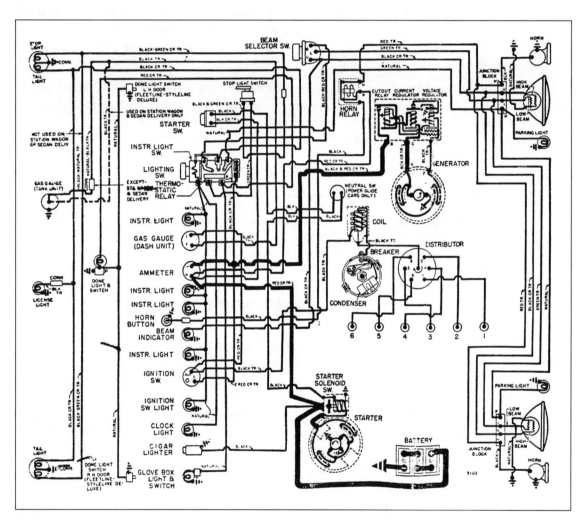

Example of a wiring diagram for early 1950s Chevy car.

Primary Wire Terminals... engineered for durability

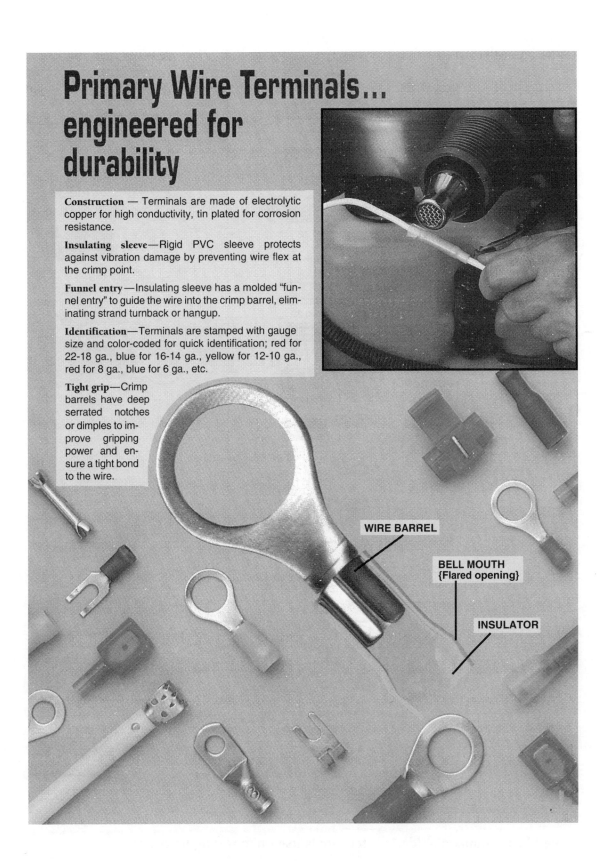

Construction — Terminals are made of electrolytic copper for high conductivity, tin plated for corrosion resistance.

Insulating sleeve—Rigid PVC sleeve protects against vibration damage by preventing wire flex at the crimp point.

Funnel entry—Insulating sleeve has a molded "funnel entry" to guide the wire into the crimp barrel, eliminating strand turnback or hangup.

Identification—Terminals are stamped with gauge size and color-coded for quick identification; red for 22-18 ga., blue for 16-14 ga., yellow for 12-10 ga., red for 8 ga., blue for 6 ga., etc.

Tight grip—Crimp barrels have deep serrated notches or dimples to improve gripping power and ensure a tight bond to the wire.

WIRE BARREL

BELL MOUTH {Flared opening}

INSULATOR

These next few pages will show the different types of wire terminals available. You may recall that in an earlier chapter I said that they color code the terminals so you know what size to buy to match the primary wire you are using. They really do that, as these next few pages will show.

RING TERMINALS

22-18 Ga.			
Std. Pkg.	Stud Sizes	Display Pack	Part No.
100	#6	ET151*	**STP151**
100	#8-10	ET120*	**STP120**
100	1/4"	ET121*	**STP121**
100	3/8"	ET122*	**STP122**

16-14 Ga.			
Std. Pkg.	Stud Sizes	Display Pack	Part No.
100	#6-8	ET123*	**STP123**
100 / 500	#10	ET124*	**STP124** / **STP124D**
100	1/4"	ET125*	**STP125**
25	5/16"		**STP157**
100	3/8"	ET126*	**STP126**

12-10 Ga.			
Std. Pkg.	Stud Sizes	Display Pack	Part No.
50	8-10	ET127*	**STP127**
50	1/4"	ET128*	**STP128**
50	5/16"		**STP168**
50	3/8"	ET129*	**STP129**
25	1/2"		**STP159**

RING TERMINALS

8 Ga.		
Std. Pkg.	Stud Sizes	Part No.
25	1/2"	**STP175**
25	1/4"	**STP188**
25	5/16"	**STP192**

6 Ga.		
Std. Pkg.	Stud Sizes	Part No.
25	1/4"	**STP187**
25	5/16"	**STP194**
25	1/2"	**STP174**

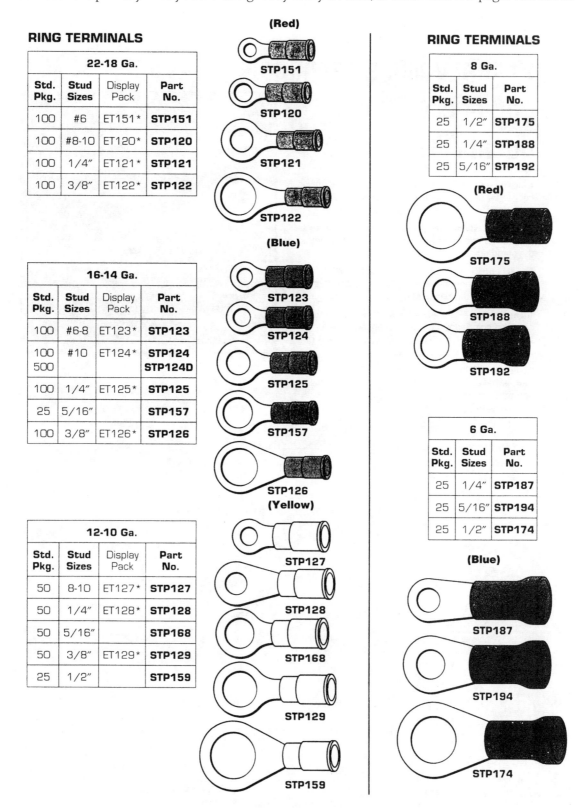

(Red)
STP151
STP120
STP121
STP122

(Blue)
STP123
STP124
STP125
STP157
STP126

(Yellow)
STP127
STP128
STP168
STP129
STP159

(Red)
STP175
STP188
STP192

(Blue)
STP187
STP194
STP174

Some of the common solderless terminals used in a wiring harness

RING TERMINAL (cont'd) (Yellow)

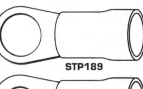
STP189

STP190

4 Ga.		
Std. Pkg.	Stud Sizes	Part No.
10	1/4"	**STP193**
10	5/16"	**STP191**
10	3/8"	**STP190**
10	1/2"	**STP189**

STP193

STP191

SPADE AND HOOK TERMINALS

22-18 Ga.			
Std. Pkg.	Stud Sizes	Display Pack	Part No.
100	#6	ET136*	**STP136**
100	#10	ET150*	**STP150**
100	#10		**STP165**

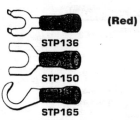
(Red)

STP136

STP150

STP165

STAR RING TERMINALS - WITH A SERRATED RING

When you tighten down on the star ring, the serrated edges pierce through paint or other coatings, biting into metal and insuring a good connection.

NEW 22-18 Ga.			
Std. Pkg.	Stud Sizes	Display Pack	Part No.
50	#10	ET91*	**STP91**
50	#8	ET92*	**STP92**
50	#6	ET93*	**STP93**

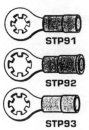
(Red)
STP91

STP92

STP93

16-14 Ga.			
Std. Pkg.	Stud Sizes	Display Pack	Part No.
100	#6	ET133*	**STP133**
100	#8	ET134*	**STP134**
100	#10	ET135*	**STP135**
50	#10		**STP155**

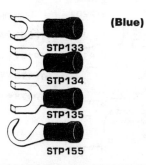
(Blue)

STP133

STP134

STP135

STP155

NEW 16-14 Ga.			
Std. Pkg.	Stud Sizes	Display Pack	Part No.
50	#10	ET94*	**STP94**
50	#8	ET95*	**STP95**
50	#6	ET96*	**STP96**

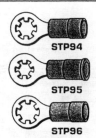
(Blue)
STP94

STP95

STP96

12-10 Ga.			
Std. Pkg.	Stud Sizes	Display Pack	Part No.
50	#10	ET208*	**STP208**
25	#10		**STP154**

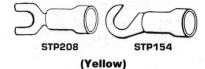

STP208   STP154
(Yellow)

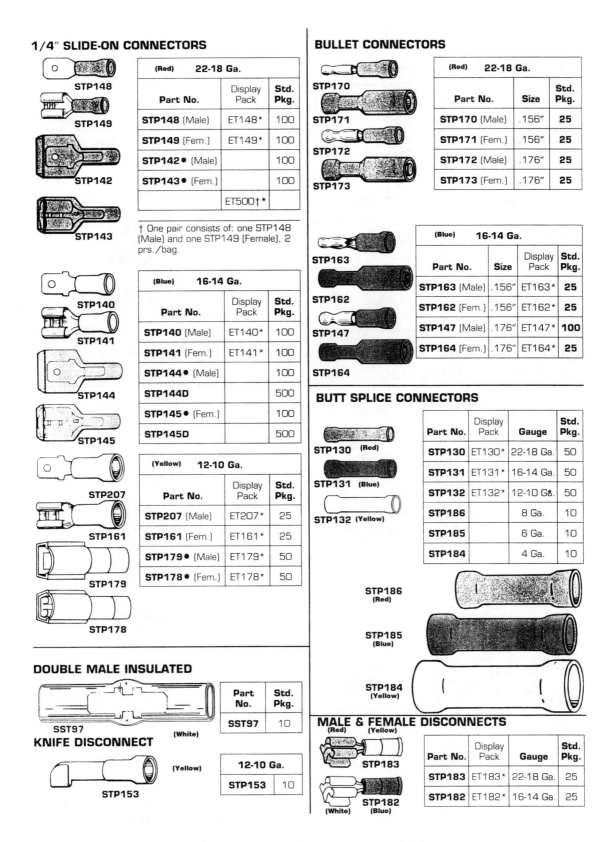

1/4″ SLIDE-ON CONNECTORS

STP148
STP149
STP142
STP143

(Red) 22-18 Ga.		
Part No.	Display Pack	**Std. Pkg.**
STP148 (Male)	ET148*	100
STP149 (Fem.)	ET149*	100
STP142 ● (Male)		100
STP143 ● (Fem.)		100
	ET500†*	

† One pair consists of: one STP148 (Male) and one STP149 (Female), 2 prs./bag.

STP140
STP141
STP144
STP145

(Blue) 16-14 Ga.		
Part No.	Display Pack	**Std. Pkg.**
STP140 (Male)	ET140*	100
STP141 (Fem.)	ET141*	100
STP144 ● (Male)		100
STP144D		500
STP145 ● (Fem.)		100
STP145D		500

STP207
STP161
STP179
STP178

(Yellow) 12-10 Ga.		
Part No.	Display Pack	**Std. Pkg.**
STP207 (Male)	ET207*	25
STP161 (Fem.)	ET161*	25
STP179 ● (Male)	ET179*	50
STP178 ● (Fem.)	ET178*	50

DOUBLE MALE INSULATED

SST97 (White)

Part No.	Std. Pkg.
SST97	10

KNIFE DISCONNECT

STP153 (Yellow)

12-10 Ga.	
STP153	10

BULLET CONNECTORS

STP170
STP171
STP172
STP173

(Red) 22-18 Ga.		
Part No.	Size	**Std. Pkg.**
STP170 (Male)	.156″	25
STP171 (Fem.)	.156″	25
STP172 (Male)	.176″	25
STP173 (Fem.)	.176″	25

STP163
STP162
STP147
STP164

(Blue) 16-14 Ga.			
Part No.	Size	Display Pack	**Std. Pkg.**
STP163 (Male)	.156″	ET163*	25
STP162 (Fem.)	.156″	ET162*	25
STP147 (Male)	.176″	ET147*	100
STP164 (Fem.)	.176″	ET164*	25

BUTT SPLICE CONNECTORS

STP130 (Red)
STP131 (Blue)
STP132 (Yellow)

Part No.	Display Pack	Gauge	Std. Pkg.
STP130	ET130*	22-18 Ga.	50
STP131	ET131*	16-14 Ga.	50
STP132	ET132*	12-10 Ga.	50
STP186		8 Ga.	10
STP185		6 Ga.	10
STP184		4 Ga.	10

STP186 (Red)
STP185 (Blue)
STP184 (Yellow)

MALE & FEMALE DISCONNECTS

STP183 (Red) (Yellow)
STP182 (White) (Blue)

Part No.	Display Pack	Gauge	Std. Pkg.
STP183	ET183*	22-18 Ga.	25
STP182	ET182*	16-14 Ga.	25

Examples of different types of solderless terminals available

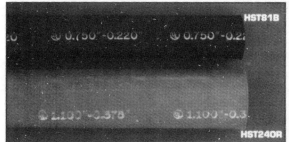

Heavy Duty Polyolefin/Double Wall—6″ Long.

● Self-sealing inner wall forms a contamination-proof seal.

Gauge	Color	I.D. Shrinks		Part No.	Std. Pkg.
		From	To		
8-1	Black	.750″	.250″	**HST81B**	5
8-1	Red	.750″	.250″	**HST81R**	5
2-4/0	Black	1.100″	.375″	**HST240B**	5
2-4/0	Red	1.100″	.375″	**HST240R**	5

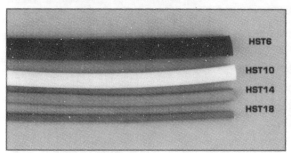

Single Wall Tubing—6″ Long

Gauge	Color	I.D. Shrinks		Part No.	Display Pack	Std. Pkg.
		From	To			
20-18	Red	.125″	.062″	**HST18**	ET18*	10
16-14	Blue	.250″	.125″	**HST14**	ET14*	10
12-10	Yellow	.316″	.156″	**HST10**	ET12*	10
8-2	Black	.500″	.250″	**HST6**	ET2*	5
Assorted Sizes	Red Blue Yellow				ET20*	5 per bag

*Contains 2 Ea. of HST18, HST14 and 1 Ea. of HST10. For more information on display pack items see pages 63 – 77.

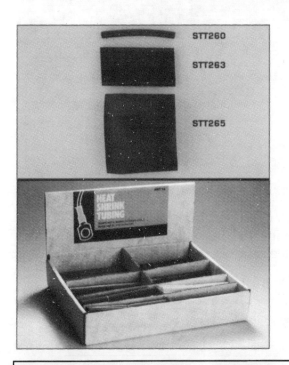

Black, Single Wall Tubing—1½″ Long

Gauge	I.D. Shrinks		Part No.	Display Pack	Std. Pkg.
	From	To			
20-18	.125″	.062″	**STT260**		25
16-14	.250″	.125″	**STT261**		25
12-10	.375″	.188″	**STT262**		25
8-2	.500″	.250″	**STT263**		10
1-2/0	.750″	.375″	**STT264**		25
2/0-4/0	1.00″	.500″	**STT265**		10
Assorted sizes				ET260*	12 per bag

*Contains 4 Ea. of SST260, SST261, STT262. For more information on display pack items see pages 63 – 77.

HST1A . . . Heat Shrink Tubing Assortment—6″ Long. Std. Pkg. 1

Qty.	Part No.	Qty.	Part No.
5	**HST6**	10	**HST14**
10	**HST10**	10	**HST18**
2	**HST81B**	2	**HST240B**
2	**HST81R**	2	**HST240R**

HOW TO USE HEAT SHRINK TUBING . . . CAUTION: Disconnect battery cables before applying heat shrink tubing!

1. Select tubing to assure a tight fit after shrinkage. Consider the outside dimension of the terminal when determining tubing diameter. Shrink ratios: 3:1 for double wall tubing; 2:1 for single wall.

2. Cover at least ½″ of the terminal barrel and 1″ of the cable.

3. Apply heat evenly to all areas of the tubing. When tubing starts to shrink, focus heat at center of tubing and move heat toward ends to eliminate any trapped air.

You can also buy assortments of wiring harness terminals in a kit that will have the most popular sizes of terminals. Most will also come with the crimper pliers (the pliers used to crimp shut the terminal on the wire to make the wiring connection). Most crimper pliers can also be used to strip back the insulation so it is ready to go into the terminal.

WIRE TIES - Wire ties are another common electrical accessory. They are just nylon wire straps that fit around a wiring harness with enough length to hold the harness in place by securing the harness to objects along the path. They are quite handy and you will find yourself using them for lots of other things besides in a wiring harness. They are sold in bundles or packages from 10-1,000 and can sometimes be bought by the pound.

AND FINALLY - Just when you thought you knew everything there is to know about primary wire, along comes **fusible links**. A fusible link is designed to replace the fuse in a circuit. A fuse has the job of protecting the circuits from current overload (high voltage).

Instead of putting a fuse in-line in the circuit, a piece of primary wire is used. Usually fusible links are 4 gauge sizes smaller than the circuit wire, and are placed in-line, in the circuit.

If there is an overload in the circuit, the fusible link will burn in two, protect-

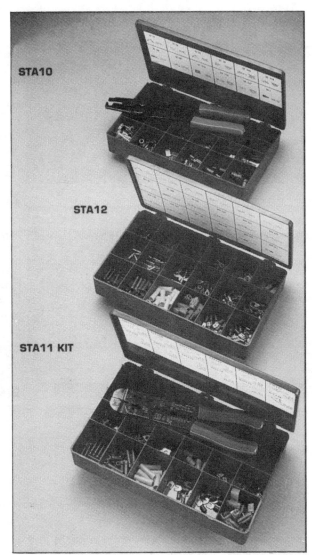

Solderless terminal kits are available that provide the most popular terminals, along with a crimper tool to install the terminals.

		Std. Pkg.	
ET30	Fusible Link 18 ga. 10½", Red (Ford)	10/1	
ET31	Fusible Link 18 ga., 8", Black (Chrysler)	10/1	
ET32	Fusible Link 14 ga., 10⅛", Green (Ford)	10/1	
ET33	Fusible Link 14 ga., 9½", Black (GM)	10/1	

These are examples of fusible links and their applications.

ET34	Fusible Link 16 ga., 8", Black (Chrysler)	10/1	
ET35	Fusible Link 16 ga., 9¼", Black (GM)	10/1	
ET36	Fusible Link 16 ga., 9⅛", Orange (Ford)	10/1	
ET37	Fusible Link 14 ga.,8", Black (Chrysler)	10/1	

More fusible links.

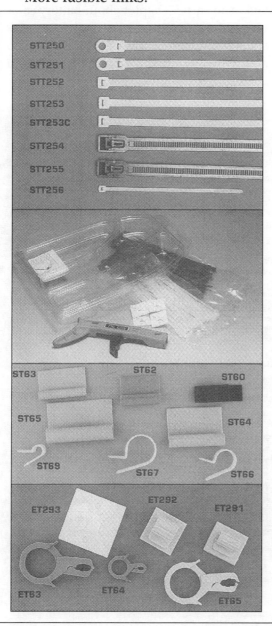

NYLON WIRE STRAPS

Std. Pkg.	Length	Mounting Hole	Releasable	Display Pack	Part No.
25	8½"	Yes	No	ET250*	STT250
25	15½"	Yes	No	ET251*	STT251
25	11¾"	No	No	ET252*	STT252
1000	11¾"	No	No		STT252M
10	14"	No	No		STT253
100	15½"	No	No		STT253C
25	5½"	No	Yes	ET254*	STT254
10	9¾"	No	Yes		STT255
100	4"	No	No	ET256*	STT256

WIRE TIE STRAP KIT & ACCESSORIES

Wire tie strap tensioning tool is easy-to-use. Helps keep electrical wires out of the way and properly routed. The tensioning tool comes as a separate unit or as part of a handy assortment.

Std. Pkg.	Description	Display Pack	Part No.
1 kit	Tensioning Tool Kit Tie Gun	ET11*	STA50

STA50 Contents: • 1 Tensioning Tool • 50 - 6" white universal tie straps • 50 - 8" black universal tie straps • 5 - mounting clips; instruction sheet.

WIRING CLIPS

Std. Pkg.	Description	Display Pack	Part No.
50	**Push-on metal wiring clip—for flat surfaces.**	ET290*	ST60
	Adhesive-backed wiring clip—		
50	1¼" L. × 3/16" I.D.	ET62*	ST62
50	1½" L. × ½" I.D.		ST63
50	1¾" L. × ⅜" I.D.		ST64
50	2" L. × ½" I.D.		ST65
	Molded nylon harness bracket—		
25	½" I.D.		ST66
25	¾" I.D.		ST67
25	¼" I.D.		ST69
	4 ea. of the ST66, ST67, ST69.	ET270*	
	Multi-colored clips on a 7" magnetic base - ¾" front jaw size (opened), (9 prs./bag).	ET63*	
	Multi-colored clips on a 14" ring. ⅜" front jaw size (opened), (16 prs./bag).	ET64*	
	Multi-colored clips on a 7" magnetic base ¾" front jaw size (opened), (9 prs./bag).	ET65*	
	¼" adhesive backed wiring clips.	ET291*	
	⅜" adhesive backed wiring clips.	ET292*	
	1½" nylon mounting base.	ET293*	

Also available are wire ties and factory-type loom material to give your job the professional look.

ing the rest of the circuit. If there is an overload in the circuit, the fusible link will burn in two, protecting the rest of the circuit.

Example: The 10-gauge wire that goes to the amp gauge in the dash from the alternator would have a fusible link made of 14-gauge wire. The fusible link became popular in the early 1970s, especially on GM pickups where they were used up until the mid-1980s.

A bit of trivia...If you are working on a wiring harness and you put power to a primary wire, how long does it take the current to get from the battery end of the wire, to the accessory end of the wire? In other words, when you turn on the power, how long do you have to wait for the power to get there? Not long, for electrical current travels through a primary wire at the speed of light, literally, which is 189,000 miles per second! At that rate of travel it takes only eight minutes for the current to travel from the sun to your driveway!

To put that in perspective, it would be the same as turning off the bedroom light, and trying to jump back into bed before the room got dark.

CUSTOM BATTERY CABLES - We also talked in an earlier chapter about battery cables and how to shop for them. Now we are going one step further and learn about how to make custom battery cables and ends. There will be some point in your life and times when you can't buy the length or size of battery cable you want already made up. So the best solution is to have one custom made.

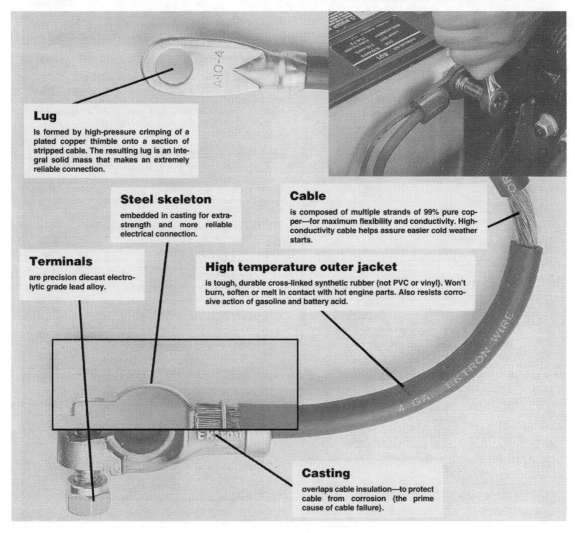

Lug
Is formed by high-pressure crimping of a plated copper thimble onto a section of stripped cable. The resulting lug is an integral solid mass that makes an extremely reliable connection.

Steel skeleton
embedded in casting for extra-strength and more reliable electrical connection.

Cable
is composed of multiple strands of 99% pure copper—for maximum flexibility and conductivity. High-conductivity cable helps assure easier cold weather starts.

Terminals
are precision diecast electrolytic grade lead alloy.

High temperature outer jacket
is tough, durable cross-linked synthetic rubber {not PVC or vinyl}. Won't burn, soften or melt in contact with hot engine parts. Also resists corrosive action of gasoline and battery acid.

Casting
overlaps cable insulation—to protect cable from corrosion {the prime cause of cable failure}.

Look for these quality features when buying a battery cable.

Let's review how a factory battery cable is made. We want to use as many of the features from the factory cables as we can, when building our custom battery cables.

The picture on the previous page shows how a factory built battery cable is made. Notice the features incorporated into a factory built battery cable, to give it a long service life.

When building a custom battery cable you should be able to identify the correct size of battery cable you want to use. Most new cable will have the size stamped on the outer insulation. As we learned earlier, and as the picture shows below, two cables can be the same physical size in outside diameter but contain completely different amounts of copper cable in the core.

When custom battery cables are made, it is necessary to use a large cable crimping tool such as that shown below. The cable's insulation will be stripped back just like it is on a piece of primary wire. The correct terminal end is selected along with a short piece of shrink tube.

First, a short piece of the correct size of shrink tube is slid onto the battery cable over the outside of the insulation. The outside insulation is then stripped back, and the bare copper cable is placed inside of the battery terminal.

Next the terminal is crimped using the large cable crimping tool. After the crimp is complete and pull tested to be sure it is tight, the short piece of shrink tube is slid up over the new crimp, and heat sealed. A heat gun or hair dryer is used to shrink the plastic tube over the joint. This creates a factory airtight connection that will provide protection against moisture, oxidation, and wear.

The picture at right shows a cable end being crimped on. The cutaway picture shows an actual cable crimp that has been sawed in half to show what a good crimp job is supposed to look like.

There is quite a wide selection of cable ends available for building custom battery cables. On the following page are a couple of cable make-up tips for common situations you will encounter.

When shopping for a pre-assembled battery cable there is quite a lot you can learn from the manufacturer's part number. The battery cable's part number will include overall length, gauge or size, terminal type, and insulation information.

Common in the "old days" were the braided ground straps. They were made of fine braided copper, then "tinned" (dipped in a coating of tin to protect the copper from moisture and corrosion). Nearly all of these ground straps were equal to a 2-gauge cable in current carrying capacity.

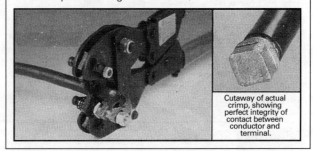

How to get a "super" crimping job . . .

- Use quality Super-Crimp terminals and quality heavy-duty crimping tools!

- Finish the job with quality heat-shrink tubing . . . for the ultimate in protection against moisture, oxidation and wear!

Cutaway of actual crimp, showing perfect integrity of contact between conductor and terminal.

A battery cable end being crimped on the cable using the correct tool. Next to that is a cable end sawed in half to show what a correct battery cable end installation looks like.

BATTERIES IN THE TRUNK are popular with street rod and some custom cars, simply because there is not any room left for a battery under the hood. If you do this be sure your battery is mounted securely, and use a battery like the OPTIMA that is sealed so you do not have to worry about vented gasses.

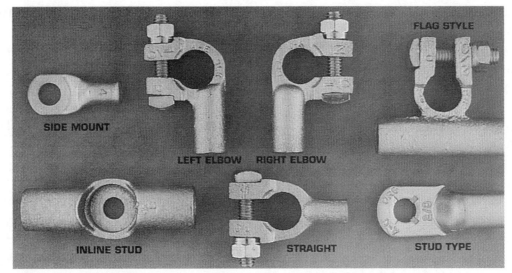

A variety of cable ends (courtesy Standard Wire and Cable).

CABLE MAKE-UP TIPS

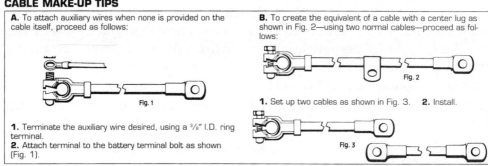

A. To attach auxiliary wires when none is provided on the cable itself, proceed as follows:

Fig. 1

1. Terminate the auxiliary wire desired, using a ³/₈″ I.D. ring terminal.
2. Attach terminal to the battery terminal bolt as shown (Fig. 1).

B. To create the equivalent of a cable with a center lug as shown in Fig. 2—using two normal cables—proceed as follows:

Fig. 2

1. Set up two cables as shown in Fig. 3.   **2.** Install.

Fig. 3

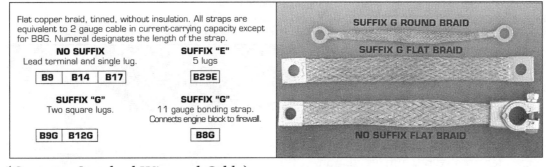

Flat copper braid, tinned, without insulation. All straps are equivalent to 2 gauge cable in current-carrying capacity except for B8G. Numeral designates the length of the strap.

NO SUFFIX Lead terminal and single lug.	**SUFFIX "E"** 5 lugs
B9 B14 B17	B29E

SUFFIX "G" Two square lugs.	**SUFFIX "G"** 11 gauge bonding strap. Connects engine block to firewall.
B9G B12G	B8G

SUFFIX G ROUND BRAID

SUFFIX G FLAT BRAID

NO SUFFIX FLAT BRAID

(Courtesy Standard Wire and Cable).

**RUNDLE'S RULES:**

Just a note about the "emergency" cable ends that are made so you can loosen a flat strap, then slide the cable under the strap and pinch or squeeze the cable under the strap to make the connection. **DON'T buy them! These are the worst cable clamps you can buy.** First of all, the cable is exposed to the moisture where it will turn green and steal your battery's cranking amps. Second, the only electrical contact surface you have with the cable is at the top and bottom of the strap and clamp. This will reduce your contact surface about 50 percent.

Or to put it another way, it is like going to work with only one shoe on. So if you are having battery cable problems, take a few minutes, and spend a few bucks, to fix it right. It will save you a mountain of trouble down the road.

Use the biggest cables you can find. 00 welding cable works well. The final flaw that trips up everyone is to not run a ground cable to the front of the car. Most people only run the ground cable down to the frame at the back of the car, and call it good. The problem with this is the ground for the starter is clear at the back of the car. As we have learned before, the closer the ground is to the starter the easier your car will start because the more of your battery's cranking amps will reach the starter. How do you think this will work when the battery ground is ten feet away from the starter and has to travel through all of the dirt and grease, or fresh paint on the frame just to get there?

I have seen race cars at the drag strip that would not start using two 800 cca batteries when the engine was warm. After convincing the owner to run a ground cable to the starter directly from the battery using the same size welding cable he used for the positive cable, his car easily started using only one battery! Seeing is believing!

Multiple Battery Hookups . . . Truck, Farm and Industrial Applications

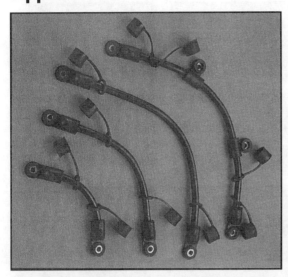

TYPICAL ASSEMBLY

STACKABLES . . .

- Universal application. Each cable can be used as a "top" or a "bottom." Cuts inventory in half . . . without sacrificing coverage.

- Precision-molded insulated end . . . provides a tight, maintenance-free seal.

- Protective cap protects against electrical shorting, corrosion and contamination.

- New, four-way cable—permits 4-battery cluster setups using only one part number: **A22-OOK.**

Only Four Part Numbers Cover Every Application

Part No.	Length	Gauge
A9-OOK	9"	2/0
A15-OOK	15"	2/0
A21-OOK	21"	2/0
A22-OOK	22" (4 Term.)	2/0

INSTALLATION TIPS

Cables are factory-assembled for use as "bottoms." To convert cable for "top" use, pry out insert with a screwdriver.

For a tight, maintenance free seal use: **BP99** stainless steel hold-down nuts. Std. pkg. 5. **BP101** black (neg.) stud nuts. Std. pkg. 5. **BP102** red (pos.) stud nuts. Std. pkg. 5.

Use **SST305**, 2/0 gauge butt splice connector to splice into O.E. cable and **HST240B** heat shrink tubing for extra protection.

(Courtesy Standard Wire and Cable).

113

CABLE HOOKUPS FOR MULTIPLE BATTERY CLUSTERS

Legend: **OEM** = OEM Starter Cable; **BC** = Butt Connector; **A9** = A9-OOK; **A15** = A15-OOK; **A21** = A21-OOK; **A22** = A22-OOK.

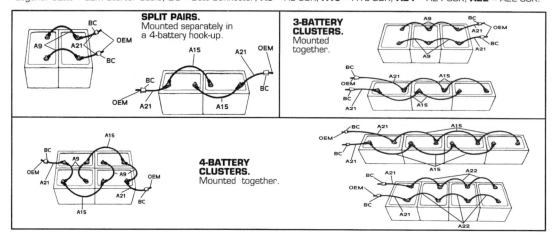

Description	Part No.
For adapting side terminal battery cable to top post batteries. (1 pos; 1neg.) Universal solid lead.	BP79
For adapting top post battery cable to side terminal battery. 3/8" threaded stud screws into negative battery terminal	BP77N
Same as BP77N—but for positive terminal.	BP77P
3/8" × 1/2" side terminal battery bolt.	BP78
3/8" × 1" extra long side terminal battery bolt. Auxiliary screw in end provides accessory hookup. Display pack (2/card).	BP78L
Stud-to-post conversion. Display pack (1pos.; 1neg./card)	BP141
Charging post,, side mount. Display pack (2/card).	BP182
Diesel side terminal battery cable bolt. For connecting 2 battery cables. Use with BP184 spacer.	BP183
Spacer required to connect diesel battery cable. Use with BP183 bolt.	BP184

BP79 BP77N

BP78 BP78L

BP141 BP182

BP183 BP184

Description	Part No.
Zinc-plated battery bolt (1 7/16" long) and nut (3/8" thick with raised shoulder).	BP40
Nut only.	BP40N
Battery post shim. Pre-formed soft lead.	BP56

BATTERY BOLTS & SHIMS

BP40 BP56

Examples of terminal adapters and hardware (courtesy Standard Wire and Cable).

Chapter 7 Review

1) 6-volt electrical systems require a minimum of 7 volts in the battery to function correctly.

2) 8-volt batteries will require a minimum of 9 volts from the charging system in order to be fully recharged.

3) 8-volt batteries will damage factory radios as well as your electrical dash gauges.

4) Because dash gauges require only a quarter of an amp to function, they must be protected when changing over to 12 volts. Most ceramic type voltage resistors have a 40 percent error rate, so a transistorized voltage drop must be used. A Runtz voltage drop offered by Fifth Avenue will do the trick.

4) Amp gauges ARE NOT voltage sensitive and do not have to be protected from 12 volts.

5) To actually reverse the polarity of an electrical system requires two things. First, reverse the battery cables. Second, reverse the wires on the amp gauge, or in the case of inductive amp gauges, simply reverse the wire loop.

6) If you plan to reverse your polarity, be sure you check with your radio man to see if your radio will make the trip. You can ask about any other electrical accessories you are not sure of.

Chapter

8

"Automotive Ignitions and Systems"

Chapter 8

Automotive Ignition And Systems

Second only to automotive wiring, ignition systems are the least understood. Like basic automotive wiring, we first need to identify the basic parts, then we can discuss what each part does and how everything is supposed to work.

A basic ignition consists of a battery, ignition coil, resistor, ignition switch, distributor, contact points, condenser, and plug wires. Let's start at the battery, which is the power source, and see what happens next.

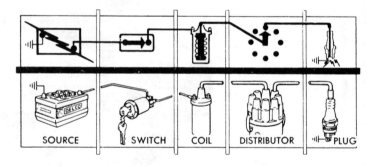

SOURCE   SWITCH   COIL   DISTRIBUTOR   PLUG

When battery power reaches the ignition switch, it will pass through the switch if the switch is closed or in the "ON" position. From there it will pass through a resistor that reduces the system voltage about 2 volts. (Voltage is reduced to lengthen the life of the contact points, just like in a voltage regulator.)

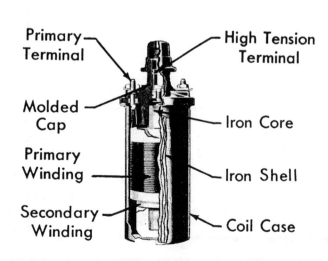

Primary Terminal

High Tension Terminal

Molded Cap

Iron Core

Primary Winding

Iron Shell

Secondary Winding

Coil Case

From there the power travels to the ignition coil. The ignition coil is actually an "autotransformer" that steps up the incoming voltage about 100 times so the voltage being sent to the distributor will be strong enough to fire a spark plug against the pressure of the compression inside of the engine cylinder. To fire a spark plug in a cylinder will usually require a minimum of 30,000 volts.

But let's back up a bit, and look at the inside of an ignition coil, and see what the inside is made of. Something pretty amazing must happen in order for the coil to be able to take the incoming voltage and boost it up over 100 times in just a fraction of a second.

The inside of an ignition coil is made up of a pole magnet, which is located in the center of the coil. To that pole magnet is connected a series of fine copper wires that are wound around the pole magnet. This inside group of fine wire that surrounds the pole magnet is called the primary windings. When the current from the battery passes through the primary windings it is stepped up or increased, to about 20 volts. (This is similar to what the field coils do inside of a generator or starter.) Then it is passed on to the contact points inside of the distributor. This circuit is called the **primary circuit**.

After the current from the primary circuit is sent to the distributor, the contact points in the distributor will open causing the magnetic field to collapse. The current is then sent back to the ignition coil, this time to the secondary windings. The secondary windings also consist of a series of fine copper wires that surround the outside of the primary windings. The secondary wires surround the primary wires and accept the magnetic field that was collapsed by the contact points. It is through the secondary windings that the voltage is increased over 100 times to approximately 30,000 volts. This voltage is then sent through the distributor to a spark plug where it ignites the fuel mixture in the cylinder.

The time that is allowed for the distributor to build up the secondary voltage to fire a spark plug is called **dwell time**. If there is not enough dwell time, the spark sent

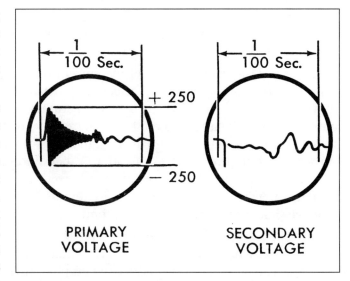

PRIMARY VOLTAGE   SECONDARY VOLTAGE

Since the primary and secondary windings are linked together magnetically, other things occur at the same time. With the collapse of the magnetic field, primary voltage, which may reach 250 volts, oscillates at a high frequency for the duration of the spark and then matches the open circuit oscillation of the current curve when the spark goes out. At the instant the magnetic field collapses, the secondary voltage may reach 25,000 volts if no spark occurs. When a spark does occur, it is usually at some lower value and secondary voltage drops back to a few thousand volts for a short interval of time.

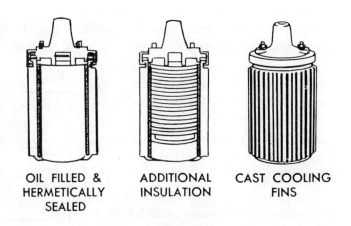

OIL FILLED & HERMETICALLY SEALED   ADDITIONAL INSULATION   CAST COOLING FINS

Heavy-duty ignition coils built with additional insulation, cast fins on the coil case, oil-filling, and other construction features help to dissipate heat faster and allow this coil to operate with less temperature increase than other coils. It can be used in hotter locations, and may be expected to provide long service under difficult conditions.

119

to the spark plug will be weak, possibly causing a misfire. At the same time this can cause the coil to overheat and fail completely. As a solution, a bigger coil can be used that would have a stronger output during the time allowed.

A coil is designed so that all of the current that enters the coil continues to flow in the same direction as long as it is in the coil. For instance, the pole magnet in a coil (such as that in a starter or generator) has current that naturally flows from north to south. Therefore, a coil is wired so that the incoming voltage from the battery enters at the north pole or + terminal. As the current continues through the coil's primary and secondary windings, it builds up strength but never changes direction. When the current is strong enough to fire a spark plug and is ready to leave the coil, the current exits out of the south terminal, the one designed to carry the current to the distributor. This is why **if you reverse the polarity of your vehicle, you need to leave the ignition coil alone.**

So what happens if you wire your coil backwards? You may experience hard starting, or in some cases a no start condition. This is because you are trying to force the current through the coil backwards. This will reduce the output of the coil about 30 percent or 5,000 volts. The reason for the drop in voltage is because you are reversing the direction of current through the coil, which will cause the currents to cancel out each other.

Meanwhile, because the ignition coil works hard at developing all of this high voltage, a lot of heat is developed. To keep the ignition coil cool and to help get rid of the excess heat, the coil is filled with a light oil. The oil will draw off the heat and extend the life of the coil. This is why, when you hook up a 6-volt coil to a 12 system (such as when you change a system over to 12-volt but forget the coil) the coil will swell up, get hot, cook all of the oil out of the inside, and cease to work! In other words you have literally cooked your 6-volt coil. Now, back to our lesson....

As we learned about the contact points in a regulator, an arc will occur when the points are opened and the current flow is suddenly stopped (just like a water faucet dripping after you turn it off). Because the contact points open and close about 12,000 times in just one mile of travel (in an eight-cylinder engine), something has to be done to take care of the arc created or the lifespan of the contact points will be short.

The **CONDENSER** has that job. The condenser prevents the arc from forming at the contact points (as they are opened) by providing a place for the current (or drip) to go. The condenser will bring the current flow to a quick controlled stop.

When this happens, the magnetic field developed by the coil is said to have COLLAPSED. This quick collapse of the magnetic field is what is sent to the secondary windings in the coil and creates the high voltage that fires the spark plug.

The picture at top, next page, shows how a condenser is constructed. If you are the curious type and cut a condenser open, you will find it made up of a cardboard-type paper insulation, wrapped in tin foil. At the base of the condenser you will find a coil spring. This spring will provide 40 pounds of pressure between the condenser wind-

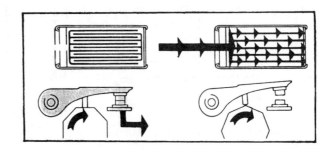

No standard automotive ignition system would function properly without a condenser. Condenser action requires high quality insulation between the two foil sheets of the winding, since high voltage is impressed on the condenser as it brings the current flow to a quick controlled stop.

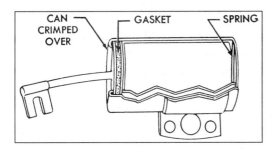

Parts of a condenser

ings and the case to ensure a good tight seal of the inner and outer gasket surfaces at all times.

Up through the 1940s condensers were prone to failure. Through industry research it was learned that the normal moisture contained in the insulation paper was the cause. So the manufactures began pre-drying the paper insulation and found that the dried paper condensers had 1,000 times the life of condensers manufactured using the non-dried insulation paper. So beginning in the mid-1940s when condensers began being constructed

using the pre-dried paper, most of the condenser troubles then disappeared, and ignition systems became much more reliable.

When a condenser fails, one of two things will happen. Either the car will become difficult to start, and/or when the engine is warm, the condenser will "leak" current (drip, just like a faucet), which will drain off some of the high voltage current from the ignition system, causing the engine to miss, especially at the higher rpm.

HEAVY DUTY CONDENSERS are necessary for some high voltage applications. Heavy-duty condensers will have thicker insulation between the foil sheets to contain the higher voltage. Since the insulation is thicker, more foil area is necessary to obtain the same condenser capacity.

Most heavy-duty condensers are made LONGER in length instead of bigger around. This is done in order to displace the heat. If the condensers were made bigger in physical diameter, the heat in the center of the condenser would build up causing the condenser to fail.

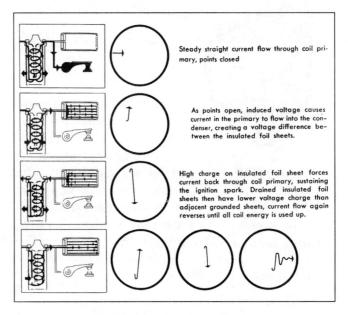

Steady straight current flow through coil primary, points closed

As points open, induced voltage causes current in the primary to flow into the condenser, creating a voltage difference between the insulated foil sheets.

High charge on insulated foil sheet forces current back through coil primary, sustaining the ignition spark. Drained insulated foil sheets then have lower voltage charge than adjacent grounded sheets, current flow again reverses until all coil energy is used up.

▼ If you are the practical joker type, you can artificially "charge" a condenser then leave it on a countertop for some unsuspecting visitor to come along and "discharge" it for you (by picking it up). While it will not hurt them, you shouldn't do it to somebody bigger than you are—unless you can outrun them.

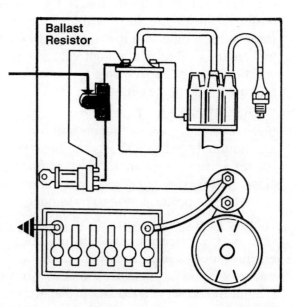

Some 12-volt systems use an ignition coil with an external series resistor assembly, the resistance of which is unaffected by changes in temperature.

121

The ignition coil will also have a resistor somewhere in the primary circuit. The resistor has the job of reducing the system voltage about 2 volts to extend the life of the contact points. In the earlier days the resistors were externally mounted, either to the coil or someplace on the battery side of the circuit. In later years they were placed inside of the coil, for this greatly increased reliability.

The **SECONDARY CIRCUIT** is the second part of the ignition system. It consists of the contact points, condenser, distributor cap, rotor, and the distributor itself.

We already know about the contact points and condenser, and their jobs. The distributor cap fits on top of the distributor and has the same number of terminals as the engine does cylinders. To these terminals are connected the spark plug wires that carry the current to the spark plugs.

The distributor cap fits over the distributor housing and on top of the rotor. The plug wire that fits into the distributor tower will have a rubber boot to seal out moisture and dirt, which can steal away part of the ignition's current.

The rotor fits under the distributor cap and spins on top of the distributor shaft. It has a brass or copper con-

RESISTOR

HIGH SIDES

ROTOR

A rotor has high sides and a special contoured surface that also reduces high tension leakage. A resistor built into the rotor serves to suppress high frequency radiation in the secondary circuit that would otherwise cause radio and TV interference. Non-resistor rotors are available when resistance type high tension cables are used.

tact tab that is able to touch the contact terminals inside of the distributor cap. The rotor spins in time with the engine so when the fuel enters a cylinder, the high voltage current will be sent to the spark plug to ignite the fuel mixture inside of the cylinder.

The **BREAKER PLATE** surrounds the breaker cam. The contact points and condenser are mounted to this plate. As the breaker cam rotates, it causes the contact plates to open and close. With every breaker cam rotation, one spark will be produced for each cylinder.

Since each cylinder fires every other revolution of the engine crankshaft (a four-cycle engine requires one crankshaft revolution for intake/compression and one crankshaft revolution for the power and exhaust cycle), the spark plug fires at the end of the compression stroke to make the power stroke. This means it is only necessary for the distributor shaft to spin at half of the engine speed.

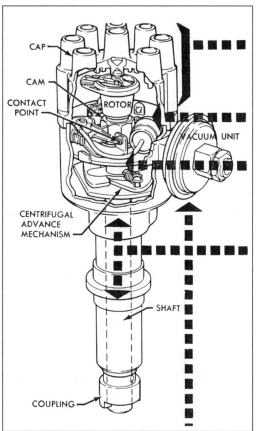

CAP

CAM

CONTACT POINT

ROTOR

VACUUM UNIT

CENTRIFUGAL ADVANCE MECHANISM

SHAFT

COUPLING

It is important that the point gap (the amount the contact points open) be measured and set accurately. Too wide or too narrow of an opening will cause difficult engine starting and poor engine performance.

From the coil, the current is carried through high tension wires, or spark plug wires to the rest of us, to the spark plug.

Many improvements have been made since the original plug wires were introduced with open terminals and cotton-wrapped plug wires. Many vintage car owners can tell tales of plug wires arcing across each other during a rainstorm when the wires got wet under the hood.

Many of the early style of spark plug wires and terminals are still available for vintage car restoration. It is also possible for you to custom build your own modern plug wires by buying the wire and terminal ends in bulk. In many antique car applications this is necessary to retain the look of the original wiring.

SPARK PLUGS are one of the most misunderstood parts of the whole ignition system. For instance, what polarity is a spark plug, and does it really matter? Yes, it does, and it is because of one of those sneaky little electrical rules which affects spark plugs: "High voltage current will flow more readily from a hot surface than from a cool one."

This brings us to an important crossroads. There are two theories on how you measure electricity. Here is a description of both.

 ## Mechanical Electron Theory

We are the practical "commonsense" people. In order to measure electricity we believe in what is called the **mechanical electron theory**. It states, "the way you measure electricity is by measuring the friction or resistance as it flows by in the opposite direction."

For instance, if you place your hand in a river or stream, you can feel the current flowing around your hand. If you begin to move your hand upstream against the current, friction is created. This friction can be measured. That is the basis of the mechanical electron theory and is the theory we use because we can measure the output. It is the theory that makes sense to us.

 ## Electron Flow Theory

The scientists and some engineers believe in another theory called **electron flow theory**. (In truth this is the "actual" way the current naturally travels.) However, just as in the example above, if you move your hand with the flow of current or in the actual direction the electricity is flowing, there is not a good way to measure the flow; in other words, you cannot measure the voltage or resistance. This is why positive ground vehicles could never have volt meters in the dash.

These two theories are partially responsible for the birth of positive ground electrical systems. As we learned earlier, when there were no accessories and magneto ignitions, the positive ground system made the most sense. The U.S. Military, to this day, still believes in the electron flow theory and many of its vehicles, even today, are positive ground, as are many heavy equipment vehicles. Any electrical theory taught to you by the military is usually electron flow theory.

Most everything in the civilian world is mechanical electron theory. As more and more accessories were developed and added to cars, a precise way of measuring the pressure behind the current was needed. This resulted in the switch to a negative ground electrical system. GM began the push in the 1940s. It is because of these two theories that many people are confused. The two theories get jumbled up, then automotive electricity makes no sense whatsoever!

Keep in mind that in this book I will use only the mechanical electron theory for any examples (as does most of the rest of the mechanical world). I just wanted to make you aware of where these stories come from, about which direction the electricity flows in a circuit, and how it is measured. There will be a few people who will argue theory with you just to confuse you, and they usually will succeed if you are not aware of what is going on.

Meanwhile, back to our spark plugs. The spark plug wire is connected to the center electrode of the spark plug. In mechanical theory, the center electrode is the positive connection from the coil and distributor. The current travels down the center of the spark plug via the electrode, and "jumps" the gap to the negative electrode, causing the electrical current to jump between the center electrode and the side electrode.

It will be this spark that ignites the fuel mixture in the cylinder. The leftover current will travel onward from the negative side electrode back to the battery via engine ground.

Because the center electrode is the hottest part of the spark plug, that is where the current from the distributor is sent. (Remember the rule that states electricity will travel easier from a hot surface than it will from a cold surface.) In fact, it will take about 5,000 less volts to fire a spark plug using the positive center electrode.

After a spark plug ignites the fuel mixture in a cylinder, and the rest of the initial current has flowed on down to the side electrode, the spark plug will also produce two or three less intense sparks using the leftover current in the spark plug's center electrode. Variations in the voltage required to fire a spark plug are due not only to engine compression, but also to engine speed, fuel mixture ratios, spark plug temperatures, width and shape of spark gap, and many other factors. The voltage available from an ignition coil also varies with engine speed. For exam-

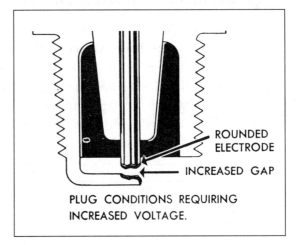

ROUNDED ELECTRODE

INCREASED GAP

PLUG CONDITIONS REQUIRING INCREASED VOLTAGE.

ple, at low speeds the contact points remain closed for a longer period of time and a high voltage is the result. At high speed the contact points remain closed a shorter period of time and a lower voltage is the result.

Misfiring will occur when the voltage required to fire the plug exceeds the voltage available from the ignition coil.

New distributor contact points make possible the highest available voltage from the coil, and new plugs have the lowest voltage requirements. Long periods of service deteriorate the contact points somewhat, lowering the minimum voltage available at all speeds. During the same period of service, a spark plug gap may increase as much as .015 of an inch, and the center electrode will usually become rounded, losing its sharp edge. These plug conditions increase the voltage required to fire by approximately 5000 volts, and thus reduce the available reserve. Filing off the rounded end of the spark plug center electrode and readjusting the gap will lower the voltage required to approximately that of a new plug.

The margin of voltage which can be obtained that is actually required to fire the spark plugs, represents the electrical reserve built into the ignition system. Installing the ignition coil close to the distributor and keeping spark plug leads as short as possible reduces the electrostatic capacity of the distribution system and thus makes a higher reserve available for the spark plugs.

❓ HOW DOES A HIGH COMPRESSION ENGINE AFFECT THE IGNITION SYSTEM?

As you might guess, a higher compression engine will create higher pressures in the cylinder, which will require a still higher voltage to ignite the fuel mixture. About 6,000 additional volts will be required. This was another reason for the changeover to 12 volts during the mid-1950s.

The introduction of Chevrolet's popular short stroke high compression V-8s is a good example. These V-8 motors reduced the dwell time of the distributor, causing a need for increased output of the coil.

By changing the electrical system over to 12 volts, the coil could provide the extra current needed as well as have a slight reserve. (Remember, when you double the voltage, it will require 50 percent less amps to do the same job. While it might appear that the 6-volt ignition system is underpowered, we have to remember that the maximum voltage is going to be required only at the instant of acceleration.)

As an interesting bit of trivia, Dodge in 1928 switched over to a 12-volt electrical system, believing it to be a better system. Even though the automaker would later be proven correct, no one else followed along, and with the lack of 12-volt replacement parts, and because Dodge used two 6-volt batteries for its 12-volt system, sales suffered. So Dodge discontinued using 12-volt electrical systems by 1930. Beginning in 1953, GM began using 12-volt systems, which had finally caught on. By 1956 all major manufacturers were using 12-volt systems.

The 6-volt system will do fine most of the time, but it will be during this slow speed acceleration time that the 6-volt system may fall short and cause the engine to misfire.

Another solution engineers used to help solve this problem was to eliminate all of the current leaks common to the old system. This resulted in the switch to high tension plug wires, replacing the cotton wrapped plug wires.

The cotton wrapped plug wires would cause problems when the car was driven in the rain. The cot-

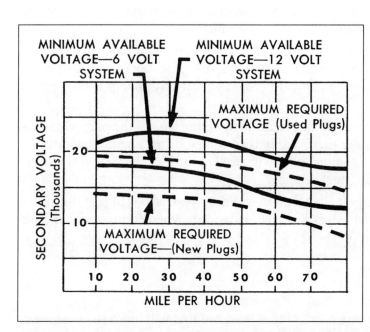

This graph shows the difference in available voltage between 6- and 12-volt ignition systems. Note the two minimum voltage curves on the chart. It is significant to note also that the 12-volt system maintains a higher ignition voltage not only over the critical low speed range, but also at high engine speeds.

ton wrap would become rain soaked causing "crossfire." (The current would "jump" between the wires because there was less resistance when the water became the carrier.) Also, the exposed outside surface of the spark plug was another source of leaks.

So by switching to a high tension plug wire, wrapped in a rubber insulation and using rubber boots to protect the spark plugs, the engineers reduced the voltage leaks of the old system by 50 percent to a measly five percent, a major improvement. So, instead of having to create more voltage by building a bigger ignition coil, the engineers simply increased the efficiency of the old system.

When we increase the size of battery cables and move the battery ground directly over to the starter from its original location on the engine block or frame, we are doing the same thing. We are increasing the efficiency of the electrical system. We are making it easier for all of the current available at the battery to be transferred to the starter motor by simply eliminating the obstructions and leaks. In other words, it is easier to run around the block if you have two tennis shoes on, instead of one tennis shoe and one sandal. While both are shoes, the tennis shoes together are more efficient than the tennis shoe and the sandal. Less effort is required, and the job is done more efficiently.

During the 1960s came the development and introduction of the resistor spark plugs. Many people assume they are popular for radio noise suppression. (They do help.) But in fact they have a completely different duty. The resistor that is placed inside of the top of a spark plug is there to stop the aftersparks or electrical "drips," much like a condenser does for the contact points. This will greatly extend the life of the spark plugs. It is for this reason that you will seldom see a nonresistor spark plug offered from the spark plug companies these days, unless it is an old number that is a low volume seller.

The resistor plug wires do help with noise suppression somewhat; however, most of the noise suppression duties have been taken care of by the radio manufacturers long ago, who learned to protect the radios from the ignition noise. Resistor spark plugs will work fine in your antique engine and should provide a longer service life.

It should also be noted that spark plugs are designed to work in a heat range of 900-1200 degrees Fahrenheit. This is the temperature at which the spark plugs are the most efficient. Spark plugs are designed differently for many different applications to help them work in their ideal heat range.

A "colder" plug will carry heat up from the electrode tip to the base of the plug where the heat will be transferred to the cylinder head, and in turn cooled by the engine coolant. This is for an engine that runs warm. A "hotter" plug will contain most of the heat at the tip of the plug to help burn off carbon and fuel deposits.

One reason spark plugs last longer today than they did 30 years ago is in part due to the use of unleaded fuel. Unleaded fuel leaves less engine deposits when compared to the old leaded fuel.

MODERN SPARK PLUGS

Every 20 years or so a revolutionary spark plug is invented that will increase horsepower and performance by some magical feat. If you will look back into automotive history, there have been a number of them, including "Jet Igniters" and many other different styles of multiple electrode plugs.

Do they work any better? In most cases, no. Here is why. Using the new split electrode plugs currently on the market, they show the flame spark or kernel splitting into two separate flames, one on each of the electrodes. This may happen for demonstration purposes, where there is no pressure from the inside of a cylinder.

But if you try to fire that same plug in a normal cylinder, under 200+ pounds of pressure, in three-thousandths of a second, the spark will take the path of least resistance, and will jump to one electrode or the other, but not both!

Piston engine aircraft have used multi-electrode spark plugs for years, simply because if a piece of carbon gets behind an electrode and grounds out that electrode, then the spark plug would not fire. No power from that cylinder and/ or any others makes flying an air-

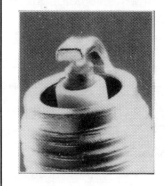

On the left is a single electrode spark plug; on the right a split or dual electrode spark plug.

craft pretty exciting! But by having multiple electrodes the flame kernel can go to one of the other electrodes, and the plug would still fire. We all know what happens to an airplane if the engine misfires and stalls under load.

The same goes for plug wires. In most cases the "extra big" center core wires will gain you very little, just as two core wire plug wires will not gain you much. Remember, your original plug wires already deliver an excess of current. Advertised sizes of 7, 8, even 9 millimeters, are common in performance wires. The size is determined by the outside diameter. The fatter outside insulation wires can help in some racing applications to prevent crossfiring. But for the average engine, there are minimal benefits.

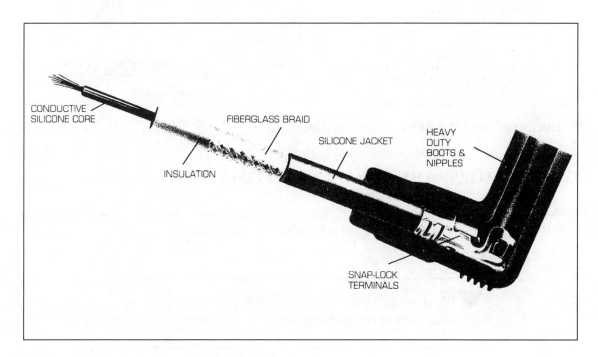

The composition of a modern spark plug wire.

When shopping for ignition wires, look for quality brass terminals and copper core wire along with a good quality flexible outside insulation. The picture below shows what features you should look for when buying ignition wires.

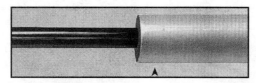

EPDM INSULATION — the inner insulation layer is EPDM rubber, rated highest at 700 volts/mil dielectric breakdown. There's no finer insulation material available. The insulating layer shields the core and offers highest protection against voltage leaks and shorts to ground.

FULL FIBERGLASS BRAID — A woven fiberglass braid around the insulation layer provides extra strength, toughness, and flexibility.

SILICONE OUTER JACKET * — Like the silicone core, the high-quality silicone outer jacket protects the wire against harsh engine compartment conditions—heat, moisture, grease, oil, road salt and other contaminants which can degrade the wire.

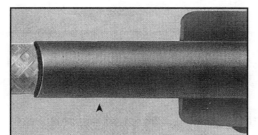

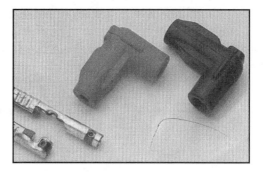

HEAVY DUTY BOOTS — Made from heat-resistant silicone*, with thick reinforcing ribs for extra strength and durability, these boots last longer and more effectively protect the critical terminal connection from outside elements. Inner "step" keeps moisture out, and locks voltage inside the boot.

CORROSION-RESISTANT SNAP-LOCK TERMINALS—Provide tight, positive connections between the wire and the spark plug, distributor cap and coil. You can hear and feel the "click" when the terminal is properly sealed. Engine vibration, rust and corrosion can't cause the terminals to "back out" or lose contact.

Features to look for when buying ignition wires.

DISTRIBUTORS - THE ADVANCE INFORMATION

We already know how the inside of the distributor works and what jobs the contact points and condenser are assigned. But what about the advance mechanisms; what do they do, and how come there are two of them?

WHAT PURPOSE DOES THE CENTRIFUGAL OR VACUUM ADVANCE HAVE WHEN IT IS CONNECTED TO THE DISTRIBUTOR?

Officially they are called distributor advance mechanisms, and they "time" the high voltage output of the coil so that it is delivered to the cylinder at the exact time the fuel mixture is ready to be ignited.

Ignition Wire Makeup Techniques

TO MAKE UP IGNITION WIRES FROM COMPONENTS:

1. Measure and cut a length of wire that is 1¼" longer than the original wire.

Slide the desired boot onto the wire, using oil or soapy water as a lubricant, check for proper orientation.

2. Using the 14 gauge "notch" on stripping tool, strip each end of the wire. Be careful not to damage the core during stripping.

3. The bare core should be ⅛" longer than of the crimping area on the terminal used.

4. Starting with the spark plug end, fold the core back over the outer jacket tightly and hold the tuck while the plug terminal is positioned so the barrel of the terminal traps the folded core against the jacket.

5. Using the notch marked "7 & 8MM", squeeze the tabs on the terminal so they encircle the wire completely. Make final crimps at several locations along the barrel of the terminal. Make sure the terminal is securely crimped and that no excess core ("tail") is exposed.

6. Slide boot over terminal.

FOR MAXIMUM PROTECTION AGAINST HEAT, MOISTURE AND CORROSION, PROCEED AS FOLLOWS:

7. Cut a section of "Cool Cover" (a heat-resistant braid) about the same length as the wire, and slip the braid over the unterminated end until the leading edge of the braid covers the edge of the boot.

8. Slide two sections of heat shrink tubing over the unterminated end of the wire, and position the leading section so that it overlaps the plug boot and the braid. (Note: The second section of heat shrink tubing will be for the distributor boot.)

9. Apply heat to the heat shrink tubing until it contracts tightly around the boot and braid.

Terminate the distributor end and push the boot over the termination.

Heat shrink the remaining section of tubing over the braid and boot.

There are two types of advance mechanisms; one that works off of vacuum and one that works mechanically. Let's take a look and see why we would need such a device in the first place.

When an engine is idling, the ignition spark is timed to ignite the fuel mixture just before the piston reaches top dead center. But at higher rpm there is less time for the fuel mixture to enter, ignite, and exit the cylinder. So that means the fuel mixture must be ignited earlier in the piston's cycle. Lost? Okay, here is an example.

EXAMPLE: Let's say the time it takes for the fuel mixture to ignite and burn in a cylinder is .003 of a second. In order for the cylinder to produce maximum power the fuel mixture must be ignited and burning at between 10-20 degrees past top dead center of piston travel. (Top dead center is when the piston is at the top of its travel in the cylinder).

At 1,000 rpm the engine crankshaft will travel 18 degrees of a cycle in .003 of a second. At 2,000 rpm the crankshaft

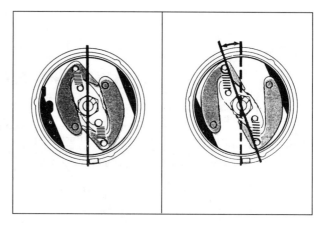

The centrifugal advance required varies considerably between various engine models. To determine the advance for a given engine, the engine is operated on a dynamometer at various speeds with wide-open throttle. Spark advance is varied at each speed until the range of advance that gives maximum power is found. The cam assembly weights and the springs are then selected to give this advance. Timing consequently varies from no advance at idle to full advance at high engine speed where the weights reach the outer limits of their travel.

travels through 36 degrees of a cycle in .003 of a second. Since the fuel mixture must be ignited and burning between 10-20 degrees after top dead center, regardless of the engine speed, it is now clear why we have to speed things up a little.

The timing of spark-to-engine speed is the job of the centrifugal advance mechanism, which is assembled on the distributor shaft. The mechanical advance, as it is usually called, is made up of two counterweights, springs, and a cam assembly. When the distributor shaft spins, the centrifugal force will separate or pull the weights apart.

When this happens, the breaker cam is rotated in the direction of the distributor's shaft rotation, causing the breaker cam to advance and make the ignition of the fuel mixture occur sooner. The higher the engine rpm, the faster the advance will occur up to a limit set by the stops, which is determined by the power curve of the engine.

 OK, IF WE HAVE A MECHANICAL ADVANCE, WHY DO WE ALSO NEED A VACUUM ADVANCE?

Because of fuel economy. Under part throttle conditions, the engine develops low vacuum in the intake manifold, resulting in a weaker fuel mixture being drawn into the cylinder. The fuel mixture is also leaner than normal, and because there is a smaller physical amount of the fuel mixture present, the mixture will not be compressed in the cylinder as much. It is because of this condition that even more additional spark advance is necessary.

This is in part because the leaner fuel mixture under less compression will burn slower. This means that the fuel mixture will have to be ignited much sooner in order to get the maximum power from the leaner mixture.

The most common type of vacuum advance is the external type. The external type was common up through the mid-1950s. This type of vacuum advance was made up of a spring-loaded airtight diaphragm connected to the carburetor via a copper or metal line. When the throttle of the carburetor opened, the vacuum change caused the diaphragm to work,

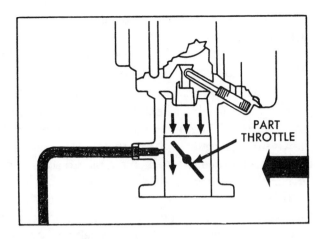

Engine vacuum

and made the breaker plate rotate just as it did with the mechanical advance. With the motor running, when the throttle is depressed the vacuum will drop, causing the advance diaphragm to move. You will physically be able to see this happen if you watch the distributor while the engine rpm rise.

A common failure of the vacuum advance unit is caused by a hole in the diaphragm. This will cause the vacuum to leak past and the advance will not work. This will show up especially during acceleration where engine rpm will be slow to increase and the engine may stumble under acceleration. Some later distributors featured internal vacuum advance mechanisms. They worked in much the same way as the external vacuum advance units.

CENTER BEARING VACUUM ADVANCE ASSEMBLY - TYPE A

The center bearing vacuum advance assembly shown is an important part of the distributor in many passenger cars. This bearing advance assembly is designed to be capable of responding quickly to the pulses of the vacuum unit that actuates it. It is extremely stable in operation, and its rugged construction makes possible long service life with accurate performance.

The construction of a Type "A" vacuum advance assembly is not complicated. It consists of a movable breaker plate, lubricating felt, support plate with side spring, and the retainers, washers, and shims necessary to maintain the assembly.

The movable breaker plate contains a bronze bearing assembled at its center. This bearing turns freely in the mating hole of the support plate. The movable plate is supported by three built-in, molded, anti-friction bearings that glide over the

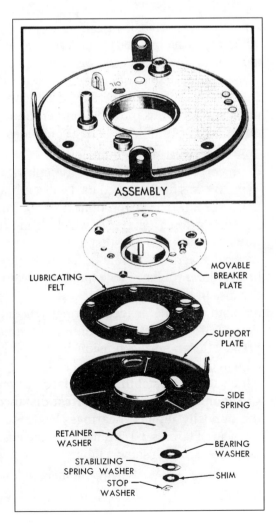

ASSEMBLY

LUBRICATING FELT

MOVABLE BREAKER PLATE

SUPPORT PLATE

SIDE SPRING

RETAINER WASHER

STABILIZING SPRING WASHER

STOP WASHER

BEARING WASHER

SHIM

upper surface of the support plate as the movable plate is rotated. The molded bearings are designed with a convex surface for minimum friction. A lubricating felt, located between the two plates, supplies constant lubrication for the three outer bearings and the center bearing. The felt also prevents dirt and dust particles from getting on the bearing surfaces.

The two plates and the lubricating felt are held together by a retainer washer that fits into a groove in the center bearing. Proper tension between the plates is maintained by a stabilizing spring washer assembly on a post extending from the lower side of the movable plate down through a slot in the support plate. The movable plate is stabilized in operation by the three support bearings which are placed so as to offset opposing thrusts of the breaker lever arm spring and the stabilizing spring washer. Sidewise motion of the upper plate while the distributor is operating is prevented by the combined action of the side spring and the breaker lever arm spring. The spring-loaded construction of the breaker plate automatically takes up looseness created by normal wear and prevents chattering. Every wearing part, in fact, has a spring take-up to maintain accurate operation.

CENTER BEARING VACUUM ADVANCE ASSEMBLY - TYPE B

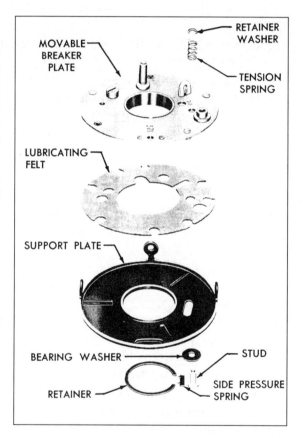

When distributors are mounted vertically so the weight of the movable breaker plate is a straight downward force, it is possible to use a much lighter stabilizing spring to prevent vibration of the breaker plate. A freer moveable plate (without play or tendency to vibrate) is desirable, of course, since it can react more quickly to the slightest vacuum impulse, and thus provide proper timing under all part-throttle operating conditions.

A center bearing vacuum advance assembly incorporating this feature, described as Type "B", was first supplied for 1953 applications (see illustration, top of next page). The amount of force (leverage) which tends to upset the stability of either center bearing vacuum advance assembly is the force at the breaker lever rubbing block multiplied by the distance from the rubbing block center line to the bottom of the molded bearings (Dimension "C"). NOTE: **It is important that breaker lever spring tension be properly adjusted. The moment of force (leverage) which tends to stabilize the plate in type "A" is the minimum force of the stabilizing spring multiplied by the shortest distance from the post to a line through the centers of the opposite molded bearings** (Dimension "A"). On the type "A" assembly, the stabilizing moment of force is 3-1/2 times the opposing force, which explains why an apparently loose fitting plate does not show a timing variation while in service.

To improve the stabilizing moment of force on the Type "B" plate with a light coil stabilizing spring, the molded bearings were spaced to obtain a greater distance between the stabilizing

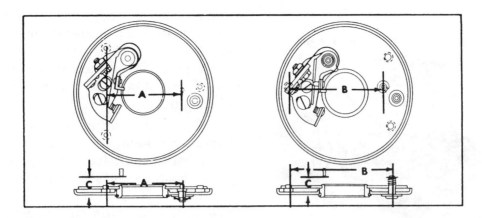

spring force and the opposite bearing (Dimension "B"). With the minimum stabilizing force of 18 ounces multiplied by the increased distance, the stabilizing moment of force is 2-1/2 times the opposing force. It should be remembered, however, that the Type "B" plate is specified only for use in distributors having vertical mountings.

EXTERNAL ADJUSTMENT DISTRIBUTOR

Greater timing accuracy has been the aim of all ignition engineers. In the external adjustment type distributor, many of the causes for variation have been eliminated, resulting in greater timing accuracy, greater durability, and simplified service.

In making these improvements, a radical change in appearance resulted and many new features were provided. The new all-weather cap encloses the breaker and automatic advance mechanisms, and is held on by two spring-loaded latch-type fasteners. The specially designed rotor serves as a cover for the advance mechanism which is above the circuit breaker mechanism. The contact point opening is set by a hexagonal wrench, and cam angle can be adjusted through a window in the cap with the engine operating.

Timing accuracy has been increased by eliminating multiple diameters on the main shaft, by lowering the circuit breaker cam to the main bearing height so that overhang does not exist, and by providing more accurate circuit breaker plate movement so that the cam always maintains its proper relationship to the rubbing block of the breaker lever.

The circuit breaker plate rides on a machined ring on the distributor casting

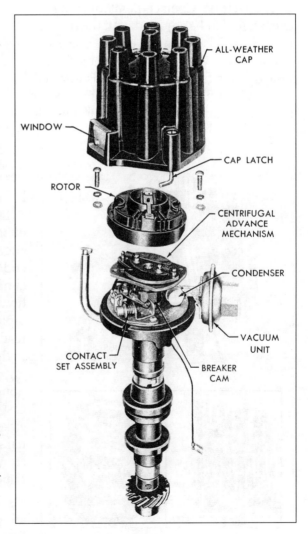

Modern distributor

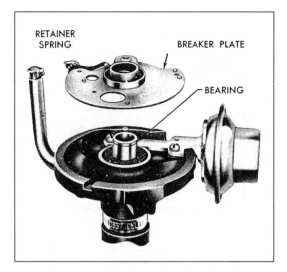

which is lubricated by a felt wick. The plate is retained by a low rate retainer spring. Elimination of friction points, spring forces, and breaker plate tilt provides timing accuracy under all part-throttle and full-throttle operating conditions.

More accurate action of the vacuum advance mechanism has been achieved by the use of a one-piece circuit breaker plate which rotates about the outside diameter of the upper main bearing, thus making the circuit breaker plate and main shaft concentric in operation.

A one-piece assembly of the circuit breaker lever and contact support, complete with adjusting screw mounts on the circuit breaker plate with two attaching screws, is shown below. Alignment of contact points is assured in manufacture by attaching the contact point to the support after the breaker lever is assembled. Spring tension is also adjusted at the factory. Contact point opening or cam angle can be adjusted with the distributor cap in place and the engine operating at idle speed. With the distributor cap window open, a hexagonal wrench is inserted in the adjusting screw and turned to obtain the specified setting. A normally difficult

operation now is accomplished in a very short period of time.

Ignition distributors on "V-8" engines are often rather inaccessible at the rear of the engine compartment. To remove the distributor and replace contact points in such a case is a chore. The external adjustment distributor, however, does not have to be removed to replace the contact point. Cap removal is readily accomplished by placing a screwdriver in the latch head slots, pressing down and turning approximately 90 degrees in either direction. This movement unhooks the cap from two cast base lugs. Loosening two contact support attaching screws, loosening the primary terminal screw, and disconnecting two terminal clips allows the complete contact assembly to be removed.

The replacement contact set is factory adjusted so that when installed the engine will run. With the engine running, point opening

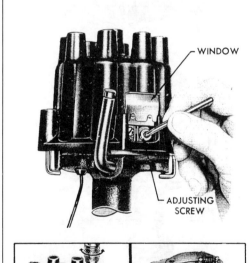

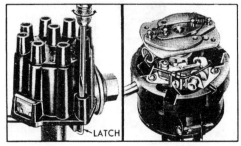

or cam angle is adjusted (through the cap window) according to specification. This operation saves valuable time for the mechanic and a perfectly adjusted distributor is supplied to the customer.

Demands imposed by special operating conditions are responsible for many design variations in distributors. Thus, heat, vibration, dust, moisture, length of service between overhauls, and many other factors must be considered when selecting component parts capable of meeting the demands of a specific installation.

Screw-type high tension terminals hold all leads in permanent contact, preventing loose connections—often a troublesome cause of ignition failure.

Distributor caps and rotors made with mica-filled molding materials retard the formation of carbonized paths when electrical leaks occur due to excessive moisture from condensation, rain, snow, etc. The addition of baffles and the changing of rib contours has decreased voltage leakage by increasing the distance between inserts and ground. These parts are also given a special insulating varnish coating that causes water to ball up and roll off the surfaces without providing a continuous path for the high tension current.

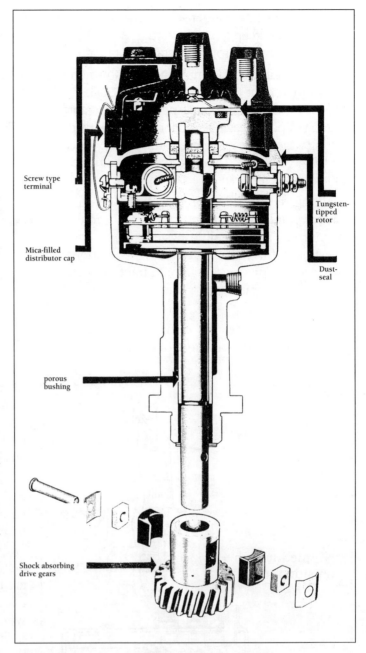

Heavy duty distributor

Built-in distributor shaft lubrication is possible by using a porous bushing extending from the upper to the lower part of a recessed housing. An oil reservoir is thereby formed between the porous bushing and casting. Oil from the reservoir seeps through the bushing to supply shaft lubrication. Only 20 W oil should be used to replenish this oil supply.

High compression engines have more torsional vibration, which causes excessive wear on distributor parts and often shears gear and coupling drive members. The use of flexible shock-absorbing drive gears and couplings when this condition occurs provides longer periods of trouble-free service. A synthetic rubber cushion between the extreme lower end of the coupling and the driven member absorbs much of the torsional vibration and reduces the transmission of shock to the internal parts of the distributor.

The heavy-duty condenser, below right, also the heavy-duty ignition coil, are hermetically sealed to keep out all moisture. A combination of these units helps prevent road failure, since moisture absorption has always been responsible for much ignition trouble.

The cam lubricator is impregnated with a non-bleeding high temperature grease to prevent oil being thrown out on the contact points. Oil should never be added to the cam lubricator. Oil thrown off onto the contact points causes rapid wearing of point material and forms a black oxide coating which adds resistance to the circuit. When the felt becomes hard and worn, the cam lubricator should be replaced.

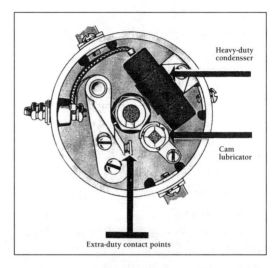

Heavy-duty condensser

Cam lubricator

Extra-duty contact points

A tungsten-tipped rotor, as well as extra-duty contact points (point having more than double the normal amount of tungsten) are a good investment for income-producing operations. Long periods of service without attention make these more durable parts ideal for truck and coach operations.

A dust seal under the distributor cap completely seals off the breaker compartment from dust or dirt, and also nitrous oxide fumes caused by sparks at the rotor tip. With the dust seal and a cam lubricator, wear of the breaker cam and rubbing block is reduced.

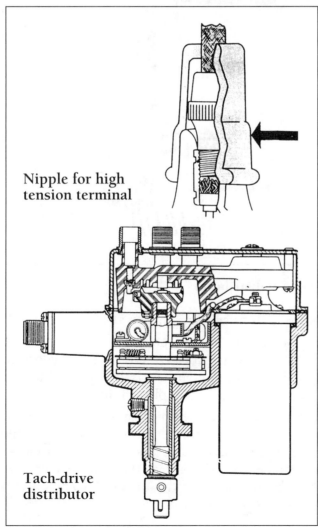

Nipple for high tension terminal

Tach-drive distributor

All high tension terminals on the coil and distributor should be fitted with nipples of a synthetic elastic compound to protect and maintain a clean surface on a portion of the towers. Moisture and dust accumulations are thereby prevented from forming a conductive path to ground which would cause engine missing. A tight fit by the nipple is required on both the cable and terminal. These precautions prevent drowning out of the ignition by water spray.

Distributors that can operate under water, and distributors with special drive shafts to provide a means of driving an engine governor or tachometer illustrate other special features available for extra-duty distributors.

This completes our chapter on ignition and wiring. If you have survived all of this so far, stop and pat yourself on the back. You have done an excellent job. The next chapter will bring us up to the modern times as we learn about alternators, and how to apply that technology to our antique vehicles. From here on out you have it made. Everything will finally start to fit together and make sense.

Chapter 8 Review

1) To greatly increase the efficiency of your starting system, move the battery ground cable so that it goes directly between the battery and a starter mounting bolt.

2) Using the correct size of battery cable will help cure most common starting problems. Increasing the physical size of the battery cable will also help cure starting problems when the engine is warm.

3) The ignition ballast resistor has the important job of reducing the system voltage by two volts, to extend the life of the contact points in the distributor. Modern coils will have this resistor built in; that eliminates a common trouble spot. Modern coils can be used to upgrade the earlier style.

4) Quality ignition components are important. Distributor caps should have brass or copper terminals, as should the contact points. Aluminum is a common substitute that often causes high resistance in the ignition circuit as the aluminum begins to corrode from the moisture present in the air. High resistance will result in hard starting and poor performance.

NOTES

Chapter 9

"Welcome to the Modern Age....Alternators"

Chapter 9

Welcome To The Modern Age: Alternators

With the addition of more and more electrical accessories, the car manufacturers of the early 1960s again found themselves in much the same spot as in the mid-1950s. The demand for electrical energy was growing steadily, while the generator charging system just about reached its design limits as far as increasing the output. It was time for a change.

The car manufacturers had been working on a new type of charging system for a number of years. Having experienced this same problem before, they knew what was coming.

So along about 1963, most of the car manufacturers introduced a new type of charging system using what is called an alternator. It was so named because this new charging system produced an alternating or "AC" current as opposed to the generator type charging system, which produced only "DC" current.

While the battery and all of the accessories still required DC current, the new charging system proved to be a winner. Let's take a look and see how alternators work, and how AC voltage is turned into DC voltage. For our example we will use a Delco system because they are probably the most common and easiest to understand.

The parts of this new alternator charging system consist of a **stator assembly**, **the rotor assembly**, **the slip ring end frame**, **and finally a drive end housing**. Let's look at each of these parts separately so we can understand just what duty each of them is supposed to perform.

The **rotor assembly** is much like the physical arrangement of the armature inside of the generator. It is made up of field windings (composed of two iron segments with interlacing fingers, called poles), the rotor shaft itself, and two slip rings.

When all of these parts are assembled together, it is called a rotor assembly. The rotor shaft rides inside of the alternator housing on two sealed bearings, as opposed to the bronze or brass bushings used in most generators.

The two **slip rings** are mounted to the rotor shaft and are what the brushes ride on. This is similar to the commutator end of the armature shaft. The slip rings, mounted to the rotor shaft, are attached to the leads from the field coils.

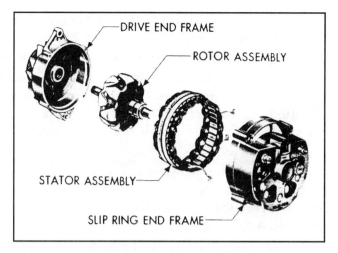

The parts of an alternator charging system.

When the ignition switch is first turned on, current from the battery passes through one brush, then through one slip ring, to the field coil. After leaving the field coil, the current flows to the other slip ring and brush before returning to the battery via the system ground. This flow of current and the path it takes is called field current.

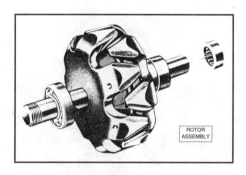
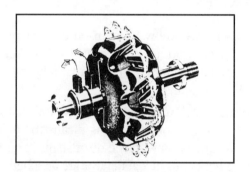

When the battery current flows through the field coil, a magnetic field is formed with a north magnetic pole in half of the rotor segments and a south magnetic pole in the other half of the segments. As the rotor turns, a spinning magnetic field is created.

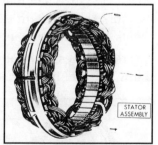

The **stator assembly** is made up of a **laminated iron frame and three output windings**, which are wound to the slots of the frame. The stator assembly is placed between two stationary end frames, or housings, that house the rotor and other assemblies. The rotor assembly fits inside of the stator assembly. A small air gap is left between the rotor poles and stator laminations. As the rotor spins, the alternate north and south poles pass each loop in the stator windings causing current to be developed in the windings.

Since the stator has both north and south poles spinning alternately, a magnetic field is created that causes the current to flow first in one direction, then in the other. This flow of current in two different directions is called alternating current or AC current. (This is the same kind of current that is used inside your house and shop.)

But our battery and accessories require only direct current or DC current. So we have to change the AC current into DC current. That is done using what are called diodes. **A diode is a simple one-way electrical valve that lets current flow in one direction only.**

An alternator will use six diodes to reverse the current flow. Three will be negative diodes mounted in the slip ring end of the alternator housing. These three diodes are often called the **diode trio**. There will also be three positive diodes mounted into a heat sink that will be insulated from the slip ring frame.

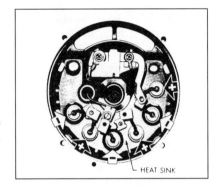

The three diodes mounted in the heat sink form what is called a rectifier bridge. The stator is in turn connected to the three studs on the **rectifier bridge** to form a complete electrical circuit.

A condenser is also mounted into the slip ring housing to protect the rectifier bridge and diode trio from high voltages. As an added benefit, the condenser also suppresses engine noise (created by the alternator) to the radio.

LET'S COMPARE APPLES TO ORANGES

Now that we know how an alternator produces current and how that current is changed to DC current from AC, let's compare the alternator to a regular generator.

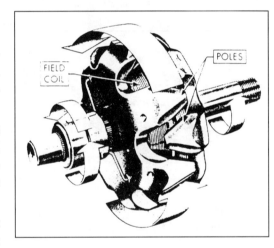

The alternator uses one large field coil that is located on the rotor shaft. This means the field coils will spin along with the rotor shaft. In contrast, the field coils in a generator are attached to the housing of the generator and are stationary.

The stator windings in an alternator are attached to the stator frame and carry the output current. They perform the same job as the segments on the armature of the generator.

The brushes in the alternator are connected in series with the field coil, and carry only a low voltage. In contrast, the brushes in a generator carry the total output from the gen-

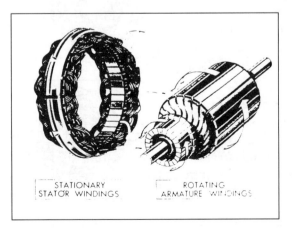

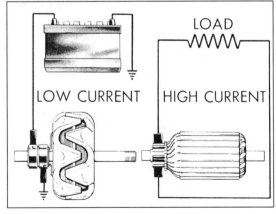

erator. The low current carried by the alternator brushes greatly extend their life over that of the generator's brushes.

The regulator used on the early alternators was much like those used by the generators. It wasn't long, however, before the external regulators became solid state. This eliminated many of the common problems inherit in all regulators in general. The temperature change, along with the arcing of the points, were two of the major problems that were overcome, resulting in a much more reliable charging system.

Along about 1973, Delco engineers figured out how to place a solid state regulator inside of the alternator. Typically, alternator output by this time was in the 60-amp range, which allowed for a good reserve capacity. Many other manufacturers did the same.

FEATURES AND BENEFITS - ALTERNATORS VS. GENERATORS

• Construction is the primary difference. In the case of a generator, the armature is the part that spins, limiting the rpm the generator can spin without damage. But an alternator, on the other hand, has the armature stationary and it's the field windings that spin, eliminating the problem of high rpm damage.

• Weight is another factor. Most 40-amp generators of the era weighed 30-plus pounds each. In contrast, a modern alternator weighs only 11 pounds and has a 60-amp output, plus the alternator has the ability to recharge the battery at idle and low rpm.

• Another obvious difference is pulley diameter. On an alternator it is not uncommon for a pulley to be one-third smaller in diameter that those found on a generator. This helps account for the alternator's strong output at engine idle because the alternator is spinning at higher rpm during idle. A smaller diameter pulley can be used on an alternator because it is more difficult to damage an alternator by too high of rotor speed. Maximum rpm for an alternator is about 12,000 rpm.

Most alternators are driven at 1.5 of engine speed. To reach maximum alternator rpm, a normal automotive engine application would have to be turning 8,000 rpm, which would not happen for long!

Alternators are usually easier to repair than a generator. There is no armature to undercut and no commutator grooves to clean. Sealed bearings used in alternator construction means most alternators are trouble free in between normal repairs. Eighty to one hundred thousand miles of use is common for most modern alternators, with little maintenance required.

UPDATING TO AN ALTERNATOR

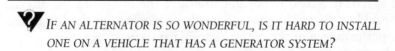

IF AN ALTERNATOR IS SO WONDERFUL, IS IT HARD TO INSTALL ONE ON A VEHICLE THAT HAS A GENERATOR SYSTEM?

Surprisingly not, if you do a little homework beforehand. Your first task will be to figure out how big of an alternator you will need for your application. To figure this out, simply add up the total amp draw of all of your accessories, including those "extra" accessories you have added or are maybe going to add in the future. To that total add 20 percent as a reserve. The total number you come up with is the smallest size your alternator's output should be.

ALTERNATOR OUTPUT RATINGS

An alternator's output is rated much like a generator's, and is the maximum output that the alternator is capable of producing for an extended period of time. Unlike a generator, however, **an alternator will normally provide 60 percent of its rated output at an idle**. This is why you add a 20 percent reserve to your total output requirements, so you won't run short of amps at idle.

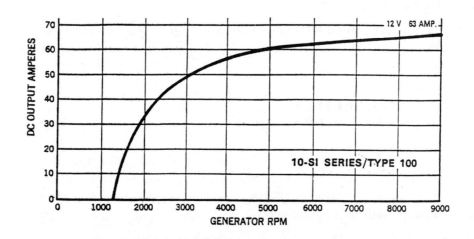

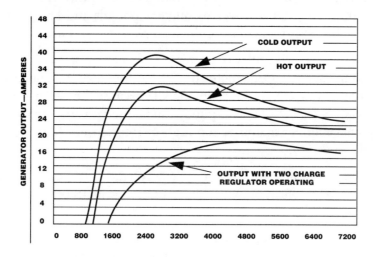

OUTPUT COMPARISON - ALTERNATOR VS. GENERATOR
Above is a comparison chart comparing the alternator to the generator system. Notice that while the alternator has a steady output at the higher rpm, the generator's output will actually fall at the higher rpm.
Keep in mind that normally alternators and generators are driven from the engine at 1-1/2 times the engine speed. It is also important to notice the output of the alternator vs. the generator at idle and low rpm. This has a considerable effect on the life of the battery in your car, and the performance of the entire charging system.
The rpm speed shown on these graphs is actual rpm of the alternators/generators.

If we use our 1950 Chevrolet car as an example as we did earlier, we know that all of the accessories together will require 36 amps. If we later on decide to add an electric fuel pump it will draw about 5 amps maximum. Maybe an electric radiator cooling fan would be nice—those draw about 6 amps max—so now we are up to 47 amps. If we add a 20 percent reserve to our 47 amps, we now have a total of 57 amps.

A common size for alternators is 63 amps. We are well within range of our output requirements. Now what we have to do is decide if we want to stay with a 6-volt system OR change over to a 12-volt system. If we change over to a 12-volt system we would need only half of our 57 amp total. But it would mean the extra expense changing all of the bulbs and related accessories, as we learned about in an earlier chapter.

If we stay with 6 volts, it would be nice to find a 6-volt alternator. But we need to be sure the alternator we buy actually puts out the amperage it is rated at. How can you be sure? One way is by looking to see how they are built.

A 6-VOLT ALTERNATOR IS A 6-VOLT ALTERNATOR...RIGHT?

This is where you get into trouble. **There are three common ways to build a 6-volt alternator**. The way your alternator is built will determine in part what output that alternator is capable of producing, and also the lifespan of your alternator.

The easiest way to build a 6-volt alternator is to place a 6-volt regulator inside of a 12-volt alternator. Using an internal regulated Delco alternator makes this quite a simple task. **But the rule of amps and volts also works in reverse**. So if you start out with a 60-amp, 12-volt alternator and then replace the regulator with a 6-volt model, not only will your voltage be reduced by 50 percent but your amperage output will also be reduced by 50 percent.

Thirty amps maximum means only 16 amps at idle. This is nearly as bad as your alternator you're trying to replace. Not much of an improvement. This style can be identified by a load test. If you see one of these installed, turn the headlights and the heater blower on high while the car is idling. This will cause the amp gauge to read discharge because you have created a 20+ amp load, and are exceeding the alternator's output at idle.

Also check the voltage at the back of the alternator. This style will typically produce 6.5 to 6.8 volts maximum at a fast idle and no load.

The next common style you will encounter will be a converted 12-volt alternator. These will look just like a regular 12-volt alternator except that they will have a small box mounted to the back of the alternator's case. This box works just like a voltage drop to create resistance, as a way of reducing the voltage.

Again, the amperage output is also reduced. In addition, a bad side effect of this method is the excess heat created through the resistance created to lower the voltage. Excess heat will shorten the lifespan of the alternator because of the extra stress placed on the internal parts. Sometimes you will see a small screw on the top of the metal/plastic box mounted on the back of the alternator. This screw is to allow you to "fine tune" the output voltage.

The third way, and the most expensive way, is to build the alternator from scratch as a true 6-volt alternator. By doing this, the output will be correct. Excess heat will not be developed, and the alternator will be reliable. A company called Fifth Avenue Antique Auto Parts, located at 415 Court Street, Clay Center, KS 67432 builds just such an alternator.

Fifth Avenue's 6-volt alternator has an output of 60 amps at 7.5 volts. The solid state regulator is built right inside of the alternator. These alternators are used by the participants in the Great American Race. You can call this company direct for more information, or to find out who your local dealer is.

This company also builds what is called a **"DA" plug**. This is necessary when you install an alternator on a vehicle that originally had a generator type charging system. Most antique vehicles prior to 1963 used what is called a "knife" type ignition switch, which had only two positions, off and on.

Because an alternator has an output at idle and low rpm, whereas the generator did not, when the ignition key was turned off, the electrical current still traveled backwards through the ignition circuit to the coil and kept the car running. Maybe this has already happened to you?

Well, it happened to the car manufacturers also. So to overcome that, they introduced the accessory-type ignition switch. By adding a third accessory post to the ignition switch, they could isolate that post from the rest of the ignition switch. This prevented the feedback from the alternator from keeping the vehicle running after the ignition key was turned off.

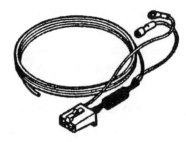

DA Plug

The DA plug, on the other hand, is a special wiring harness that allows the car to be started and stopped using the original style of ignition switch. They are standard on Fifth Avenue's alternators, and are available separately. They are designed to work with any GM internal regulated alternator built between 1973 and 1985. The DA plugs will work with both 6- and 12-volt applications.

TIME-SAVING TIP: When shopping for an alternator, look at the specifications carefully. Especially on many high amp output alternators (80+ amps), the output curve will show that the high output is only produced when the alternator is spinning at high rpm (highway speeds). **In many cases these high output alternators will produce less current at idle and through the mid range than a standard lower output alternator**. If your application is going to require a high amp alternator, be sure the output will occur when you need it.

Also, **watch the cooling fans on the front of the alternator**. The fan on the front of an alternator is designed to draw outside air through the alternator to cool the internal components. It is quite common when installing an alternator on an older vehicle to have the alternator rotating in the opposite direction for which it was assembled. When this happens the cooling fan on the front of the alternator spins backwards and doesn't provide much cooling. The result is an alternator that runs hot and overheats just like a car engine. The final result is an early alternator failure.

Note: For some alternators you can purchase or specify a "bi-directional" fan that will cool the alternator regardless of which way it spins. Normally there is little or no additional cost for this style of fan; you just have to ask for it.

12-SI SERIES/TYPE 100 D. C. AMPERES OUTPUT		
VOLTAGE	RATED OUTPUT	GENERATOR OUTPUT AT APPROX. 1600 RPM
12V	66 Amps	23 Amps
	78 Amps	30 Amps
	94 Amps	30 Amps
Weight: 5.1Kg (11.2 lbs.)		

Amperage output at alternator idle speed.

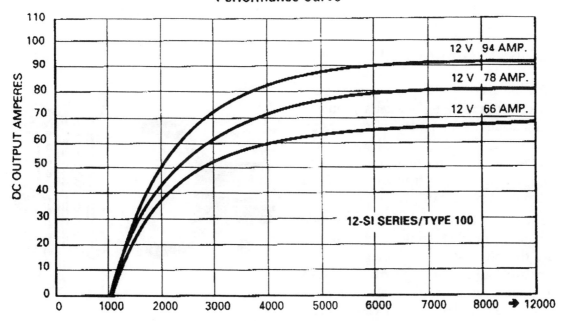

Performance Curve

12 V 94 AMP.

12 V 78 AMP.

12 V 66 AMP.

12-SI SERIES/TYPE 100

High amp alternator output.

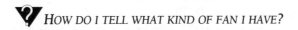

HOW DO I TELL WHAT KIND OF FAN I HAVE?

When looking down into the fan blades from a top view, **a counter-clockwise rotation fan (ccw) will have the blade on the RIGHT-HAND portion of the welded-on blade. In contrast a clockwise fan (cw) will have the blade on the LEFT-HAND portion of the welded-on blade.** Be sure when you purchase an alternator that the cooling fan will match the direction of rotation of your application.

PULLEY SIZES

Two different styles of machine steel pulleys. The left one is a standard 3/8 single groove; the right a two-groove pulley. For longer life, machine steel pulleys are preferred over pressed tin pulleys.

When shopping for an alternator, be sure you look for one that has the correct diameter of pulley. You want one that is smaller in diameter than the one that was on your generator. (Remember that the faster your alternator spins at idle, the greater the output will be.) There is also a wide selection of special pulleys available so you can run accessories from your alternator. This way you do not have to try to find a multi-groove crankshaft pulley. (You do not want to use the original pulley off of your generator even if it fits, as the diameter is too large.)

Some of the pulley combinations available include standard 3/8, two groove 3/8, two groove 1/2, wide width 1/2, width 3/4 size, and finally a two groove 1/2 and 3/8 combination. It is quite a handy trick to run your power steering or your a/c compressor from the alternator.

MOUNTING BRACKETS

For the majority of applications there is a replacement mounting bracket available to mount an alternator in place of a generator. This is by far the easiest and cheapest in the long run. If you are the home improvement type, you can sometimes modify or build a replacement bracket of your own.

The two rules you must follow include making the bracket strong enough to support the alternator, and being sure the alternator pulley lines up with the rest of the pulleys. Be sure, also, that you allow enough room to clear any obstacles or accessories when building your own bracket.

Fifth Avenue carries a wide selection of alternator mounting brackets for a number of popular applications including 1928-

Two different types of alternator mounting brackets.

1953 Ford cars and trucks as well as 1937-1962 Chevrolet cars and trucks. In addition, they have a number of specialty brackets available to cover most any application.

ONE WIRE ALTERNATORS became popular in the early 1970s. Instead of having two wires coming out of the top of the alternator via the little white plug, there is a rubber plug where the wiring harness normally is. The only connection you have to make to the alternator is the "BATT" wire that connects to the 10/32 stud on the back of the alternator. (Hence, the one wire name.)

How do they work? By the use of a special regulator, the alternator uses the electrical current stored inside of the rotor to "self-excite" itself. This is done when the alternator rpm reach about 1200 rpm engine speed, the internal current is released and the alternator will begin to charge. (The higher the output of the alternator, the faster or higher the engagement speed will be.)

This style of alternator works great on the modern style V-8 engines for which it was designed. The idle speed of these engines is near to the alternator's engagement speed. But when they are used on early antique engines, you will have trouble making the alternator engage and begin to charge.

The reason for this is because your antique engine has an idle speed of between 600 and 800 rpm whereas the alternator requires a minimum of 1200 rpm engine speed to begin to charge.

This may not happen for a few minutes, so in the meantime you use the battery for electrical energy. Then when the engagement rpm is reached, the electrical load is "dumped" onto the alternator all at once. This will place an extra strain on the alternator. (Like revving the motor up in your car, then dumping the clutch.) In short, these one-wire alternators work great for the applications they were designed for, but they do not work so well on the older vehicles. Some of you, no doubt, had one of these alternators and have had this experience.

Selecting an alternator for your application is not difficult; you simply have to do a little homework to obtain the results you want.

Another thing you want to decide is what "clock" position you want your alternator to have. The clock position is simply the location where the wiring harness plugs into the alternator. As you might guess, this is determined by looking at the front of the alternator and seeing where the harness plug is located. It is just like the face of a clock. Twelve o'clock is straight up. To the right a quarter of a turn is the 3 o'clock position, etc. Pretty simple.

With the clock position of your alternator at 12 o'clock, this will allow your wiring harness to plug into the alternator on top. You can ask for any clock position you want to match your application; the clock position can be changed fairly easily either by someone at the auto parts store or your local alternator shop.

WIRING THE ALTERNATOR

Most of you will use the GM style alternator we talked about earlier. Wiring this alternator is simple. First, you remove the "BATT" wire from the old regulator and connect it to the 10/32 stud on the back of the alternator marked "Batt." You can tape all of the rest of the wires from the old voltage regulator back into the original harness, for future generations to use when restoring your vehicle.

The plug-in harness that plugs into the top of the alternator will have two wires coming out of it. The red "load" wire also goes to the 10/32 stud at the back of the alternator. (It is internally connected to the regulator.) The white wire is the "exciter" wire.

The white wire takes about 1.5 volts from the battery, when the ignition switch is first turned to the on position, and sends it to the alternator's field

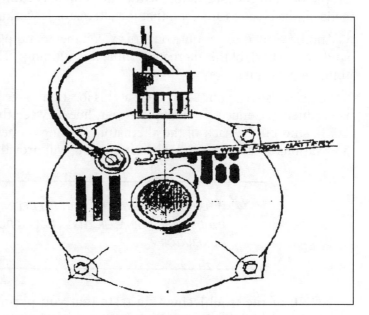

Typical alternator wiring installation.

149

circuit. This field current tells the alternator to begin charging regardless of the rpm the engine is running.

This is why a two-wire system works so much better on the vintage car applications. The second wire will excite the alternator and make it begin to charge regardless of the engine rpm. This will even work on cars and trucks of the early 1930s that have an idle speed of just 400-500 rpm.

WHAT IS THE "R" TERMINAL OF THE ALTERNATOR FOR?

The "R" terminal or Relay terminal as it is sometimes called, provided some of the alternator's output and was used to power electric tachometers, a dash light, hour meters, or other modern accessories. In some applications it was connected to the dash light to give notice if the alternator was failing to charge.

The "R" terminal was simply a necessity of modern times; the newer cars no longer have an amp gauge or volt meter in the dash. There has to be some way of keeping track of what is going on.

By the way, did you ever wonder which car company was the first to introduce the "idiot" lights in the dash that replaced mechanical gauges? That honor belongs to the Hudson Automobile Company, who began the practice in the early 1950s.

IS THERE ANY SIMPLE WAY TO CHECK MY ALTERNATOR TO SEE IF IT IS WORKING?

Yes, there is! **The easiest way is to touch a screwdriver to the smooth-bearing surface on the back of the alternator, while the vehicle is running**. If that bearing surface is magnetized, the chances are good that the alternator is working.

Another way is to get out your trusty volt meter and place the positive lead on the 10/32 stud on the back of the alternator (while it is running). The resulting voltage will tell you if things are working okay.

You can also use your amp gauge at this location to see what kind of amps your alternator is producing. Connect your amp gauge in-line between the load wire from the dash and the 10/32 stud on the back of the alternator. Turning on headlights and heater blower motor and various accessories while the car is idling will provide a sufficient amperage load.

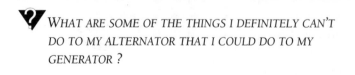

WHAT ARE SOME OF THE THINGS I DEFINITELY CAN'T DO TO MY ALTERNATOR THAT I COULD DO TO MY GENERATOR ?

NONE of the troubleshooting tests that you performed on a DC charging system generator will work on an AC alternator type charging system! Here are the most common mistakes, in the order of their appearance.

RUNDLE'S RULES:

1) Don't ever try to polarize an alternator.

2) Do not take one battery cable off of the battery while the vehicle is running to see if the alternator is charging! This is the same as running your vehicle's engine wide open in neutral.

3) Do not short across OR ground any of the terminals on the alternator OR the regulator.

4) When jump-starting your vehicle BE SURE you connect positive post to positive post and negative post to negative post. Also remember RED is always the positive and the BLACK is always the negative. This same rule also applies when you are connecting your battery to a charger. ANY transistorized device (this includes your alternator) is not forgiving if you hook up your battery connections backwards. Consider yourself forewarned!

5) Do not overtighten the drive belt. About one-half inch of play in the middle of the belt at a point located at the center of the distance between the alternator and the next accessory is just fine. A belt that is too tight will wear out the front bearing of the alternator before it's time.

6) Be sure you have a good engine to frame ground, and a good battery to frame ground. Also be sure your alternator is grounded to the engine well! In some applications it is necessary to run a short ground strap from the back of the alternator case, over to the engine block. (If this is the case, a threaded hole is provided on the back of the alternator case at about the 5 o'clock position.)

Alternators, like generators, are usually grounded through the engine block via the mounting bracket. But on some applications where both the mounting bracket and the engine block have been painted, the alternator will not be grounded. This will sometimes show up as an intermittent charging problem. The simple solution is to run a color matched short 18-gauge wire from the back of the alternator to the engine block, like a bolt on the manifold. Be sure you have a clean metal-to-metal contact.

HOW DO YOU CHECK AN ALTERNATOR CHARGING SYSTEM?

First let's check the alternator with the external regulator. It is really quite simple. Again we will use a GM style alternator and regulator as an example because they are the most common. If you have another application just follow along in your shop manual. Many of the procedures will be the same.

The first thing to check at the sign of a charging problem is the wiring. **Check for damaged or frayed insulation, as well as loose or corroded connections. Terminal ends should be cleaned and tightened as necessary. Be sure the alternator drive belt is not loose.**

You can check the voltage at the battery and the alternator output stud to confirm you have a charging problem. Also check to make sure there is not a problem with a poor ground, or a loose wire at either the regulator or the alternator. Most alternator charging systems are for the most part trouble free.

To check the output of the alternator, place your amp gauge between the load wire and the "BATT" stud on the back of the alternator. Start the engine and turn on headlights and a heater motor. The amp gauge should show a positive charge. If it does not, the alternator should be checked.

If an overcharge condition exists when you must add water to the battery on a regular basis, you should check the battery for a shorted cell in the battery. The low charge in that one cell will tell the regulator that a low voltage condition exists.

CHECKING THE REGULATOR

You can remove the cover of the early style regulators and check to see if the points are working (closing when the accessory load is being turned on). Carefully check to be sure the points are not burnt or stuck together. You can check your service manual for further help, but if the points are not working properly, then you know the regulator is partly at fault.

INTERNAL REGULATED ALTERNATORS are even easier to check. First, as you would for any system, check for loose wires and corroded connections, dirty terminals, a poor ground, or a loose drive belt. To check the regulator of an internal regulated alternator is quite simple. All that you need to do is **carefully** insert a small screwdriver in the "D" shaped hole on the back of the alternator. This "D" shaped hole is located about the 2 o'clock position on the back of the alternator.

Carefully, slide a small screwdriver into the hole until you just touch the small metal tab. Now, carefully touch this tab with the screwdriver, then touch the screwdriver shaft to the edge of the alternator housing.

This procedure will bypass the regulator to tell you if the alternator itself is charging. **You will only want to do this for a brief time**. If your alternator shows an increased output when you bypass the regulator, the chances are the regulator itself is at fault. If there is no increased output, then the alternator is in need of attention.

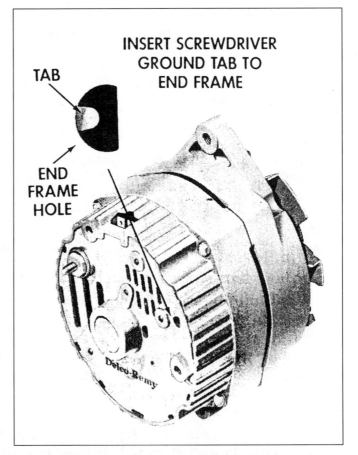

Grounding generator field winding.

Because of their design and the way they are built, alternator charging systems, regardless of brand, are for the most part trouble free and require little maintenance. They all work using the same basic principles, which you now understand. Following instructions in a service manual should be no problem.

Chapter 9 Review

1) One of the main advantages of an alternator over a generator is that the alternator will produce current at idle and low rpm; the generator is unable to do that.

2) Alternators will readily accept a higher working rpm, therefore they can provide a greater output at idle and low rpm. Alternators can run up to about 12,000 rpm alternator speed without damage.

3) Alternator output at idle will typically be 50 percent of the maximum rated output.

4) A "DA" plug will allow you to keep your original ignition switch when updating to an alternator.

5) One-wire alternators work well on modern V-8 engines that have an idle speed of 1100 rpm or greater. On the other hand, most antique engines have an idle speed of 500-800 rpm, which is too slow to engage a one wire alternator that requires an engine speed of at least 1100 rpm.

6) DO NOT remove one cable from the battery while your vehicle is running to see if your alternator is charging. This practice will cause serious damage to your alternator.

7) The smooth-bearing surface on the back of an alternator is one place to check to see if your alternator is charging. If this surface is magnetized while your car is running, the chances are good your alternator is working.

8) You can also use your volt meter at either the 10/32 stud on the back of the alternator or at the battery to check your alternator's output. You can also place your amp gauge in-line between the 10/32 stud on the alternator and the load wire. Then by turning on accessories you can measure the amperage output of the alternator.

Chapter
10

"Adding More Accessories"

Chapter 10

Adding More Accessories

There are a number of accessories that have become popular in the last few years. In this chapter we will discuss some of those accessories, explain what results you can expect from them, and how to figure out if your charging system has enough amps to power them.

HALOGEN LIGHTS have become one of the more popular accessories in recent years. Both headlights as well as taillights are available for both 6- and 12-volt applications. The halogen lights do provide a brighter and softer light. But keep in mind if your original head-

General Electric lighting test car; a 1936 Buick.

lamps are dim because of a low output from your charging system, replacing your sealed beams with halogens WILL NOT solve your problem.

Chances are that if your headlights are dim now, it is because the generator is not keeping up, especially at an idle. **Halogen headlights will require one-third more amperage than a conventional sealed beam**. So adding a greater amp load to your electrical system will not give you brighter headlights. You need to fix your original problem first—the lack of sufficient voltage to power the headlights you already have. I know it says right on the package that your lights will be 33 percent brighter if you install the halogen bulbs. But that is if you have the amps available to run them. If you were to change over to an alternator-type charging system that could produce the extra amps needed, then your newly installed halogen bulbs would indeed be at least 33 percent brighter than the stock headlamps.

In part because of the advertising, many people believe that by installing halogen bulbs, their dim headlights will be gone. Again, this will be true ONLY if there is enough amperage available to power them. In many cases, if there was enough amperage available to power the original headlamps, they would be more than bright enough.

CELLULAR PHONES have also become quite popular over these last few years. But if you have a 6-volt system, how do you run a cellular telephone? By use of a **regulated** power supply that boosts up the voltage from 6 to 12 volts.

The secret is it has to be a REGULATED power supply! The majority of power supplies are NOT regulated. If 6 volts, plus or minus, is supplied to the input side, then the output side of the inverter will yield 12 volts, plus or minus.

Transistorized radios and telephones and the like (as we learned earlier) must have a constant, even power supply or they will be "toast" in a short amount of time. All transistorized accessories are voltage and polarity sensitive. Two companies that offer such a power supply include Fifth Avenue Antique Auto Parts, of Clay Center, Kansas, and Antique Automobile Radio, Inc. of Palm Harbor, Florida. (See the Source List at the end of this book for complete addresses.)

The power supply that these two companies offer also has available a cigarette lighter plug attachment. This can be used to power a large selection of 12-volt accessories. One popular combination used with this power supply is the Sony brand portable CD player with the remote speakers. The remote speakers are placed in each corner of the dash during driving, with the player residing on the front seat.

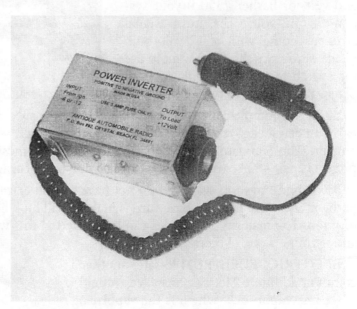

The clear crisp sound of a CD can be enjoyed while driving, and you will not have to change the dash or interior in any way. When you arrive at your destination you simply remove the speakers, unplug the CD player, and store it in the glove box or trunk. The power supply remains up under the dash out of sight. Oh, the luxury of it all!

A 6/12 regulated power supply for use with cellular phones and car stereos.

ADDING TURN SIGNALS is another popular task. While hand signals are still legal in most states, the younger generation will tend to ignore you, and there is that chance that your arm will go home in another car. The solution, of course, is to add turn signals. But how do you do it so they look like they belong there? Here is one solution:

Example of a turn signal switch that mounts on the steering column of the vehicle.

1) Your first duty is to change the park lights in the grille into both park and turn signals. To do this you need to simply remove the **single contact filament wire** at the base of the lamp socket and replace it with a **two filament contact wire**.

2) You also need to replace the bulb with one that has two contacts in it. Now you have turn signals and park lights in the same fixture and there are no other modifications necessary. Be sure and label your wires—the original park lens will connect just as it did before; the new wire will connect to your turn signal switch.

3) For the taillights you simply need to locate the taillight socket inside of the housing. Most older cars had one socket for taillight(s) and one socket for brake light(s). **Again, you will remove the single contact taillight socket, and replace it with a two wire contact.** The original taillight wire will be the same. The new turn signal wire will go up to the new turn signal switch. The same procedure goes for both taillight assemblies.

4) Now for a turn signal switch. One of the nicest ones available is a chrome one that mounts on the steering column just as they did in the 1940s and 1950s. It is a Part #901 manufactured by the Signal-Stat Corp. This switch will work with both 6- and 12-volt applications.

This kit also requires a flasher wiring harness part # 263. The flasher you need will be a #535 if your system is 6-volt, or flasher #550 if your system is 12-volt. The turn signal switches come with a 12-volt bulb inside of the switch. If you want to use the switch for a 6-volt application, simply swap out the #53 twelve-volt bulb for a #55 six-volt bulb.

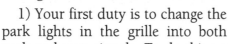

There are complete instructions for wiring up the switch to your system. The two contact socket replacements are available through your Standard ignition retailer. The Standard brand part number you will most likely use for this project is part #S24 or part #S26N. Check with your local auto parts retailer.

By doing things this way, you do not have to drill extra holes in the body or add extra lights to have turn signals. It will look like a factory job. The majority of vehicles can be converted this way, and if yours is one of them, you're set!

ELECTRIC FUEL PUMPS are another common addition. Most are installed to help overcome vapor lock (which is the vaporizing of the fuel before it gets to the carburetor). This normally occurs between the gas tank and the mechanical fuel pump. This is something we

A turn signal flasher and the wiring harness it plugs into.

haven't had to deal with for quite a number of years, but is becoming more of a problem in recent years. The reason is the change in the way gasoline is being refined.

First a little history lesson. Along about the mid-1970s came

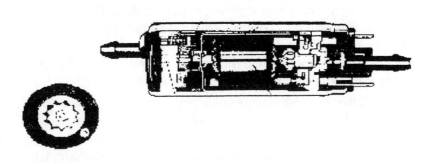

A gear-driven electric fuel pump.

the switch to unleaded gasoline. This affected us in a couple of ways. In the old days we used the lead in gasoline as an upper cylinder lubricant and as a cushion between the valve and the valve seats in the cylinder head.

Modern engines use what are called "hardened seats" that are tempered and do not require any lubricant or cushion between the valve and seats. Hardened valve seats are available for most older engines. The engineers say if you have quite a few miles on your engine using leaded fuel, chances are you have nothing to worry about. There is enough residue leftover to last the life of your engine.

The good that comes from unleaded fuel is that there are fewer deposits remaining on the spark plugs, which make sparks plugs last much longer and burn cleaner. Some of the engineers say that if you are concerned about the lack of upper cylinder lubricant, you can add a pint of diesel fuel to a tank full of gasoline to replace your lost upper cylinder lubricant.

The other thing that happened was the octane rating of fuel dropped about 10 points. (The octane in the fuel is what helps prevent pre-ignition of the fuel in the cylinder before the piston reaches top dead center. Pre-ignition is the knocking or pinging sound heard under hard acceleration.)

Back in the 1960s there was a gasoline fuel additive called ethyl that really boosted the octane rating of gasoline. It was common during the muscle car era of the 1960s to drive into a gas station and buy 100+ octane fuel for less than a dollar a gallon! Most "regular" fuel today is around 80-85 octane, with premium being close to 90 octane.

❓ WHAT ABOUT THE GASOLINE IN THE OLD DAYS?

The gasoline sold in the 1940s and 1950s did have the lead additive, but did not have the high octane because the cars did not have the high compression and did not need it. By the way, did you know **gasoline was originally a by-product of the refinery process used to make kerosene and fuel oil, and was once considered waste**? As a result, it was common practice during the 1920s and 1930s to have to filter the gasoline as you filled your tank (to strain out the impurities) at the service station. Chamois was the common filter material used.

Also, if you will remember in those days, all of the pump nozzles were made of brass. Did you ever stop to wonder why? The reason for service station nozzles on gasoline pumps of the era being made of brass was to prevent a spark of static electricity from occurring when you bumped the edge of your gas tank while filling up. (Brass was soft and would not create a spark if it was bumped against the fill neck of a gas tank.)

Static electricity was a real problem in the old days. For instance, static was created when the fuel was dumped into the underground storage tank. It was also created when the fuel stored underground was pumped to the surface and into the glass cylinder of the visible gas pump. It was also created when the fuel left the pump nozzle and entered the car's gas tank. The danger of a stray spark causing a fire was everywhere.

The spark from a metal nozzle while you were filling up would no doubt relocate you and the entire station straight to the moon! Modern pumps of today are internally grounded through the wire mesh in the fill hose and there is no static discharge available at the nozzle. In addition, modern pumps are grounded throughout the system, to prevent static discharge from being a problem.

Additional trivia: The old visible measure pumps of the 1920s and 1930s hand pumped the fuel from an underground storage tank up to the visible cylinder where it was measured. Did you ever notice that the fuel entered the bottom of the cylinder instead of the top, as you would normally fill a bucket? Why was this?

As the fuel was being pumped through the fill pipe, static electricity was being created. If the glass cylinder was filled from the top, the distance from the end of the fill pipe to the surface of the fuel would be exposed to the air in the cylinder. As fuel dropped from the fill pipe to the surface of the fuel, lots of static electricity would be created as the fuel left the fill pipe.

Also, the air space remaining in the cylinder would contain the explosive fumes of the gasoline. The additional static electricity created by filling up the glass cylinder would be discharged into the inside of the cylinder. Any stray spark of static electricity could ignite the gas fumes in the cylinder and follow it down into the underground storage tank. The result would again cause a major relocation of the service station. And, because the storage tank is never completely full, there would be plenty of air on hand to feed the fire and help with the explosion underground.

By filling the glass cylinder from the bottom there is less static created, and less gasoline fumes being discharged into the air space inside of the cylinder. Most of the fumes are contained in the fuel itself, which is submerged under the gasoline and is not exposed to the air.

Refueling an automobile during this era was quite a dangerous thing. Besides the station taking all of these precautions in handling the fuel, there was still the static that developed in the car while it was traveling down the road. Because the original tires were made of pure rubber, they insulated the car from the road, preventing the static buildup from being discharged. Motorists of the day had to be awfully careful when they pulled into a service station for a fill up. The first one to exit the car discharged the static electricity. You had to be careful not to lean against the gas pump as you got out of the car.

WELCOME TO THE '90s

Beginning in the 1980s, in the interest of cleaner burning fuels and less pollution from automobiles, the gasoline refining process was changed. Today's gasoline is being aerated. This blending of air into the fuel is supposed to result in a cleaner burning fuel. This new fuel was designed to work in modern cars that have fuel injection and will carry 30+ pounds of fuel pressure. But for the rest of us that drive antique cars that use mechanical fuel pumps boasting three to four pounds of fuel pump pressure, it is difficult for us to pump this new fuel, especially when a good part of it is air. This becomes evident on a hot summer day in July when the temperatures are in the 90s. This explains why we are having more trouble with vapor lock today than we have had in the past 15 years or so.

NOW IT'S LEGAL TO RUN MOONSHINE

There is another factor we also need to be concerned with. Beginning in the mid-1980s, many areas of the country began adding an alcohol called ethanol to their gasoline. (A by-product of corn. Yep, that's what they used to tell the revenue agent.) Again this was/is done to provide a cleaner burning fuel. But for older antique vehicles this alcohol in the fuel can create quite a problem. Alcohol will swell natural rubber seals and gaskets, causing problems with mechanical fuel pumps and carburetors. It can also dissolve some gas tank sealers. It was also during this time that all of the lead additives were removed from gasoline. You'll remember that lead was used as a cushion between the exhaust valve and the seat in the cylinder head.

Remember back in the 1960s when gasoline was a reddish orange color? It normally had a shelf life of six to eight months. The down side of this was when this gas went bad, it turned to "varnish" and really made a mess of things. It would gum up carburetors, fuel pumps, and even plug up fuel lines. Many of you have removed the gas cap of an old car that has been parked five or six years with what was a partial tank of gas leftover in the tank. That smell is the smell of stale gas—gas that has gone bad.

Once you have smelled that smell your nose gets sensitive to it and you can smell it right away, as you walk up to an old car in storage, without removing any gas cap. What you are smelling is the lead additive in the fuel. Modern gasoline will have a shelf life of about six months. It does not smell nearly as bad as the old stuff, but will still gum up fuel pumps, fuel lines, and carburetors.

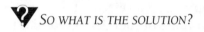 *SO WHAT IS THE SOLUTION?*

Most components can be rebuilt using alcohol resistant seals and gaskets. A gasket material called neopherene will resist the swelling caused by alcohol and is commonly used as a replacement gasket material. It is not difficult to overcome this problem IF you know ahead of time that the problem exists. Most carburetor and fuel pump rebuilders already use this type of gasket. If you are having this type of work done, simply ask the rebuilder what type of gasket material he uses, and tell him you want to use the alcohol resistant gaskets.

Keep in mind that in many states the oil companies are not required to label the gasoline pump if the gasoline is mixed with LESS than 10 percent alcohol. Many times the only way you will find out is at your next fill up. This sometimes can create a real hassle. Ten percent alcohol is enough alcohol to cause you problems if your fuel system contains the older all-natural rubber gaskets.

While a modern electric fuel pump seems like the obvious solution, you need to be sure the pump you buy will pump alcohol. Unlike modern mechanical fuel pumps, many after-market universal electric fuel pumps WILL NOT pump alcohol fuel. You will need to read the directions and specifications carefully before you buy a pump. Most electric pumps will state clearly: "not to be used with alcohol fuel."

Also, some fuel additives will affect these pumps. If you are in the habit of adding a small amount of diesel fuel to your gasoline to replace the benefits of lead, keep in mind some electric pumps will not pump diesel fuel even in small amounts. It pays to do a little homework before you buy a pump so you will not be disappointed later on.

Let's spend a few minutes and talk about the different kinds of electric fuel pumps and what results you can expect from them. While most of us don't plan to purchase alcohol fuel on a regular basis, sometimes accidents will happen. You need to know how your fuel system will react.

There are three common types of electric fuel pumps sold today: **diaphragm, rotary vein,** and **gear driven**. Guess which ones do not make good social drinkers? Right, the diaphragm and the rotary vein styles.

The diaphragm in a diaphragm pump will swell up, causing the pump to fail, just like it does inside of your carburetor. This can happen with as little as 10 percent alcohol in the fuel, in just a few tankfuls. (It is the same as when you were in high school and put the five-buckle overshoes in the carburetor cleaner overnight in shop class. When you returned the next day, they were hip waders.) Diaphragm pumps are also noisy, sounding like a machine gun on the front line. The instructions will tell you not to install them in the trunk for safety reasons (in case of a fuel leak) but if you think they're noisy now, enclose one in a trunk sometime!

Because the alcohol in the fuel makes the fuel drier, it also takes away part of the lubricative properties of the fuel. Most rotary vein pumps depend on the lubricative properties of the fuel to extend the life of the veins. So the alcohol will shorten the life of this style of pump also. Rotary vein pumps are fairly quiet; they make a whirring noise while operating.

The most durable type of electric fuel pump you can buy is a gear driven fuel pump. These pumps will pump alcohol and most any fuel additive. They are quiet and small in size. Another benefit of a gear driven electric fuel pump is they overcome vapor lock by increasing the VOLUME of fuel delivered while still using the ORIGINAL fuel pump pressure. This prevents problems from occurring with the needle and seat in the carburetor, and would allow the electric fuel pump to be used along with the original mechanical pump. This style of electric fuel pump works just like the oil pump inside of your engine.

Ask a few questions when shopping for an electric fuel pump. **Find out what the pump's working pressure is, and the volume of fuel delivered**. For the antique car applications, low pressure and high volume is what you're looking for.

If you drive your car locally, you can pick and choose the station you buy fuel from. Word of mouth and your own experience tells you which gas stations to avoid. But suppose you were traveling across the United States like the participants in the Great American Race. What about buying fuel?

This is one of the major problems faced by The Great Racers. What if you get a tankful of alcohol gas? You can prepare everything except your electric fuel pump. Your electric pump either is, or is not, a social drinker, but you better know before you leave home. Unlike you, who know the stations, the Great Racers have to buy fuel along their route usually as quickly and conveniently as possible. They have to prepare for the worst. Their electric fuel pump must be able to pump alcohol fuel in an emergency.

Fifth Avenue Antique Auto Parts does offer a gear driven electric fuel pump that will pump alcohol, and does overcome vapor lock by delivering an increased volume of fuel, while still maintaining the original fuel pump pressure. This pump is gear driven and works much like the oil pump inside of your engine.

Fifth Avenue offers this style of pump for both 6- and 12-volt applications, in either positive (+) or negative (-) ground models. These pumps were developed in part for the participants that race in the Great American Race.

 OKAY, WE KNOW ALL ABOUT ELECTRIC FUEL PUMPS EXCEPT HOW MUCH ELECTRICITY THEY USE.

D	8"	10"	11"	12"	13"	14"	16"
H	$2^1/_4$	$2^1/_4$	$2^1/_4$	$2^1/_4$	$2^1/_4$ - 3	$2^1/_4$ - 3	$3^1/_{16}$
X	$10^7/_8$	$10^7/_8$	12	$12^5/_8$	$13^1/_8$	$14^3/_4$	$16^3/_8$
Y	$4^1/_4$	$4^7/_8$	$5^1/_4$	$5^7/_8$	$7^1/_8$	$7^1/_8$	$8^1/_8$
C	**Vertical edge height on all fans is $1^1/_4$ inches**						

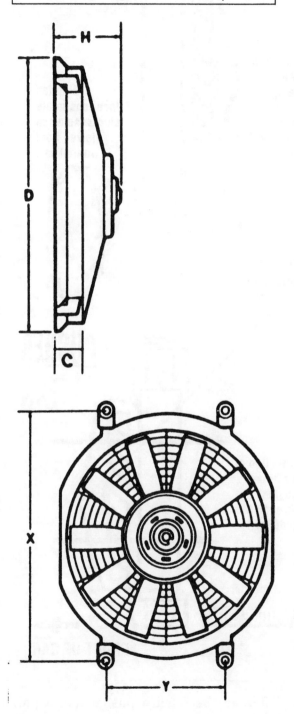

How to measure for an electric radiator cooling fan.

Most electric fuel pumps are pretty efficient and will use 2-3 amps when working. Most will have an inline fuse rated at 5 amps, so it is safe to figure a 5-amp draw when checking to see if your charging system can power this accessory. Your instructions that come with the pump will give you the power requirements. You were planning on reading the instructions, weren't you? Of course.

Be sure that when you wire in your new fuel pump, it is wired so that it turns OFF and ON with the ignition switch (Do not use the ignition coil!). Make sure there is no power to the pump when the ignition switch is in the off position!

Be sure the pump is mounted in a secure position and the fuel line is free of any moving parts or sharp edges. After you install your pump be sure to check for leaks. It is better to be safe than sorry!

Electric radiator cooling fan.

ELECTRIC RADIATOR COOLING FANS are another popular accessory. But, how do you shop for one and what do you look for?

First you need to determine the size you need based on the width of your radiator. The cooling fan will do the best job if it is mounted as close to the TOP of the radiator as possible. This is where the warm coolant enters the radiator.

You need to measure the width of your radiator at the top. The common sizes, in inches, for electric radiator cooling fans include: 8, 10, 12, 14, and 16. These sizes usually include the fan's outside housing measurements.

The next thing you will want to measure is the width of the space you have between the radiator and any brackets or braces. Four inches is normally the minimum width or (depth) most fans will require. You will need both of these figures when shopping for a cooling fan.

PUSHER VS PULLER STYLES

The last thing you need to decide is if you want a "pusher" or a "puller" style of fan. A pusher style mounts on the front side of the radiator behind the grille, and pushes air through the radiator. A puller style of cooling fan mounts on the engine side of the radiator, and usually replaces the original fan. This style of fan pulls the air through the radiator.

Because most electric radiator cooling fans are efficient, it really does not matter which style you use. Normally the style you use is determined by your space limitations.

? *WHAT DO YOU LOOK FOR WHEN BUYING AN ELECTRIC RADIATOR COOLING FAN ?*

First **look for a large motor**. Look at the specifications and see what kind of amperage draw and horsepower rating the motor has . A large motor will do a better job, be more efficient, last much longer, and draw less amperage than a smaller motor that is underpowered for the job, and always under a constant strain.

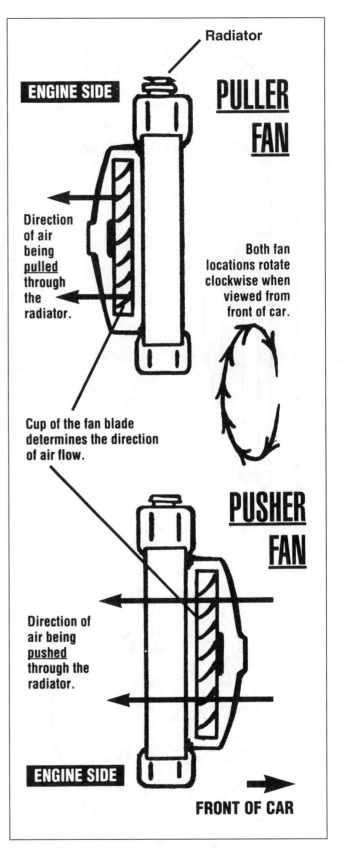

The difference between a pusher and a puller style of electric fan.

When it comes to cooling fan motors **bigger is better**. Some of the more powerful motors on the large diameter fans will draw 6-10 amps. In most applications, however, a 14-inch fan is more than big enough to do the job. Using a 14-inch cooling fan as an example, it should move approximately 1,125 cubic feet of air per minute (CFM rating) if it has the correct size motor and blade combination.

COOLING FAN BLADES are the next most important feature you want to look at. You should to be able to identify the style of fan you're looking at, as either a pusher or a puller style. That is done by looking at the blades. **REMEMBER: regardless of the style, the curvature of the blade ALWAYS faces the engine.** So by looking at the blades and the mounting shroud you can easily identify the style of electric cooling fan you are looking at.

The number of blades is important also. It is common to see anywhere from four to ten blades on a fan. Again, you are in the air moving business, so the more blades you have, with the correct pitch, the more air you can move—if you have the horsepower to move those blades.

Along with the number of blades, look at the curvature or pitch of the blades, The deeper the curvature and the more aggressive the pitch, the more air the fan will move, and the more horsepower will be required from the motor.

Some electric cooling fans will advertise universal blades that will work for either style of fan. These are not nearly as efficient as those made specifically for one style or the other. The universal blades tend to have a flatter, less aggressive pitch and will move a much smaller quantity of air. They will also require less horsepower to run.

Something that happens quite often is an antique car owner will go down to the local discount auto parts store and buy an electric cooling fan kit. In most cases this will be one with the universal flat style blades. The counterperson will say, "Those are universal electric fan kits, it doesn't matter which direction they run. To change the direction just reverse the wires on the motor...."

If that were actually true, why go to the work of installing the fan on your radiator in the first place? If it truly doesn't matter which way the blades turn, the fan isn't going to move much air! It may make a lot of noise and sound like a Kansas tornado, but what you need to be concerned with is how much air is actually moving through the radiator. After all, isn't that why you are installing an electric cooling fan in the first place?

Many times you will hear car owners say, "Yeah, I put one of those electric cooling fans on my car, and it didn't do a dang bit of good! Fact is my motor runs hotter now than it did before I installed the fan!" What do you suppose he did wrong?

As you are walking through your next car show event, take a look at cooling fans, especially blades. It is not uncommon to see fans with the pitch backwards. This tells you someone doesn't understand how a cooling fan works. Many of the people that complain about how worthless their cooling fan is—"that it doesn't cool worth a darn"—have their fan mounted backwards or have one with the universal style of blades, neither of which moves much air.

I am not a big fan of the new "S" shaped blades either. I believe them to be another form of a universal style blade. We can learn the most from aircraft propellers. Their job is to move a vast amount of air. If they do not, the airplane doesn't fly. Then there are helicopters....

The last thing you need to be aware of is the installation kit. It should contain all of the hardware to mount your fan, as well as all of the wiring necessary, and the switches. Some fans will come with a temp sender switch to turn the fan off and on automatically. These are mounted in the radiator or engine block. I am not a fan of these either because most of them are not accurate. I believe you should control the fan yourself and turn it off and on when you need it.

If your fan is efficient, and capable of doing its job, it should have no problem cooling down your engine, while the car is running. Also, having your fan run after you shut the car off is not a good idea, especially if you are going to go off and leave it. The temp sensors will sometimes keep the fan running for 15-20 minutes after the engine is turned off. This will put a pretty good drain on your battery. Just for safety's sake, I do not want anything running on my car if I'm not around.

In summary, I believe "you" should control when your cooling fan is turned off and on, and I also believe that it should be wired so that it is turned off with the ignition switch. If your cooling fan is efficient enough, this arrangement should be no problem.

ENGINE COOLING TIP: Sometimes we make things harder than they have to be. For instance, cars prior to the mid-1950s were built using the theory that the coolant had to circulate rapidly in order to cool the engine. Most car owners today use a blend of 50/50 permanent antifreeze year-round, in their antique car just as they do in their modern car. So what's wrong with that?

Think back to the days when your car was new; there was not any permanent antifreeze. In the summertime you ran straight water; in the winter, alcohol based antifreeze. If you stop and think about it, straight plain water is the best disperser of heat. Modern antifreeze is heavier than water.

What happens in most old car cooling systems, with a 50/50 mix of permanent antifreeze, is that the antifreeze is heavier than water so when it enters the top of the radiator it falls quickly to the bottom. Because the cooling system is designed to circulate quickly, the antifreeze provides little or no cooling effect.

Also, because the antifreeze is thicker than water, the air cannot circulate through the antifreeze as easily. The result is a car that runs warmer than it should. So what's the solution? In the summertime, run straight water and a pint of rust inhibitor. In the winter you can go back to 50/50 antifreeze to protect things from freezing.

Does straight water over a mixture of 50/50 permanent antifreeze really make a difference? YOU BET IT DOES! I have seen the same car run 30 degrees cooler using straight water vs. the 50/50 permanent antifreeze it replaced. I watched this happen to a flathead Ford running in the Great American Race. Seeing is believing! (Thanks to Rex Gardner, Great American Racer from Stillwell, Kansas, who understands and showed me what it takes to keep a flathead Ford from losing its cool.)

A trick left over from the old days that is still very effective today is to add a teaspoon of common household baking soda to the radiator for every gallon of coolant. So, if your cooling system holds four gallons of water, then you need to add four teaspoons of baking soda to it. This dissolves the lime from the inside of the radiator core and suspends it in the water where it came from in the first place.

Along the same line—did you ever wonder what they used to put in the radiator during Depression times to stop a leak? The following remedies are supposedly tried and true. Just remember, that was then and this is now, and some of these are pretty desperate measures:

1) Black pepper - no doubt because it was always available and cheap.

2) Oatmeal - If you grew up in the Depression, it was what you ate for breakfast each and every day. Bet you didn't realize how much you had in common with an old car radiator.

3) Raw egg - The story goes that all you really needed was the whites of the egg, but why not toss in the rest for good measure. Besides, how are you going to separate things along the roadside?

4) Cow pie - The rule here is that you had to have a fairly fresh one—one that was crusty on the outside but fresh in the middle. I suppose it was what the cow ate more than the pie itself that did the trick. Very little research has been conducted in this area I'm told.

A little clarification is in order here, depending on which part of the country you are from. Cow pies, meadow muffins, and sun cookies are all the same thing, and are from the cow family. These did work in your radiator. Road apples and horse hedge balls are of the horse family and were not usually used in the radiator except in the case of an extreme emergency.

 *By the way...*

Remember desert water bags? First you filled them with water, then soaked the outside. As you drove in the heat of the day the water on the outside of the bag evaporated, keeping your drinking water cool. Did you ever notice that in the old days those canvas bags were always hung at the front of the car close to the radiator? Why? Because as the water evaporated from the canvas bag, the cool air was drawn through the radiator. Guess what? They still work just as good today as they did in the old days.

A desert water bag is available from Fifth Avenue Antique Auto Parts.

ACCESSORIES IN GENERAL are usually pretty simple to install. If there is a question about your charging system being able to handle the extra load, take a few minutes and figure it out. Most instruction sheets will have a specification list and will list the amount of amps required to run the accessory.

Some accessories, such as radios, for instance, will give their ratings in watts. Remember, all that you have to do to change watts into amps is divide the watts by the system voltage!

For example, you're looking at a car stereo that has a 50-watt rating, and you want to install it in your 1950 Chevy car that now has a 12-volt charging system. How many amps will this radio require? Right ! Just a shade over 4 amps, which means it should have a 5 amp fuse in line...but, you already knew that.

Quite often the advice you get is to install a 100+ amp alternator on your car, "because that is what everyone else is doing." But if you stop and ask "everyone else" why they are doing it, most of them can't tell you. So you ask a simple question: "How many amps does your system now require?" Often their reply will be along the line of, "Well, er, ah, I dunno?" In most cases they install big alternators because that's what the new cars use, or they saw one that big on a car in a magazine.

The reason most of us don't need that big of an alternator is because we don't have to run all of the "stuff" such as the computer sensors, memory chips, and related components that are on a new car. Most of the solid state components that we install as accessories today are many times more efficient and require a whole lot less electrical energy than the same accessory did when our cars were new.

We actually have the best of both worlds. We can take advantage of modern technology and install the accessories we want, while at the same time avoid all of the complicated things that go bump in the night.

We have no real need for a giant alternator. In most cases a 60-amp alternator will more than do the trick for all of us. We can be sure our alternator is big enough because we know how to sit down and figure out what our electrical load is, then we simply buy the alternator we need for the job. What could be more simple.

Example of a high output alternator.

ORIGINAL FACTORY RADIOS

In the next chapter we will learn about factory radios. Like most everything else, if you understand the basics of how things work, you can troubleshoot your own radio problems. Many of us still have the original radios in the dash and they sound beautiful (better than the mother-in-law in the back seat) and work great most of the time. But what do you do when they quit working and how do you check things out?

This next chapter is compliments of "Handy Dan" Schulz of Antique Automobile Radio, Inc. of Palm Harbor, Florida. Dan is an all-around good guy who understands vintage car radios and accessories better than most anyone else in the country. He has no doubt forgotten more about old radios that the rest of us will ever know.

Dan will tell us the do's and don'ts of radio ownership, as well as the RIGHT way to update your radio to 12 volts, or add FM, to your original radio (yes, it can be done). Dan will also give us a few hints on installing radios and antennas, and how to find the source of that annoying static squeal coming from your radio. Please pay attention here because Dan is doing us a good turn.

NOTES

Chapter 11

"Original Factory Radios"

Chapter 11

Original Factory Radios

by Dan Schulz

First a little history. The generally accepted beginning of the age of radios in automobiles is 1932. There were a few radios built specifically for cars before 1932, but they are the rare exception rather than the rule. Stutz motor cars offered a factory radio as early as 1929. Cadillac/LaSalle offered a Delco-Remy radio in late 1929 or early 1930. There were several technical problems as well as logistical ones that prevented car radios from being widely accepted before 1932.

Radio as a commercial means of entertainment was only a few years old at the time. In 1922 there were only 60 licensed broadcasting stations in the United States. Unless you lived in a metropolitan area, and drove your car during the evening hours when the stations were on the air (most did not broadcast during the daytime hours), there was little incentive to install a radio in your car.

During the 1930s, however, there was a large increase in the number of radio stations across America. This made the idea of owning a car radio more appealing to the average car owner. But one of the problems that had to be overcome, was all of the early car radios used vacuum tubes to "pull voices from the sky." All vacuum tubes require a fairly high voltage (typically 90 to 350 volts) to operate.

Unlike most home radios (which could use house current to provide the high voltage to run the vacuum tubes), the problem with car radios was how to obtain a steady supply of high voltage current from a 6-volt electrical system. As a result, all car radios built before 1932 either had a special battery box to hold high voltage batteries or they used what is called a dyna-motor, which was a special 6-volt motor that drove a special high voltage generator. Neither of these solutions was practical and was not affordable by the average car owner.

In 1932, William Lear (more famous for his Lear Jet, and 8-track tape players) invented the radio vibrator. This clever device used a vibrating reed or wafer to open and close a set of points, which in turn could drive a step-up power transformer that could provide the high voltage needed for the radio. The vibrator works a lot like the ignition coil and contact points in the distributor of your car.

By the end of 1932, most every car manufacturer was offering a radio. By 1933 Hudson Terraplanes had a radio as standard equipment. Radios became popular during these years;

by 1935 the number of radios produced yearly was more than ten times what it was in 1932. These early radios were rugged and well built and had good sound quality for the times. Most early radios were built inside of a large metal box mounted to the firewall, with a separate speaker and control head mounted on the steering column or dash.

Every new year brought new radio innovations, better methods of production, and more features. In 1938 Chevrolet introduced push-button tuning. By 1939, everybody offered push-button tuning. Ford used a Roto-matic tuner that provided five preset stations with only one push button. In 1947 Delco obtained a patent for the first Signal-Seeking radio. Delco, however, did not offer this radio as a factory option until 1950.

Miniature tubes began to appear about 1950, which made radios much smaller and lighter. The development of the transistor radio in the mid-1950s was to have the greatest impact on radio manufacturing. It was Chrysler in 1956 that offered the first all transistor radio. Most automobile electrical systems were 12-volt by then; that encouraged the development of hybrid radios. These hybrid radios used special tubes that did not require high voltage to operate, and used power transistors for the output stage.

By 1957 most manufacturers had switched to this design, and by 1958 there was no more vibrator powered radios. The last year for vacuum tube radios was 1962, although some Delco signal-seeking radios used one tube for that function as late as 1963. Other related "firsts" include:

1955 First Mopar Signal-Seeking Radio.

1956 First FoMoCo Signal-Seeking Radio.

1956 First year printed circuits were commonly found in radios.

1956 Chrysler introduces the automobile record player The Highway Hi-Fi.

1958 Delco introduces a series of portable all transistor radios which could be plugged into the dash and used as a car radio.

1958 Lincoln introduces the first FM receiver in car radios. FM was not offered by anyone else until 1963.

1959 RCA introduces a 45 rpm record player for automobiles that would play a stack of 14 records on an automatic turntable.

1964 The 4-track and later 8-track were introduced, which killed the car record player market.

1967 The compact cassette made its debut in the United States, and quickly killed the 8-track market.

A common question in my business is "What year did they start using the CONELRAD civil defense symbols on radio dials?" (the little triangles on the dial from the "duck and cover" era). Studebaker and all Chrysler products began using them in 1954. Ford, including Lincoln and Mercury, along with Hudson, began in 1955. All General Motors products, along with Packard, first used them in 1956.

THE NEW FORD RADIO RECEIVER

SOLD EXCLUSIVELY BY FORD DEALERS

The New Ford Auto Radio Incorporates:

New advanced principles of circuit and tube design. A totally new idea in sound distribution and musical fidelity is built into a dynamic speaker located above the occupants' heads in the headerbar of the car.

veloped Automatic Volume control, illuminated custom-built instrument panel control mounting in the ash receptacle opening.

The Receiver is mounted directly above the steering column out of sight and out of the way. This installation does not interfere with the installation of either a hot water

FIGURE 1

Other features of the set are two unit construction with separate speaker, highly de-

or hot air heater and does not cramp leg room.

Many Happy Miles With A Ford Auto Radio

Ford offered this radio package for the 1935 model year.

Chrysler Imperial ad for an early 1930s radio. This radio, like many other early radios of the era, didn't make it big. Note the retail price. As an incentive for the dealers to promote these radios, their cost was only $24.50 each.

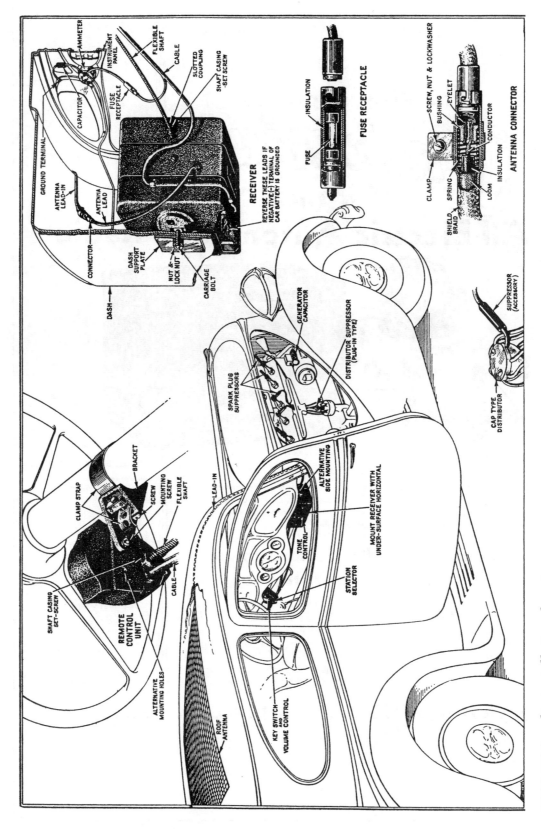

1933 RCA radio installation drawing.

An example of a car Hi-Fi.

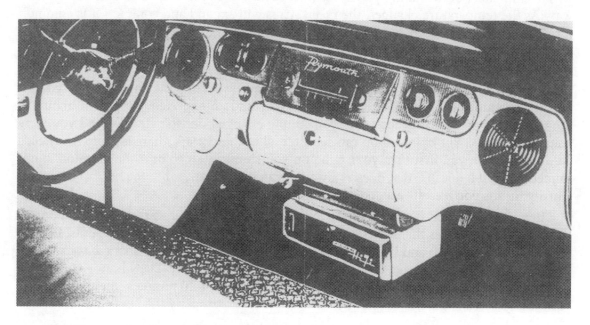

In 1956 Plymouth offered the first Highway Hi-Fi.

If you have ever looked inside an old tube/vibrator radio, you have seen a large collection of many different parts and materials. This collection of materials belongs in four different groups: **tubes, inductors, resistors, and capacitors.** As a group, tubes have the best survival rate. They are built to withstand shock and vibration and their critical elements are sealed in vacuum under glass, which also protects them from moisture and dirt. Tubes are designed to operate many thousands of hours without failure, usually in excess of the radio's service life. They can, however, be damaged (especially rectifier tubes) by overloading caused by other defective components.

INDUCTORS, which include transformers and chokes as well as tuner coils, generally survive as long as they are kept dry. Because most inductors require a ferrous core (this usually means iron or untreated steel) and are often insulated with paper, dampness and moisture are their greatest enemy. Resistors (especially prewar types) are made of compressed carbon, and as they age will change values quite dramatically. Again, moisture speeds up this process.

CAPACITORS are made using several different processes, for different applications. Most types used in car radios have a rated life of 10 years. The most common style of capacitors used in older car radios are either electrolyte, which are used in the power supply section, or paper foil types that are used everywhere else.

The electrolyte capacitors are made with a chemical called electrolyte, the same type used in batteries. This electrolyte dries out over time, which causes the electrode inside of the capacitor to deform, causing the capacitor to fail. Heat will greatly speed up this process. Even brand new old original electrolyte capacitors should be suspect.

The paper foil capacitors are usually damaged by thermal cycling. If you were to disassemble one or two of these capacitors, you would find two long thin strips of metal foil with a thin sheet of insulating paper between them. This assembly is usually sealed with wax. As the temperature changes, the metal strips will expand and contract. It is common for these capacitors to go through a 100-degree temperature change during a 24-hour period, especially in winter. Eventually this wears through the insulating layer and the capacitor fails.

When your car was in its prime, and the radio quit working, the chances were good it was the vibrator. An original mechanical vibrator had an expected lifespan of about 18 months of regular use. In those days you simply changed out the vibrator and you were back in business. But by now you can see after all of these years, there is more that needs attention. When you first turn your radio on you should start to hear the vibrator "hum" immediately. If it doesn't, that doesn't always mean it is defective, but the hum of a vibrator usually means you are off to a good start.

Often a vibrator that has been sitting for quite a while will not start due to oxidation of the points. Many times the points can be cleared by running the car engine at fast idle (to raise the input voltage) and by switching the radio off and on quickly about 20 times. The rapid impulses may be all that is needed to make the vibrator start. The vibrator's operation may be shaky at first, but if you leave the radio on for 15 or 20 minutes, the points in the vibrator will clean themselves and the vibrator will start properly the next time.

Some adventurous tinkerers will disassemble the vibrator and file the points. But when you file the points you are filing on points made of soft brass that have a thin silver coating. So when you file the points, you are filing away the thin silver coating. This exposes the brass which will burn away quickly, usually within a few hours. You can guess the result.

The solution is a modern solid state vibrator. There is one made for most every car radio ever built. A solid state vibrator does the switching using transistors instead of points. They are much more reliable and have a much longer lifespan.

SPEAKERS are another magical device. Speakers are made with a paper cone that is glued to a small voice coil electromagnet. The changing magnetic flux in the coil

These are some of the solid state vibrators manufactured by Dan Schulz of Antique Automobile Radio Company, Inc. This company is the world's largest manufacturer of solid state radio vibrators.

causes the paper to vibrate and produce sound. Imagine a piece of paper, sitting in your car for decades, exposed to the sun and humidity, then pushed and pulled many times each second as it acts as a speaker. This will explain why your speaker will rattle and not faithfully reproduce all of the sounds you should be hearing.

Most original speakers can be reconed (the term for replacing the paper) but in most cases you would be better off replacing the speaker with a new one. Prior to World War II, the technology for making high quality permanent speakers cheaply did not exist.

Radios built until the early 1950s used electrodynamic speakers that required a large electromagnet to

energize the pole piece. This system required an extra amp of power from the radio to work properly. By replacing this old style speaker with a modern one, you will reduce the power consumption of the radio, and have a better sounding radio.

So which kind of speaker do you have? All electrodynamic speakers use three wires. Yellow is the field wire. Green goes to the voice coil, and black, brown, or bare braid is ground. A permanent magnet speaker requires only two wires: voice coil, and ground. To replace your old style speaker with a new one, simply tape off and do not use the yellow wire. (Do not forget to tape the yellow wire as it was/is a hot wire.) Simply connect the ground wire and the green wire to your new speaker, and you're in business. Nearly all replacement speakers will be 4 ohms, and a 10-watt rating will be more than enough.

> **NOTE OF CAUTION:** Most of the tube type radios used 4-ohm speakers. With the introduction of transistorized radios in the late 1950s, manufacturers "went nuts" using all sorts of speaker combinations. For instance Nash used both 20- and 40-ohm speakers depending on the model of the radio. Motorola manufactured radios using 4-, 8-, 20-, and 40-ohm speakers. Chevrolet car buyers in 1957 were offered four different radios, and the ohms rating of the speakers in each was different and will not interchange.

In later years things became standardized, and 8-ohm speakers are the rule to this day. When replacing the speakers in your radio or adding speakers, be sure your new speaker has the correct ohms rating, or you could damage your radio.

ANTENNAS are the most misunderstood part of any car radio system, but one of the most important. The "stick" antenna we are familiar with today was not used on cars until solid metal roofs became popular about 1937. Until that time most enclosed cars actually used the roof insert as the antenna. The roof insert was generally made of wooden bows with the headliner tacked to the inside, and a fabric material on the outside. The fabric was supported by "chicken wire" that was nailed to the wooden bows. As long as the chicken wire didn't touch any metal, it made an excellent antenna. Most car manufacturers simply attached a shielded wire to the chicken wire, and routed it over and down the windshield post when the car was being built.

This antenna was being offered before 1931, long before radios were common. But the manufacturers were able to advertise that the car was "wired for radio," which seemed to put them on the cutting edge of technology. Cars with wooden roofs used a copper screen tacked to the inside of the roof as the antenna.

Another solution for radio antennas was the side mount spare tires. The theory was simple. If you had a spare tire mounted on the side or rear of your car, all you had to do was insulate the metal parts from the car body, then attach a wire to your tire rim. These antennas did give excellent performance. And if you had dual sidemounts, you could have dual antennas! If your sidemounts had a metal cover, you simply insulated the cover, then attached a wire to the cover.

Other variations of this theme included Cadillac's trunk lid antenna where the trunk hinges were insulated and the antenna wire was attached to the trunk lid. Buick used a similar idea during the 1937 through 1939 model years.

During the late 1930s the stick or "fish pole" antenna was becoming popular. But there was no set location for this new antenna. Left side, right side, above the windshield, side mount on the cowl, on the fender, on the trunk, nobody agreed where this new antenna should be mounted. If you look at cars today in the mall parking lot, it is plain to see nobody has figured it out some 40 years later.

But the antenna plays a big part in how well your radio works. Your antenna, regardless of style, must be tuned to your radio, and the antenna lead-in wire must be grounded well at both ends. If you get a lot of ignition noise in your radio, the first place to look is the antenna. There are only two ways engine noise can get into your radio. The obvious way is the hot wire, but most manufacturers have taken care of that long ago through various noise suppression devices. The only other source is the antenna. It is, of course, difficult to filter noise from an antenna without removing some of the signal.

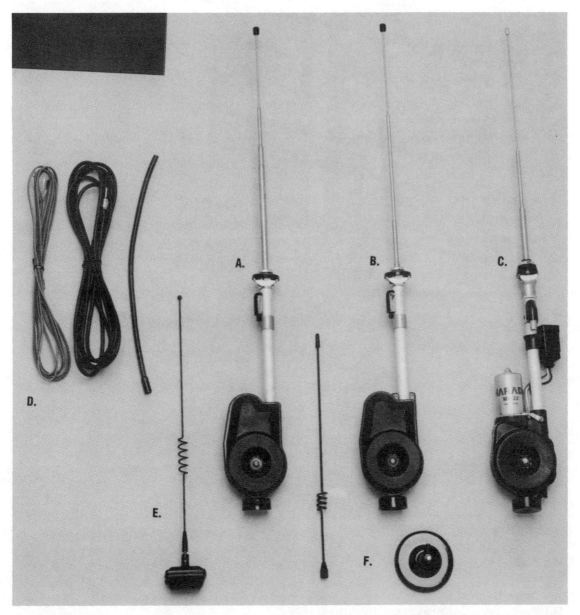

Examples labeled A, B & C are power antennas, E & F are cellular antennas and D is power cables.

181

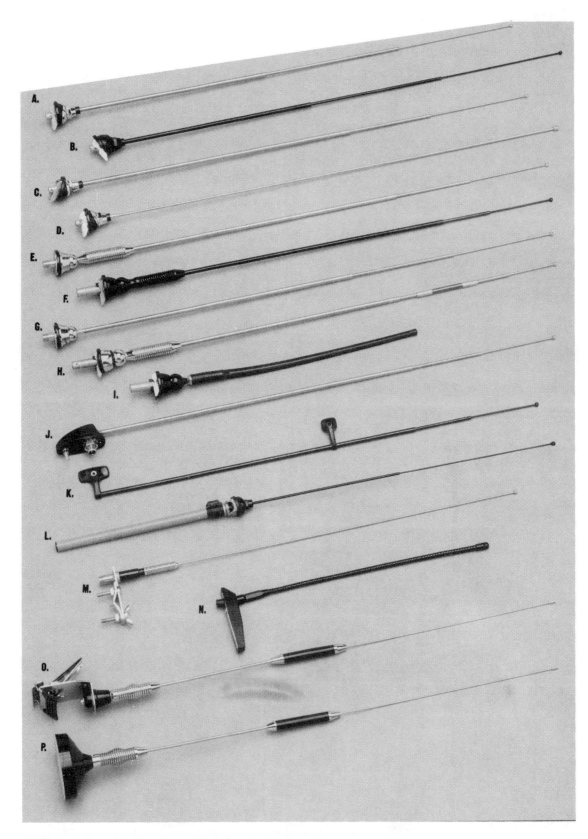

Different types of universal antennas.

OVER-CAR ANTENNA

Philco Part No. 45-2292

Studebaker Stock No. AC436

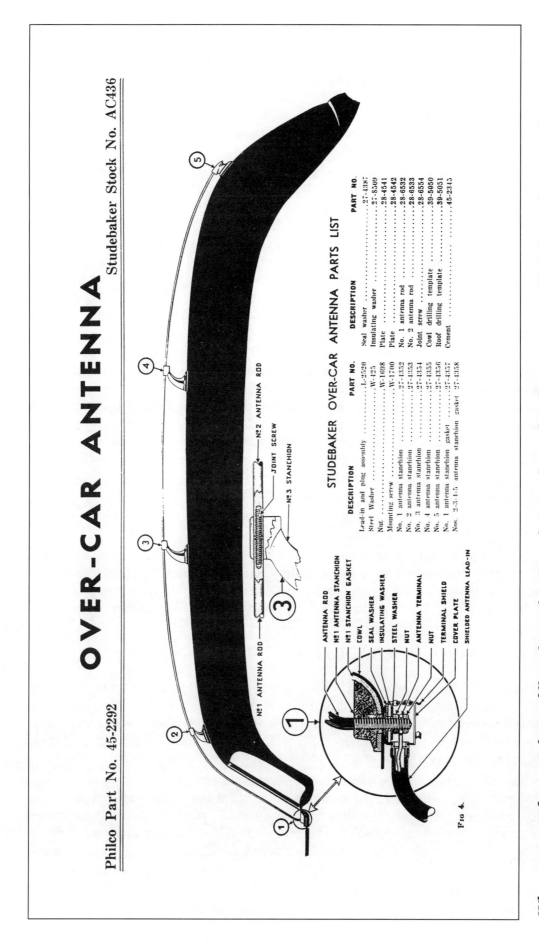

FIG. 4.

STUDEBAKER OVER-CAR ANTENNA PARTS LIST

DESCRIPTION	PART NO.	DESCRIPTION	PART NO.
Lead-in and plug assembly	L-2520	Seal washer	27-4387
Steel Washer	W-425	Insulating washer	27-8309
Nut	W-1698	Plate	28-4541
Mounting screw	W-1700	Plate	28-4542
No. 1 antenna stanchion	27-4352	No. 1 antenna rod	28-6532
No. 2 antenna stanchion	27-4353	No. 2 antenna rod	28-6533
No. 3 antenna stanchion	27-4354	Joint screw	28-6554
No. 4 antenna stanchion	27-4355	Cowl drilling template	39-5050
No. 5 antenna stanchion	27-4356	Roof drilling template	39-5051
No. 1 antenna stanchion gasket	27-4357	Cement	45-2345
Nos. 2-3-4-5 antenna stanchion gasket	27-4358		

When car manufacturers began filling the roof section of cars with metal, radio antennas could no longer be a part of the roof material. Studebaker chose this as its solution to the radio antenna problem.

Many a car owner never has any radio problems until he has his car painted. Generally that car owner will spend far more time and effort on his paint job than the factory ever did. He has cleaned, primered, and painted surfaces that the factory never did. As a result the place where the antenna base touches the underneath side of the fender now has a fresh coat of primer and paint. The antenna is no longer grounded on this end. The antenna base must have good metal-to-metal contact to work properly.

Most all radios will have a trimmer adjustment. **The function of this trimmer is to match the antenna input to the characteristics of the antenna and the car body. This adjustment cannot be made by a radio technician at the shop, or be preset at the factory, it must be done with the radio in the car and the antenna extended at the height it will be used**. This adjustment will have a definite effect on overall sensitivity of the radio and on signal seeking radios, for it determines how many stations the tuner will stop on, or if it will stop at all.

This adjustment is simple, and many radios built after 1950 have a thumbscrew, so no tools are required. Tune the radio to a weak station at the top of the AM band (usually around 1400kc), then turn the antenna trim screw in or out until the station is the loudest. Then gently tighten the trim screw and you are done.

This adjustment is easily done. However, it is best to locate the trim knob before you install the radio. Sometimes it is not out in plain sight. For instance, 1942-1948 Ford cars have the trim screw behind the tuning knob. On 1942 through 1947 Hudsons, you have to remove the ashtray to get to it. While a simple procedure, it is still an important one.

MODERNIZING OLDER RADIOS

Any radio can be converted to 12 volts without destroying the original character of the radio. If you have converted your electrical system to 12 volts, you should convert your radio as well. Using a voltage drop has several drawbacks. Voltage drops or resistors reduce the voltage based on the amount of current the radio draws. All radios are not created equal so one size resistor cannot fit all.

Second of all, in order to drop the voltage enough, the resistor must dissipate the same amount of power the radio uses. This means your electrical system has to supply twice the power the radio uses. And finally, radios that use solenoid operated tuners will be starved for voltage when the high current solenoid is activated, so it will not function properly.

The correct way to convert a 6-volt radio to 12-volt is to replace the 6-volt power transformer with a 12-volt unit. Also you must replace the vibrator, dial lights, and other 6-volt parts, with the 12-volt replacements. Vacuum tubes and solenoids should also be replaced. If your radio uses a dynamic speaker it must be changed to a permanent magnet type. The good side of all of this is your radio will now require one half the voltage to operate than it did before. So if your radio required 7 amps on 6 volts, it will now require 3.5 amps on 12 volts.

CHANGING THE POLARITY OF THE RADIO

If you are considering changing the polarity of your electrical system you should first make sure such a change is compatible with your radio. Generally a radio with a mechanical vibrator and no solid state devices (transistors) will work equally well using either polarity.

If you are using a solid state vibrator you only need to replace it with one of the correct polarity. There are a few radios, however, that do not take the reversing of polarity well. 1955 Chrysler products with signal-seeking radio will not work on reverse polarity. The signal-seeking motor will run backwards and jam. To correct this problem, the motor windings must be reversed.

Many prewar radios used synchronous vibrators. These vibrators will NOT work with reversed polarity. The high voltage they produce will be negative instead of positive and the result will be a large bang after a minute of operation. The bang is caused by the electrolytic capacitor turning inside out—not a pretty sight.

If your vibrator has more than four pins on the base or your radio does not have a rectifier tube, it is no doubt a synchronous vibrator. Some radios will allow you to rotate the vibrator and plug it in the other direction to reverse the polarity. (Remember this when you are changing your own vibrator—pay attention to which way you took it apart.) You can install a solid state vibrator of the correct polarity if the original vibrator is not reversible.

EIGHT-VOLT BATTERIES - The high side voltage of your radio requires 200 to 300 volts to operate. The absolute maximum rating for most tubes and electrolytic capacitors is 350 volts. In order to produce the high voltage, the vibrator multiplies the input voltage by 40. A 6-volt system can be expected to vary in voltage between 5 and 7.6 volts, giving a high voltage range between 200 and 304 volts.

In order to keep an 8-volt battery charged at the same rate as a 6-volt battery, the voltage input to the radio must now be 7 to 10.1 volts, which in return will produce a high side voltage of between 280 and 405 volts! This is far in excess of the components ratings. In fact, if you use an 8-volt battery in your electrical system, you are operating the entire car at 135 percent above its design rating. If your car will not start or run properly on the original 6-volt system the problem should be located and corrected, not covered up by raising the voltage!

QUESTIONS - I will be glad to answer any questions about restoring or updating your radio. I would rather have you ask a few questions first, than have you destroy your radio by experimentation.

One last thing...the ball on top of your car antenna; what purpose does it serve? A) decoration B) protection from the sharp end, or C) static discharge.

The correct answer is C. While you're driving down the road, static will build up and collect on your radio antenna. Without the ball on top of the antenna the static will collect at the end of the antenna and form a ball of static, sometimes referred to as "St. Elmo's fire" or a "corona discharge." This static will discharge through the radio speaker, causing a pop-pop-popping sound, that you will hear through the speaker on a dry cold night.

The ball on top of the antenna prevents this accumulation of static at the top of the antenna. By the way, this same static buildup can also occur on accessory curb feelers where you can actually see sparks coming from the end of the feelers on a dry cold night.

Dan Schulz

NOTES

NOTES

Chapter 12

"Wiring Your Car Trailer For Lights"

Chapter 12

Wiring Your Car Trailer For Lights

Car trailers and lights seem to be a conflict of interest. Neither seem to work well together and oftentimes it seems there is a plot by the trailer to disarm your trailer lights.

See if this sounds familiar. You go out early Saturday morning to hook up to the car trailer so you can go retrieve your latest "good deal." After you hook up the trailer and safety chains, you are out plugging in the trailer lights. The connector plug is a little rusty; maybe you shouldn't have let it lay on the ground all winter long.

So you clean out the plug as best you can, then spray a little WD-40 in the terminals (that usually does it), and plug everything in. Now to check your lights, a tap here, a wiggle the wire there, and a good smack of the RH taillight housing and everything works.

You're off down the road looking forward to a stop at the quick mart for a coffee and a donut. Life can't possibly get any better than this. You're doing just what you want to do on a Saturday off.

Six miles later you make the turn into the convenience store, only to hear that dreaded click noise, followed by the smell of burnt something. You look down at the dash and see the turn signals are no longer flashing.

Now you remember not to use the turn signals when towing the car trailer because there is a short in the wiring harness that you never quite got around to fixing.

So you will have some lights; you go through your tool box and the truck's glove box looking for a fuse. Darn, can't find one. Now it is off to the quick mart for coffee, donuts, and a $5 fuse assortment, just to get the one fuse you need. Your day off suddenly isn't going so well.

Let's back up a bit and see if we can fix some of our problems. Even if you buy a car trailer new, it is not uncommon to have problems like this. In the interest of speed and economy it is quite common to see the trailer's taillight primary wires stapled to the underside of the middle of the trailer. One of two things has/will happen. When the wires were stapled to the underneath side of the trailer, the staples pierced the insulation of the wiring, which will or already did cause a short in the trailer wiring harness. The other scenario is the first ice storm

FLAT MULTI-CONDUCTOR AUTOMOTIVE CABLE

AWG	Conductors Colors	Stranding	Std. Pkg.	Part No.
16	4 (Red/Black/ Green/White)	19 × 29	100 Ft. Spool	**C16-4E**
16	4 (Red/Black/ Green/White)	19 × 29	25 Ft. Spool	**C16-4V**
14	4 (Yellow/Brown/ Green/White)	19 × 27	100 Ft. Spool	**C14-4E**
12	4 (Yellow/Brown/ Green/White)	19 × 25	100 Ft. Spool	**C12-4E**
16	3 (Brown/Yellow, Green)	19 × 29	25 Ft. Spool	**C16-3V**
16	3 (Red/Black/ Green)	19 × 29	100 Ft. Spool	**C16-3E**
16	3 (Brown/Green/ Yellow)	19 × 29	100 Ft. Spool	**C16-3B**
14	3 (Brown/Green/ Yellow)	19 × 27	100 Ft. Spool	**C14-3E**
16	2 (Black/White)	19 × 29	100 Ft. Spool	**C16-2E**
14	2 (Black/White)	19 × 27	100 Ft. Spool	**C14-2E**
12	2 (Black/White or Black/Green)	19 × 25	100 Ft. Spool	**C12-2E**

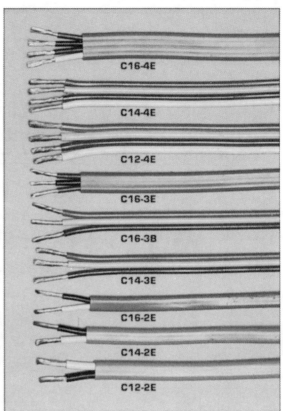

Trailer wiring that is preassembled in a harness.

in or mud road you travel down pulls loose the wires and the connections on the underneath side of the trailer. You already know about the rest.

So what is the solution to all of this? The first order of business is to fix it like it should have been done in the first place. You can start by measuring the distance from the front of your trailer hitch along a path that goes down and along the left-hand outside of your trailer, back to the rear of the trailer. Add to that, the distance across the back of the trailer. Now you are ready to go to the auto parts store.

When you arrive at the auto parts store you want to ask for trailer wiring loom. It is available with 2, 3, 4, 6 ,7, or 9 wires, all color coded, and comes inside an all-weather protected coating, much like the wiring harness in your car. Look under the brand names of Standard or Belden. (Ask your auto parts guy to look it up in the wire and cable book.)

For most applications, you want to buy the four-wire harness. This will accommodate

Example of trailer plug with metal housings.

190

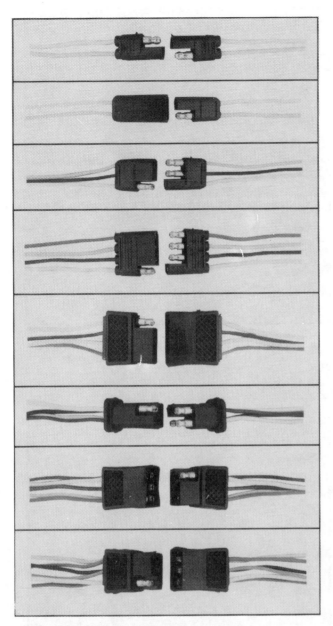

Examples of trailer plugs with molded rubber housings.

stop lights, turn signals, taillights, and ground. (Note: Your application will require the five-wire harness and connectors if your system has separate stop lights and turn signals.) The six-wire combination is required if your system has both electric brakes and separate stop lights and turn signals. Be sure that you add a couple of extra feet in length to your purchase to allow for any human error that might have occurred during the measurement of your trailer.

Next on your shopping list is the "male" and "female" connector plugs. Buy the ones with the metal housings and brass terminals inside. They have an alignment groove so you cannot connect the plug backwards. Again, you want to buy the connector plugs to match your harness. (Remember, one wire in the system is always ground, that you will get from the tow vehicle, so you do not depend on the trailer hitch ball for ground).

Many a car trailer owner has greased the trailer hitch ball only to find that the trailer lights no longer work. The grease took away the metal-to-metal contact between the ball and the trailer hitch, the only source of ground. No ground, no lights.

Along with all of this you will also need to buy the related solderless terminals so you can make your wiring connections. It is also an excellent idea to borrow your brother-in-law's soldering gun and solder all of the wiring connections to ensure a trouble-free system. Finally, you will want to buy a supply of shrink tubing (just as we used on our custom battery ends) to place over all of your wiring connections, to seal out the dirt and moisture.

You should also purchase a big supply of the wire holders called wiring harness brackets. They simply fit around the wire loom and have a hole at the end tab so a screw or bolt can be used to mount the bracket. These are available in rubber coated metal, or nylon. This will hold the wiring harness in place without damaging the harness itself. Metal lasts longer; either one is better than a staple over the primary wire. These brackets are quite inexpensive and will come in handy for a lot of things besides wiring projects.

When you get home unroll your wiring harness and get ready to secure it to the trailer. Starting at the back and leaving yourself some extra length, secure the trailer harness about every 18 inches or so. Secure the harness underneath the trailer, clear at the back, protected by a rear support angle if possible. Run the harness along the back, across to the left-hand side and up along the left-hand side of the trailer.

Be sure your harness clears the trailer suspension and any other moving parts. Tucked up behind the angle of the trailer sides is a good location. When you get to the front of the trailer follow along the edge underneath until you get to the hitch. You can then follow the inside of the trailer hitch to the front of the hitch. Be sure when you measure and cut off the extra harness at the front of the hitch that you allow enough extra length in the harness for turning corners and traveling over uneven ground.

Now you can go back to the rear of the trailer and make the lighting connections. Strip back only the insulation you need to make the connection. Write down on a piece of paper as you make the connections, what color code the wires are. Remember, taillight and turn will be one wire, brake light will be one wire, and the ground wire will be another.

For the left side, it is just the same. Taillight and turn signal is one wire. The brake light will be one wire and will be connected to the right-hand brakelight wire. The ground will be one wire and should be connected to the ground wire from the right-hand side.

Now simply move to the front of the trailer and make the same connections you just completed at the rear of the trailer. The female end of the connector is what is usually mounted to the trailer harness. It's the male end that has the pole terminals exposed. When you remove the outside cover, all of the terminals will be marked.

For most modern cars and trucks you can buy a plug-in wiring harness for a trailer adapter. These adapters are available at most any full-line auto parts store. If none are available for your application you need to carefully cut and mark each wire as you connect it to

Solderless terminal wiring kit with crimper pliers.

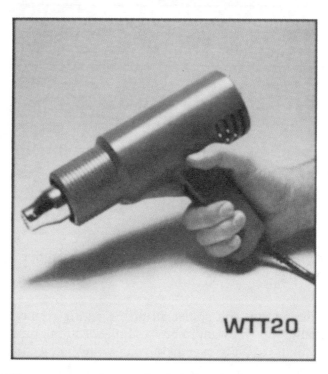

Heat gun used to melt shrink tubing.

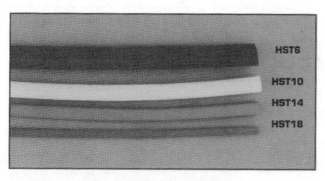

Examples of heat shrink tubing.

the female plug. Do only one wire at a time, making sure you have a good connection.

Be sure to solder and use shrink tube on all of your connections at the tow vehicle, just like you did on the trailer, to keep out dirt and moisture. To insure good connections and prevent corrosion over time, put a light coating of diaelectric grease on the terminals of the connector plug. This will help prevent corrosion and moisture from affecting your connections. This is the same white grease they use for the GM high-energy ignitions. It is available at most any full-line auto parts store.

Last but not least, be sure you check your flasher to be sure it is heavy enough to flash the extra lights. The majority of the modern original equipment flashers will do the job, but check the rating of yours to be sure. The specifications will tell you how many bulbs the flasher is capable of flashing. If you have done all of this, you now have a car trailer with a dependable lighting system. It will make going after old cars a lot more fun. It will make your attitude much better, and even the dog will start to like you more.

NOTES

Chapter

14

"The Checkered Flag!"

Chapter 14

The Checkered Flag!!

As you may have noticed, we do not have a Chapter 13. This is a trick we learned from the motel people. This chapter will be a history/trivia fun chapter. Sometimes we seem to have it tough, but remember there were also some rough times for the manufacturers and the aftermarket. If hindsight is 20/20 a lot could be learned from the past. And we can appreciate the present a little more if we understand what happened in the past to get us where we are today.

STATIC ELECTRICITY was one of the big obstacles the early engineers and car manufacturers had to overcome. For instance, in the early days tires were made of natural rubber. They acted as an insulator between the car and the road. During long trips static would build up on the car and could not be discharged to the ground because of the tires. The result: the first one to exit the car and touch the ground was the one that discharged the static electricity. As a courtesy, mothers-in-law usually got out first.

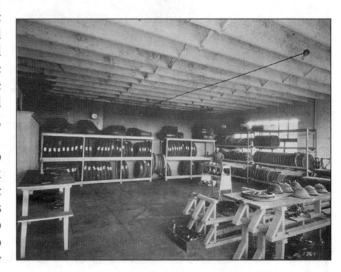

In later years, carbon was added to the composition of tires, and that allowed for the discharge of the static buildup in the car. During the 1940s powdered carbon was also added to the inside of inner tubes in cars to help eliminate some of the static electricity that was affecting radios. Delco had a kit for this task where the carbon was installed into the inner tube using a syringe. It made having a blowout not the ideal thing when you were dressed in your Sunday best.

THE AFTERMARKET PARTS COMPANIES

The Standard Motor Products Company, as we know it today, was begun in April of 1919 in New York City. The company originally bought finished products in bulk and repackaged them in glass jars for distribution. Piston rings, ignition parts, as well as starter and generator brushes were the company's first products. Still in business today, the company celebrated its 75th anniversary in 1994. They are one of the few surviving original aftermarket companies.

Early Standard Products display.

THE RIGHT TO REPAIR

In 1932 Delco-Remy, a subsidiary of General Motors, initiated a law suit against P & D, a popular aftermarket manufacturer of ignition parts. The suit claimed infringement of Delco's design patents. Standard Motor Products joined in the suit on behalf of P & D, knowing a victory for Delco would mean the end of aftermarket parts sales.

The lawsuit dragged on for years and finally ended up in the Supreme Court. In a landmark decision the aftermarket won. The result established the doctrine of Right to Repair stating that "the owner of a vehicle had a right to take his vehicle to any repair shop he chooses, and in turn the repair shop may purchase parts from any source they choose." After this, it was common for the "OEM" equipment reps and dealers to refer to the aftermarket parts as "imitation parts" or "gyp-ignition" parts.

THE ESTABLISHMENT OF JOBBER WAREHOUSES

In the 1940s large jobbers who maintained large parts inventories were reselling parts to smaller local jobbers. So the manufacturers established rebates to the larger jobbers based on the volume of parts they purchased. But in 1949 the Federal Trade Commission served citations against five companies, including Standard Motor Co., claiming the rebate system was illegal. Standard fought the case for 20 years. None of the other manufacturers got involved, knowing that if the case was lost, they, too, would have to give up their rebate system.

But in the course of the proceedings, all of the other manufacturers were cited and they gave up their rebate system. Standard continued to fight and kept their rebate system. Standard eventually won, making them the only company who could legally offer a rebate program. This landmark decision on cost justification is now cited in the legal textbooks as "The Standard Motor Products Case."

P & D IGNITION PRODUCTS COMPANY

P & D Ignition Products Co. was named after the company founders, Messrs. Piffath and Danziger. Established in the 1920s, it was once one of the largest suppliers of aftermarket ignition parts. In the 1970s the company was sold to Bendix Corporation, a division of Allied Signal. The company closed in 1980.

EIS BRAKE COMPANY

EIS Brake Co. was founded by Ernest I. Schwarz in 1932. Still in business today, it is now owned by Standard Motor Products Co., which purchased the company in 1986. The hydraulic brake system had been invented by Malcom Loughhead (later to be called the Lockheed Co.), who held all of the patents during the 1920s.

Wagner Electric held the exclusive market-ing rights to the hydraulic braking system. However, in 1929 Schwarz found a way around the patents and began manufacturing hose cou-plings for the system. In 1932 the EIS company was founded and production of brake hose couplings was expanded. Shortly thereafter the company began blending its own brake fluid as well as manufacturing their own friction parts and materials. EIS remained an independent family-owned company until 1978 when it was  purchased by the Parker Hannifin Co. In November of 1986 EIS Brake Parts became a part of Standard Motor Products, where it remains today.

THE SAGA OF THE TUCKER RADIOS

Sometimes things aren't what they seem. Take for instance, Tucker cars. Preston Tucker had every intention of putting his cars into production. His goal was to produce 100,000 of his Tor-pedos in the first year. As is standard practice in the industry, Preston ordered materials, espe-cially long lead items, well in advance of production. Motorola was the company chosen to manufacture radios for the Tucker automobiles. Motorola geared up and made as many as 10,000 radios under contract in anticipation of a strong sales year.

As it turns out, only 51 Tucker automobiles were completed. All were equipped with radios. Rumor has it that all but two of the original 51 Tucker cars survive. One was hit by a train; the other was destroyed in a fire. But what became of all of those radios?

In the early 1950s when the assets of the Tucker empire were being liquidated, the McGee Radio Company of Kansas City, Missouri, bought the entire inventory of leftover Tucker radios for the approximate sum of a dollar each. They began selling the radios, new in the box, with antenna, via mail order for $20.00 each. They were advertised as aftermarket or pickup truck radios. A few years after these radios went on sale, the carmakers changed over to 12-volt elec-trical systems, which hurt the market of an already doomed radio once again.

Many years later a fire destroyed the McGee warehouse that housed the remaining Tucker radios. Even so, many of the radios went into circulation new in the box, with antenna. Many people are under the assumption that there were not many more radios built than there were cars built. Nobody wished that to be true more than Motorola did during those later years. As a result, the value of these radios is not as great as many people think. There are, without a doubt, several new spares on the shelf for each of the remaining 49 Tucker automobiles.

Daniel R. Schulz

THE DELCO-REMY COMPANY

The Remy Company, as it was first known, was started by two brothers, Frank and Perry Remy. When they first started, a house wiring business was the plan. But the two brothers couldn't help notice there were 11 car manufacturers in Anderson, Indiana in 1903. It seemed that the auto industry was going places, so the brothers decided to get involved.

Their first product was a magneto ignition for automobiles. The product was a success and production was up to 50,000 magnetos a year by 1910. But by 1912 the days of magnetos were looking to be numbered. The switch was on to a battery-type ignition. Not up to the battles of big business, the boys sold out to Fletcher Savings and Trust Co., who kept the name but expanded the product line to include cranking motors, generators, and distributors.

Competition was fierce, especially from the Dayton Engineering Laboratories Co., better known as the Delco Company. The two companies struggled along until they were both bought within the same year by United Motors Corporation in 1916. Their separate but equal status remained, even when United Motors became a part of General Motors in 1918. In 1924 Remy Electric's fate was up for grabs, due to a business slump right after World War I.

The saving grace turned out to be Klaxon horns. The Remy Company convinced Detroit that they could build Klaxon horns cheaper than the Klaxon Co. of Newark, New Jersey. The Klaxon plant in New Jersey conceded and all of the equipment was shipped to Anderson, Indiana.

In 1926 the Delco Co. and the Remy Co. consolidated, and become a single division of General Motors. In 1928 the division began battery production. Also, Guide Motor Lamp Co. was purchased and moved to Anderson. Soon after in 1933, the Packard Cable Co. was bought, and the equipment and inventory was also transferred to Anderson, Indiana.

In 1936 the Delco-Remy Division began producing car radios. During World War II, 85 projects, and 673 products were assigned to the Delco-Remy Division. The end of the war and the 50th anniversary of Delco-Remy Electric coincided.

Later on, in the early 1960s, Delco introduced the Delcotron alternating current generator. Caterpillar was their first customer. From there...the rest is history. The Delco-Remy Division continues to this day to play an important part in the history of General Motors, its parent company.

AND FINALLY, WHO UNDERSTANDS ELECTRICITY BETTER, YOU OR YOUR FRIENDS?

After you study automotive electricity for a while you get the urge to demonstrate to your friends how much you know about the subject. While they usually don't share your devoted interest, there are ways of getting their attention and letting them know that you indeed understand automotive electricity better than they do.

Case in point: When I was growing up there was Doc Chartier's Repair Garage in Oakhill, Kansas. Like most old garages that have been around since the beginning of time, every visit resulted in a learning experience. One of my earliest learning experiences concerning automotive electricity occurred at Doc's Garage.

In the office of Doc's garage was an old potbelly stove that burned wood, paper, cardboard, and an occasional half a cup of coffee. Next to the wood stove was an old barroom chair with (as I later learned) two 16 penny nails in the seat about two cheeks apart.

Had I been more observant I would have noticed the old cotton-wrapped wire lying on the floor partially covered up by the old books and magazines and the diverse selection of old used auto parts. But when you come inside from the cold zero degree winter day outside, your mind is in neutral, and all you can think about is getting warm. The neighborhood gang is all sitting in the office telling tall stories. They are more than glad to offer you a warm seat by the stove, which you gladly accept.

Ten minutes or so later, along comes old Doc. Knowing what I know now, he knows he has a victim, and I am about to get Case Tractor Magneto 101, the abridged edition. Doc walks over to his old rolltop desk and sits down, pretending to be writing out a bill, while carrying on a conversation with all of us.

Doc reaches down to one of the lower drawers of the desk—I assume to reach for an envelope. Next thing I know I am getting the heck shocked out of me, and I am jumping up and down. Everybody else is having a good laugh. Old Doc just grins and walks back to the shop and goes to work.

When things return to normal somewhat, I went back to ask Doc if he would explain how a magneto works—especially the one in his lower desk drawer. From that day forward I never forgot what ground was and how much 40,000 volts is.

Over the years, I have experienced many such lessons in life. They make quite an impression on you, and you will remember them a lot longer than any lesson you read from a book.

The following list is a few lessons in electricity. Some of these I have taught and with some of these, I was the student. What you do, or which you are, is up to you.

Did you ever wire a Model T Ford coil to the body of your car so anyone leaning on your car got shocked? Remember having to jump up on the running board so you yourself didn't get shocked?

Did you ever hook up a Model T coil in the tail pipes so you could shoot fire out the exhaust on Saturday night, and impress your girlfriend's Dad?

Did you ever visit an antique auto parts store that has a countertop made of 16-gauge sheet metal? Did you ever wonder if a Model T coil was hooked to that countertop? Stop by sometime, and I will be glad to answer that question. I will also be glad to explain about ground and ignition spark. I have a good memory for that sort of thing.

Finally, the best Model T coil trick I ever saw was in an old-time mechanic's garage that was run by two brothers and looked on the inside like it was about 1935. Skylights in the roof were dark, not letting much light in. The shop had only a half-dozen 60-watt bulbs for light. The office and the bathroom were side by side.

Their trick with a Model T coil was that they had run a small copper wire through the wall, under the toilet tank and down into the water about three inches. The copper wire was corroded and had turned black, matching the rest of the bathroom decor. You had to look really hard to see it in the dim light.

While I was not the victim of this lesson, I did hear the results and I enjoyed a good laugh. I guess my early lesson in life wasn't so bad after all.

NOTES

Chapter 15

"IT'S EASY TO BE AN EXPERT..."

"Does All of This Really Happen in Real Life"

15

Does All of This Really Happen in Real Life?

Congratulations for surviving reading this book! You are now among the elite experts, and will become more popular—especially at car club meetings as people discover your intimate knowledge of electricity. Carry your burden proudly.

To start you off on your journey as "keeper of the knowledge," let's go through some of the scenarios you are likely to encounter. As usually happens, the oddest problems will occur during the first few months. Don't worry—the problems will become the normal, garden variety soon enough.

Be prepared, and tackle the situations as you feel comfortable. It is not your job to solve every electrical problem in the state in the next sixty days. Remember that some of those problems have been around for a couple of years—at least.

The first time someone asks you why his or her car won't start, you are likely to assume the cause is an electrical problem. Experience will soon teach you to not assume anything. Even if your friend did put gas in just yesterday, how much did he put in? Three gallons in a 25 gallon tank may not be enough to reach the pickup tube in the bottom of the tank—assuming that the pickup tube is in fact at the bottom of the tank.

Some are not. This is so that the water and dirt remain on the bottom of the tank and the gas is sucked up from a higher level above that—but let's assume all of that is OK.

Keep in mind that even though you are being a good guy and offering your observations and technical advice *for free,* it is not without some risk. You are expected to know it all. Let me assure you: you don't. While you may have the best intentions, you should know that *if* you have misdiagnosed the problem, your new-found credibility will be tarnished.

Also, some people will attempt merely to test your knowledge and embarrass you. If you are not careful they will get the job done. Proceed with caution and all should go well. If you encounter a problem you don't understand don't be afraid to say, "I don't understand this problem, but let's go find someone who does. . . ."

Back to our story: You believe the gas bit, and by removing the air cleaner and manually working the linkage you can see there is indeed gas at the carburetor. What should you do now?

It looks as though this might actually be an electrical problem. Start by checking the ignition switch. Many older vehicles will "crank" the motor over without the ignition key in the "on" position. Without the key in this position there will be no voltage to the ignition coil. . . and you know the rest. This happens quite often, sometimes by accident, and sometimes to see how smart you really are.

If the key is in the on position, check the ignition coil itself. Is there voltage there? Is it *enough* voltage? Remember there should be at the very least two volts less than system voltage if there is a ballast resistor in the circuit, and full system voltage if the coil itself has an internal resistor.

Suppose you are working on a 1955 Chevy car, for instance. The coil shows only 8 volts at the (+) terminal. What does that tell you? Either the battery is discharged, which is causing low voltage at the coil, *or* the ballast resistor mounted on the firewall could be at fault. How are you going to figure that one out?

Of course, by first checking the battery voltage at the battery with your trusty volt meter. If the battery checks out OK then you are going to check the voltage at the input side of the ballast resistor.

If the input side reads 12 volts you know everything is OK up to that point. Now check the output side of the ballast resistor. Hey, it shows only 8 volts. I think we are on to something here. We have isolated the problem between the input side and the output side of the ballast resistor.

This would suggest that the ballast resistor itself is the problem. The coil is receiving only 8 volts because the output side of the ballast resistor is providing only 8 volts.

You have done it! You have isolated the problem and solved the mystery. You replace the ballast resistor and the car starts. You recheck everything and all is well. As a result the happy owner takes you downtown and buys you supper at McDonalds—a Happy Meal, of course.

Suppose the ballast resistor checked out OK. What would you do then? Right—check the output terminal of the coil (-) and see what voltage is present. From there you can remove the distributor cap and see if you have "spark" at the ignition points, and so on, down to the plug wires.

It becomes pretty easy to isolate a problem if you can find where the voltage stops, or is weak. Then you know the problem is between where you have voltage and where you do not.

The 1955 Chevrolet car was an easy lesson. Now let's try one that is a little more difficult and see how you get along.

Positive Ground Cars

This is an all-too common occurrence. Many antique car owners are unaware that there was even such a thing as a positive ground electrical system. When the owner replaces the battery, he simply connects the battery cables to the battery posts as if it were negative ground. Even though he has not paid any attention to the original battery cables and posts, the car owner might think he has done everything correctly. Little does he know.

Meanwhile, what about the poor generator and regulator? They are still trying to be positive ground. That is going to make things pretty difficult for the charging system to work correctly. It is at this point that you will most likely be called upon to fix a charging problem.

If you suspect a polarity problem, you should check right away to see if the points in the regulator are arcing. You can usually hear this, without removing the cover from the voltage regulator. Other signs something is wrong: the amp gauge in the dash will either show no charge; or the needle will be going back and forth, trying to decide what is going on. In short, the electrical charging system will be in a state of confusion.

A friend may say to you, "my generator used to work, but when I replaced my battery, the generator seemed to quit charging." Check the polarity then the battery to see which way he installed the cables. More often than not they are backwards, even though he may have had to stretch the heck out of the cables.

It also may be necessary to repolarize the generator after you install the battery the correct way, in order to get everything working together again.

While you are at it, check the voltage regulator. Many times car owners that are having charging problems will replace the battery first because it is the easiest to replace and they already know how to do it.

If the battery doesn't do it, next in line is usually the voltage regulator because "that usually fixes it." You know this is not the way to determine the problem. The deeds have been done and the parts are installed, but still nothing works—so it is up to you to fit it. What now?

First check the voltage regulator. If the car owner didn't know he had a positive ground system he may just have installed a negative ground regulator. If the customer didn't specify at the local auto parts store for a "6 volt voltage regulator" more often than not he will get a negative ground regulator, no questions asked. This is because the younger guys that work at the counter have never heard of positive ground either.

Most positive ground regulators will be stamped on the bottom or on the outside of the cover. If in fact your friend does have the correct polarity of regulator, check all of his wiring, making sure all of the connections are on the right terminals.

If this all checks out, ask him if he read the directions where it said to "polarize" the regulator to the generator after installation. If he gives you a "blank" look and you find the dog chewing on the instructions, you can assume the worst. At last polarizing his generator should get him going.

But *what if* he bought a negative ground regulator for his positive ground car. Can he return it to the auto parts store? Not likely. Most auto parts store will not accept returns on electrical parts—for obvious reasons.

So can you adapt a negative ground regulator to his system? Yes. But only if you change his system to a negative ground system, which, you know, is not difficult. Reverse his battery cables and wires on the amp gauge, also don't forget to polarize his generator.

Check his radio, if he has one, to make sure it will still work OK, (most will) and leave a note for the next guy explaining that his system has been changed to negative ground.

Remember, the next guy could be you. Meanwhile explain to your friend the importance of getting exact replacement parts, and the wisdom of taking the old part in for identification.

What Else Is Going to Happen to Me in the Real World?

Hot Start Problems

This is by far the most common problem you will encounter. You may have gone through this experience on your own cars and may have fixed your problems by what you have learned in this book. As a simple reminder here are the most important things to check.

Battery cable size—as you know by now, the size of the battery cable greatly affects how well your vehicle starts. It is very common to see 8 gauge cables on 6 volt systems—the modern replacement. Also watch for the cables with the fat insulation and small gauge wire inside. Finally, you may also see aluminum battery cables.

The aluminum battery cables, as you know, are the source of high resistance, especially when they are hot. You know the rest of this story.

Also watch rebuilt starters. Copper is very expensive these days. It was common a few years ago for a few starter rebuilders to substitute aluminum field coils in place of the original copper. As you already know, this does not work very well; especially when the car is hot, the aluminum field coils create high resistance, making the vehicle difficult to start.

The owner is quite sure it is not the starter at fault because it was newly rebuilt! It has been my experience that it is always better to take your generator or starter to a quality rebuilder and have it rebuilt. This way you know what you are getting back. Also—let's face it—the quality of the older original parts will in most cases exceed what the modern replacement offers. If you doubt this, look how long things lasted in the first place.

So you physically checked the cables and while you were at it checked the ground and moved it to the starter mounting bolt or some place close by. Now you need to check to see if the battery is in good shape. This you know how to do: check voltage, check cells if possible, etc. All seems good.

Now what about the cables between the battery and the starter. Are they good? Remember our little trick: turning on the headlights before you crank over the motor? We learned that if the lights go clear out when the motor is cranking, there are poor or dirty connections between the battery starter. Dim lights mean everything is OK.

What about the starter itself? How much voltage is at the starter when the motor is cranking? Remember we also learned that there should not be more than half a volt drop between the battery and the starter post during cranking.

Also, what about the starter itself? A factory or shop manual will tell you how many amps the starter should require for cranking. Usually it is not much more than 175 amps. Suppose you check this starter and find it is drawing 240 amps while cranking over the motor. That should tell you the starter itself is in need of some attention. Maybe the bushings are worn and the armature is rubbing on the field coils: a common occurrence. There is usually an internal defect of some kind if the starter is drawing excessive amps during cranking.

Also some cars will have the exhaust running down right next to the starter, which will cause the starter and especially the starter solenoid to soak up the heat from the exhaust. One solution is to buy or make a heat shield that deflects the heat away from the starter.

Another solution is to move the starter solenoid up and away from the source of heat. GM cars of the sixties can benefit from replacing the GM starter solenoid with a Ford type that mounts up on the firewall away from the heat. You may recall learning this trick in the chapter on starters. This is a popular fix-up for race cars and performance street vehicles.

Ground: Body, Frame and Engine

Let's say one of the guys in the car club just finished a body restoration of a 1936 Ford Coupe. He has installed a new wiring harness and everything else is new from front to back. Even the frame is detailed with a nice glossy coat of Chassis Black paint.

Upon his first trip around the block, however, he discovers that when he applies the brakes, the horn honks; when he turns on the taillights, the headlights and brake lights also come on. After he doublechecks all of the wiring, he asks for your help.

Do you have a clue? Right, you should suspect the ground—or in this case, the lack of it. There needs to be a return path for the ground to follow. If there is not, ground will find it's own path, which may not be consistent. It can also be dangerous.

As we learned earlier in this book, paint is an excellent insulator of electricity. So with the fresh layers of paint on the frame and the new body webbing, etc., the chances are good there is little or no path for the ground to follow. As a result, the ground is finding it's own path, which as we also learned is the path of least resistance.

The solution of course is to correct the ground path. You can do this by making sure there is a good body-to-frame ground. This may require scraping some of that new glossy paint off the frame, until you get down to bare metal. You can also bolt a fender washer to the frame before it is painted to protect your ground path.

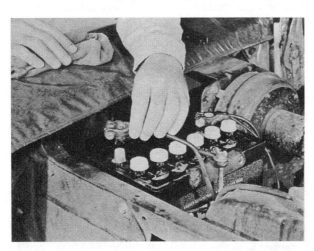

Next on your agenda is to check the body-to-engine ground. Again the same rules apply. If the engine is all detailed out and freshly painted but the generator isn't working, then maybe the generator itself is not properly grounded. The paint on the generator bracket and the paint on the engine have taken away the ground. This is often true when the voltage regulator is mounted to the firewall. The ground usually comes from the firewall via the mounting screws.

Sheetmetal grounds can sometimes cause lots of grief. For instance, headlights mounted to the radiator cowling will often flicker just like the old silent movies. The problem is a poor ground. The sheetmetal shifts in relations to the frame causing a poor ground path. Also, the connections were usually exposed partly to the elements, and corroded easily, which caused high resistance. High resistance will often result in short bulb life.

One easy solution is to run a ground wire from the headlight bulb housing down directly to the frame. This should eliminate the flickering of the headlights and extend the bulb life at the same time.

The final ground problem you will incur is engine-to-frame. Again, this is important to assure all of the accessories mounted to the engine will work as they should. This is one of the most important grounds.

The lack of engine-to-frame ground can cause a fire. With no path to follow, the ground will find it's own path, which can be the throttle return spring on the carburetor. The result is usually a fire and a big surprise for the driver who has no clue what is going on under the hood.

As we learned earlier in this book, the Chevrolet Corvette is one of the cars in which ground is very important. With an all-fiberglass body, the Corvette will have more than 100 ground straps to provide a return path. Leaving any one of those straps out will result in a break in the electrical highway. The result can be something simple like an accessory that does not work, or something serious like a fire under the hood.

For those of you restoring a Corvette, it may seem crazy to have so many ground straps. You might think leaving off a couple really shouldn't make that much difference. Ask someone who has been there—they will tell you otherwise.

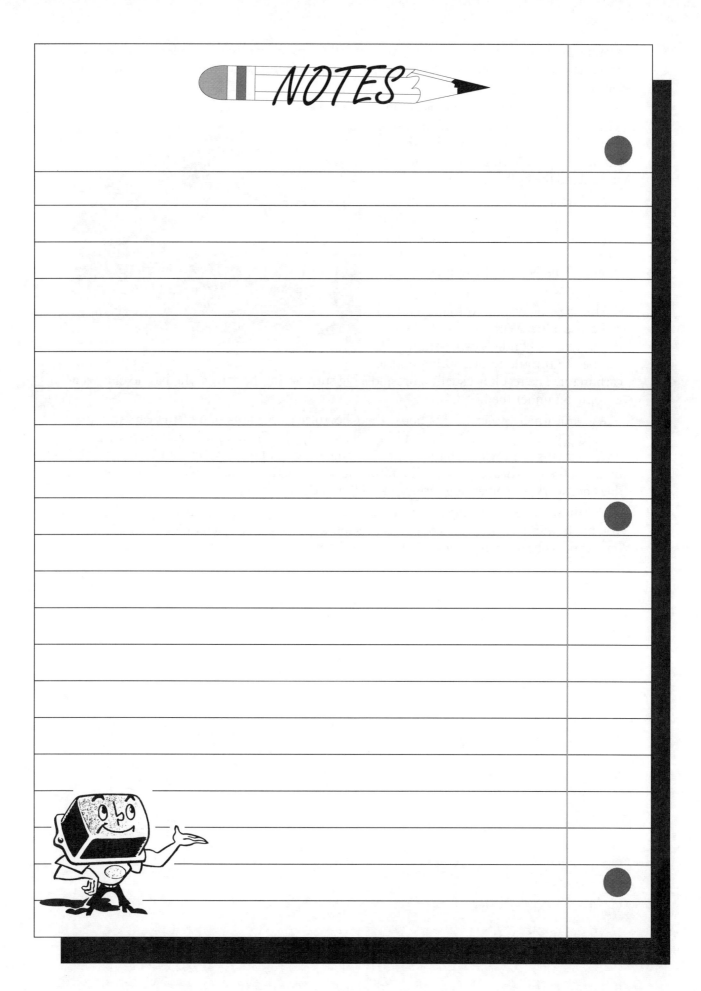

Epilogue

I hope some of these real life adventures will be of help to you. I remember reading lots of electrical books that explained all of this stuff in technical terms. While they seemed clear and I thought I understood everything, when I opened up the hood of my car nothing there seemed to relate to what I had just read.

So I did what everyone else does: closed the hood, went in the house, and placed the electrical wiring book on the shelf, only to use it later for a plant coaster.

I hope this book, in contrast, has made life easier for you and you have learned enough to make it worth your time. Most of all, I hope you don't use this book for a plant coaster.

Finally, even though you may never do automotive electrical projects for a living, I hope you have learned enough to take care of your own problems and help a few friends. If so, you and I have both done well.

Source List

Below are the full names and addresses of the businesses that I named in the book. In some chapters I gave addresses and some I did not. Not to worry; here is the complete list. There is even space in the book so you can add your own sources. Writing them on the back of the phone book is not a good idea because if you are like everybody else, you throw the old phone book away as soon as you get the new one, which means you threw your own listings away and have to start all over. It's kind of like what your mother used to tell you about keeping track of your homework.

Antique Automobile Radio, Inc.
Mailing address:
P.O. Box 892
Crystal Beach, FL 34681
700 Tampa Road
Palm Harbor, FL 50256
Phone: 1-800-WE-FIX-AM
FAX: 813-789-0283
Contact: Dan Schulz

Store hours: Monday through Friday, 8-4:30 Eastern time.
Payment accepted includes Visa, MasterCard, Discover, and COD.

1932-1962 radio repairs and restorations, FM conversions, voltage conversions, polarity conversions, 6-12 regulated power inverters. They are also the largest manufacturer in the world of solid state radio vibrators. They provide excellent service and are very knowledgeable. Catalog available upon request.

Fifth Avenue Antique Auto Parts
415 Court Street
Clay Center, KS 67432
Phone: 913-632-3450
FAX: 913-632-6154
Contact: Randy Rundle

Store hours: Monday through Friday, 9-6 Central time. Saturday by chance. Payment accepted includes Visa, MasterCard, money orders, good checks. Alternator dealerships are available to qualified established businesses; please inquire.

Fifth Avenue manufactures their own 6- and 12-volt alternators. They also are the originators of the "DA" plug for alternators and have one of the largest selections of mounting brackets and alternator drive pulleys found anywhere. They are famous for their wide selection of 6-volt accessories. It was Fifth Avenue and Antique Automobile Radio that developed together the "Runtz voltage drops."

Fifth Avenue is well-known to the participants of the Interstate Batteries Great American Race, where their products have been tested and proven extensively.

OPTIMA Batteries are available from Fifth Avenue Auto Parts, as well as many local distributors from coast to coast. Check the Yellow Pages for the dealer nearest you.

Electric Radiator Cooling Fans are available from Fifth Avenue Auto Parts. They have radiator cooling fans available in both 6- and 12-volt models, in pusher or puller styles, in a wide variety of sizes.

Gear Driven Electric Fuel Pumps are also available from Fifth Avenue Auto Parts. Six- and 12-volt models are available.

Interstate Batteries are sold locally by service stations and repair garages coast to coast. Watch for an Interstate Batteries sign on display or check the Yellow Pages for the 800 number listing all the local Interstate battery dealers.

Standard Motor Products are available through your local full-line auto parts jobber such as Big A and CarQuest Auto Parts Stores, which are located nationwide.

"Runtz" Transistorized Voltage Drops for dash gauges are available from Fifth Avenue Auto Parts.

Also mentioned in the book are a number of popular name-brand aftermarket parts manufacturers. Some of these included:

Delco

Signal - Stat

Ideal brand (flashers)

Wagner lighting

Most any of these name brands can be found at your local full-line auto parts stores such as NAPA, CarQuest, and Big A. You can simply call them and say "By the way, do you carry Wagner Lighting products?" If they do, then you already know what is available from them. This same example will work for most any other application or brand name.

Suppose you are looking for a trailer wiring harness. You already know from reading this book what is available and what to look for when buying the related hardware. All you have to do is pick out what you want from the catalog they show you. Again, you already know what everything does and how many wires you need in your harness and the number of feet required. Because you are this good, maybe you should pay yourself about $25 an hour.

Index

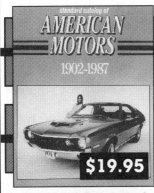

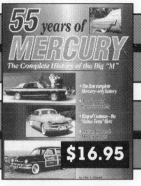

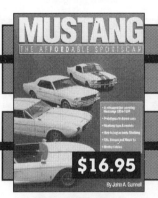
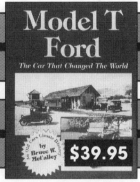
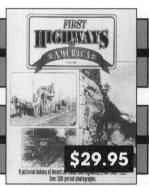

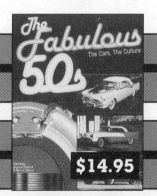